Texts in Computing

Volume 18

What Is a Computer and What Can It Do?

An Algorithms-Oriented Introduction to
the Theory of Computation

Volume 5
Bridges from Classical to Nonmonotonic Reasoning
David Makinson

Volume 6
Automata and Dictionaries
Denis Maurel and Franz Guenthner

Volume 7
Learn Prolog Now!
Patrick Blackburn, Johan Bos and Kristina Striegnitz

Volume 8
A Meeting of the Minds: Proceedings of the Workshop on Logic, Rationality and Interaction
Beijing 2007
Johan van Benthem, Shier Jun and Frank Veltman, eds.

Volume 9
Logic for Artificial Intelligence & Information Technology
Dov M. Gabbay

Volume 10
Foundations of Logic and Theory of Computation
Amílcar Sernadas and Cristina Sernadas

Volume 11
Invariants: A Generative Approach to Programming
Daniel Zingaro

Volume 12
The Mathematics of the Models of Reference
Francesco Berto, Gabriele Rossi and Jacopo Tagliabue

Volume 13
Picturing Programs
Stephen Bloch

Volume 14
JAVA: Just in Time
John Latham

Volume 15
Design and Analysis of Purely Functional Programs
Christian Rinderknecht

Volume 16
Implementing Programming Languages. An Introduction to Compilers and Interpreters
Aarne Ranta, with an appendix coauthored by Markus Forsberg

Volume 17
Acts of the Programme *Semantics and Syntax*. Isaac Newton Institute for the Mathematical
Sciences, January to July 2012.
Arnold Beckmann and Benedikt Löwe, eds.

Volume 18
What Is a Computer and What Can It Do?   An Algorithms-Oriented Introduction to the
Theory of Computation
Thomas C. O'Connell

Texts in Computing Series Editor
Ian Mackie   mackie@lix.polytechni

What Is a Computer and What Can It Do?

An Algorithms-Oriented Introduction to the Theory of Computation

Thomas C. O'Connell

ISBN 978-1-84890-098-1

College Publications
Scientific Director: Dov Gabbay
Managing Director: Jane Spurr

http://www.collegepublications.co.uk

Cover produced by Laraine Welch
Printed by Lightning Source, Milton Keynes, UK

Contents

Preface   **ix**

1   **Introduction**   **1**
    1.1   A simple question 1
    1.2   Decision problems 2
    1.3   What is a computer? 8
    1.4   Recap 12

2   **Finite State Machines**   **15**
    2.1   Introduction 15
    2.2   Focus on the states 17
    2.3   Deciding $\{0^n1^n : n \geq 0\}$ using a finite number of states... or not   21

3   **Turing Machines**   **23**
    3.1   Introduction 23
    3.2   Turing machines can count! 31
    3.3   The Church-Turing Thesis 35
    3.4   So what exactly is a computer anyway? 37

4   **Unsolvable Problems**   **39**
    4.1   Introduction 39
    4.2   Reductions 43
    4.3   Rice's Theorem 49
    4.4   Exercises 50

5   **Nondeterminism**   **53**
    5.1   Introduction 53
    5.2   Nondeterminstic search algorithms 55

5.3 Nondeterministic finite automata 60

5.4 Free will is useless 66

6 Computational Complexity   **73**

6.1 Introduction 73

6.2 Time 76

6.3 Combinatorial explosions 79

6.4 Polynomial time reductions 86

6.5 NP-complete problems. 91

6.6 Proof of the Cook-Levin Theorem 93

7 Reduce, Reuse, Recycle!   **101**

7.1 Introduction 101

7.2 Three is a crowd. 102

7.3 First grade math. 107

7.4 HAMILTONIAN CYCLE is NP-complete 117

8 Is it Better to Be a Pig? Approximation Algorithms   **123**

8.1 Introduction 123

8.2 Optimization problems 129

8.3 Approximately optimal solutions to hard problems 130

8.4 Fully polynomial time approximation schemes 135

8.5 Finding good enough solutions is not always easy. 145

9 Is It Better To Be an Ant? Heuristics For Hard Problems   **149**

9.1 Introduction 149

9.2 Local Search 150

9.3 SAT Solvers 152

10 Space   **163**

10.1 Introduction 163

10.2 Hierarchy Theorems 171

10.3 Relating Space, Time, and Everything Else 175

11 Conclusion   **181**

Solutions to Exercises   **183**

   Solutions for Chapter 1: Introduction 183

   Solutions for Chapter 2: Finite Automata 185

   Solutions for Chapter 3: Turing Machines 189

   Solutions for Chapter 4: Unsolvable Problems 213

   Solutions for Chapter 5: Nondeterminism 221

   Solutions for Chapter 6: Computational Complexity 223

   Solutions for Chapter 7: Reduce, Reuse, Recycle 231

   Solutions for Chapter 8: Approximation Algorithms 251

   Solutions for Chapter 9: Heuristics 265

   Solutions for Chapter 10: Space 269

Chapter Notes   **279**

   Notes on Chapter 1: Introduction 279

   Notes on Chapter 2: Finite Automata 279

   Notes on Chapter 3: Turing Machines 279

   Notes on Chapter 4: Unsolvable Problems 280

   Notes on Chapter 5: Nondeterminism 280

   Notes on Chapter 6: Computational Complexity 280

   Notes on Chapter 7: Reduce, Reuse, Recycle 281

   Notes on Chapter 8: Approximation Algorithms 281

   Notes on Chapter 9: Heuristics 281

   Notes on Chapter 10: Space 282

Stuff you need to know   **283**

   Miscellaneous 283

   Algorithms 283

Acknowledgements   **289**

Bibliography   **291**

Index   **295**

Preface

I took a bus home from the airport one morning a long time ago. After I sat down, a scary looking guy got on the bus, came up to my seat, and in a somewhat less than pleasant voice said, "You look like one of them POT smokers." Simultaneously searching for a response and for something large and heavy with which to defend myself, I replied, "Nope."

Scary Dude: "You sure you're not one of them POT smokers?"

Me: "Yep."

Unconvinced, he walked to the other end of the bus while I began to reconsider my decision not to join a martial arts class with a friend the week before. Scary Dude sat next to a student from the University of Texas. The student was reading a book for a literature class. Scary Dude asked, "What ya readin?" I couldn't hear much of the reply. For some reason, I mostly heard Scary Dude's part of the conversation. Then he said, "I read a book once, and it was *Charlotte's Web*."

Most of the computer science students I have taught are a lot like the scary dude on the bus – they don't read. At least, they don't read their textbooks. I can sympathize with them. Even with good books, I find myself getting too bogged down in the details and losing the story. I am hoping this book will be more like *Charlotte's Web*. Not that I expect this to be an easy read or for it to include any pigs or spiders, but I want to stick to the story even if that means skipping over some details . . . and if I can figure out how to include a pig and a spider, I will. With that in mind, I intend to keep the main part of the book short. I do plan, however, to include a number of solved problems that would likely appear as theorems and examples in other books. Some of these problems will be much harder than others. Even if a problem seems incredibly difficult, at least think about the approach you would take in solving it before looking at the solution in the book.

Instructors using this book for a course may wish to use supplemental material to explore some topics more deeply. The book may be particularly useful for independent study, especially when the goal is to quickly develop an understanding of the central topics in the theory of computation. I would certainly not recommend using it to defend yourself on the bus ride home from the airport. Other, more comprehensive, computer science texts are much better suited for that purpose.

Thomas C. O'Connell
Skidmore College
Saratoga Springs, NY
October 2013

Chapter 1

Introduction

1.1 A simple question

What is a computer and what can it do? This sounds like a simple enough question. We all know what a computer is and we see them do lots of things. Imagine, however, that you are on a college admissions tour. You meet with an admissions officer who asks you what major you are likely to choose in college. You confidently respond, "Philosophy." He says, "Hm, let me ask you a few questions." After typing your responses into his computer, he triumphantly hits the return key. The computer promptly announces, "Computer science is the best major for this student."

Can a computer do that? Can a computer decide what major is best for you? Even after you graduate, how would you be sure that you had the best possible major in college? Maybe if you had majored in philosophy instead of computer science, you would have been happier. Maybe if you had majored in chemistry, you would have gotten a higher paying job when you graduated but would have blown yourself up in an industrial accident.

The way we measure the success of the selection might have a big impact on whether or not a computer can solve the problem. For example, it might be unrealistic for us to expect a computer to predict that you would get blown up in a chemistry lab several years after college. On the other hand, maybe it would be reasonable to expect a computer to predict that you would be "happiest" as a philosophy major if it was given a list of your favorite books and the list included everything Plato ever wrote.

The question of what a computer can and cannot do might get pretty complicated if we have to worry too much about measuring things like "best" and "happiest." For the moment, let's concentrate on things that are a little more concrete than determining what your major should be. Can we write a computer program that can determine whether any given scientific theory is correct? If so, we could input the theory of relativity or even the theory of evolution to the computer and it would tell us whether the theory is correct. We might save a lot of lawsuits and school board arguments if we could write such a program.

Scientific theories might be a little cumbersome to input to a computer, but what about mathematical statements? For example, suppose we were given the problem of proving or disproving that n^2 is $\Theta(n \log n)$. (It is not. See the Stuff You Need To Know at the end of the book.) If I had a computer that could take any mathematical statement and determine whether it was true or false, it would certainly have saved me a lot of trouble on the prove or disprove questions in my discrete math class. (Who needs proof by induction? I've got an iPad.) *Can a computer determine the validity of any mathematical statement?* This question is especially significant because it was the question that in many ways started theoretical computer science as a field of study.

The mathematical statement problem is no more straightforward than the problem of determining the best major for each student, or is it? In the case of the major, it is not clear how we determine whether the computer was successful. The question of whether a mathematical statement is true, however, has a definite yes or no answer. The statement is either true or it is false. These are the types of problems we want to consider first. Not that other types of problems are uninteresting, but we need to start somewhere and it is best to start simply. Problems that require a yes or no answer are called **decision problems**.

Definition 1.1 *A* **decision problem** *is a problem that requires a yes or no answer.*

I just said that.

1.2 Decision problems

You have probably written programs to solve decision problems before. Maybe not too many, though, since we usually prefer writing programs to do cooler stuff than simply returning yes or no answers to questions.

Here are some examples of decision problems:

1. Given a list of names and a query name, determine whether or not the query name in the list.

2. Given a graph and two vertices, s and t, determine whether or not it possible to reach t starting from s.

3. Given a mathematical statement, determine whether or not the statement is true.

It is easy to see that the first two of these problems can be solved with a computer. A sequential search will find a member of a list. A breadth-first search will find all of the vertices reachable from a starting vertex. I have no clue how to solve the mathematical statement problem in general but neither does anyone else, so I don't feel too bad.

For simplicity, we have changed our question of "What is a computer and what can it do?" to "What is a computer and what decision problems can a computer solve?" This question should be simple enough to answer, right?

Consider the following algorithm for the list membership problem:

isMember(L,q)

```
1    Initialize i to 0
2    while L[i] ≠ q
3        Increment i
4    end while
5    if L[i] is q
6        then return YES
7        else return NO
```

Would a computer executing this algorithm solve the list membership problem? Suppose the computer is given an **instance** of the problem for which the correct answer is YES. In other words, the computer is given particular values for L and q such that q is in L. For example, when $L = [\text{"}Joe\text{"}, \text{"}Ted\text{"}]$ and $q = \text{"}Ted\text{"}$, the computer will certainly return YES. But what if the computer is given an instance for which the correct answer is NO? For example, suppose $L = [\text{"Willie"}]$ and $q = \text{"Hank"}$. The computer will start at the first element of the list, which is "Willie", and compare it to q, which is "Hank". They are not equal, so the computer will enter the body of the loop. The index i will be incremented. Now the computer will evaluate the loop condition using the next element of the list. There is no next element, but we must not care because our algorithm doesn't check. In some languages, like Java, the program will crash. In other languages, like C++, the program will just keep running forever or until something really bad happens. In either case, we would not say that this algorithm solves the list membership problem even though it solves it correctly for all instances of the problem for which YES is the correct output. We want our programs to work correctly for all instances of the problem, so we'll say a program solves a problem if it is guaranteed to return the correct answer for every instance.

Definition 1.2 *A computer* **solves** *a decision problem if it halts and returns the correct answer for every instance of the problem.*

That certainly seems like an obvious definition with an inordinate amount of preceding justification. However, if we are careful in setting things up, our lives will be a lot easier in the long run.

Now that we have decided that what we mean by "What can it do?" is "What decision problems can it solve?", you may think we have finished defining our question. However, there is more to do. For one thing, we need to understand how the inputs are presented to the computer. We have lots of different input devices: keyboards, mice, touch screens, hard disks, flash drives, DVDs, microphones, digital video cameras, etc. All input devices have one thing in common; they present information to the computer using some kind of encoding, usually some kind of binary encoding like ASCII or UNICODE. The keys that I touch on this keyboard are translated into signals that represent symbols. DVDs contain information encoded in binary. Video cameras take visual signals and "digitize" them. The actual encoding really doesn't matter much to us. What matters is that the input is encoded as a string of symbols and the computer is able to decode these strings.

We call the set of symbols that a computer might be given an **alphabet**. A sequence of symbols from an alphabet is called a **string over the alphabet**.

Definition 1.3 *An* **alphabet** *is a finite set of symbols. For example,* $\{0,1\}$ *and* $\{a,b,c\}$ *are two different alphabets. We will usually use the symbol* Σ *to represent the alphabet from which strings are formed.*

Definition 1.4 *A* **string over an alphabet** Σ *is a finite sequence of symbols from* Σ. *For example,* 0101 *is a string over both* $\{0,1\}$ *and* $\{0,1,2\}$, *but it* *is not a string over $\{a,b,c\}$. We use Σ^* to denote the set of all strings over alphabet Σ. If $\Sigma = \{0,1\}$, then $\Sigma^* = \{0,1\}^*$ is the set of all binary strings, including the empty string. The* **empty string,** *which we denote by ε, is a string defined over any alphabet. The empty string consists of zero symbols.*

Let's think again about a computer that solves a decision problem. It is given a string over some alphabet as input. It must answer YES if that string encodes a problem instance for which the correct answer is YES; it must answer NO otherwise. In other words, we can think of a decision problem as partitioning the set of problem instances into two subsets: the set of YES instances and the set of NO instances. The computer's job is to determine which of these two subsets contains the instance encoded by the input string.

For example, consider the following decision problem:

GIVEN: A string over $\{0,1\}$.

QUESTION: Is the string a valid ASCII encoding of the letter 'D' in either lower or upper case?

The set of YES instances is $\{01000100, 01100100\}$. The computer should answer YES when given a string from this set. For this problem, the alphabet, Σ, is $\{0,1\}$, while Σ^* is the set of all possible binary strings.

When talking about decision problems, we usually refer to a set of strings as a **language**.

Definition 1.5 *A* **language L over an alphabet Σ** *is a subset of Σ^*.*

Each of the following is a language over the alphabet $\Sigma = \{0,1\}$:

1. $L = \{0,01,11\}$.

2. $L = \{x : x \in \{0,1\}^*$ and x begins with $0\}$.

3. $L = \{0^n 1^n : n \geq 0\}$.

   (Wow, where did that $0^n 1^n$ notation come from? We use exponents to mean that a symbol is repeated a specified number of times. So 0^n means we have n 0's. The language $\{0^n 1^n : n \geq 0\}$ is the set of all strings consisting of some number of 0's followed by the same number of 1's. For example, $\varepsilon, 01, 0011$ and 000111 are all in the language, while 1, 011, and 0101 are not in the language.)

4. $L = \{G : G$ is a binary encoding of a directed graph with six vertices$\}$.

5. $L = \emptyset$.

   (This is the language, called the **empty language**, containing no strings whatsoever.)

6. $L = \{\varepsilon\}$.

   (It is important to notice that this language is not the empty language. The empty language contains no strings, while this language contains one string, namely the empty string. This will undoubtedly confuse you many times before you get used to it.)

If a computer solves a decision problem, then we say it **decides** the corresponding language of YES instances.

Definition 1.6 *A computer **decides a language** if for every given input string, the computer returns* YES *if the input string is in the language and* NO *if the input string is not in the language. Because of the correspondence between a language and a decision problem, we also say that the computer **decides the decision problem** described by the language.*

For example, consider the following decision problem:

GIVEN: A directed graph G.

QUESTION: Is there a cycle in G?

This problem can be described by the language consisting of strings G such that G is an encoding of a directed graph and the graph represented by G contains a cycle. In set notation, we would write this language as:

$L = \{G : G$ is a string that represents a graph containing a cycle.$\}$.

More specifically, we might encode a graph as an adjacency list with vertex numbers written in binary. For example, $[10,11][01][01,10]$ is an encoding of the graph in Figure 1.1, using an alphabet consisting of five symbols: 0, 1, a comma, a left square bracket, and a right square bracket. The first list enclosed in square brackets indicates that there are edges from vertex 1 to vertices 2 and 3, where the numbers are encoded in binary. The second list indicates that there

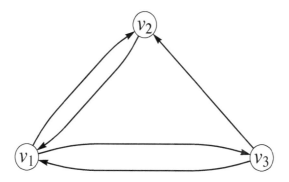

Figure 1.1: A directed graph that contains a cycle.

is an edge from vertex 2 to vertex 1. In general, we will leave the encoding scheme for a problem unspecified and simply assume that some reasonable encoding scheme is being used.

Can a computer decide the language corresponding to the cycle detection decision problem? We have to be more careful about what we mean by computer. For any graph G, can the computer I have at home tell whether G has a cycle? My computer has 8MB of RAM. What if the encoding of G is bigger? We could use the hard disk to store G. My computer has a 200MB hard disk. What if G is bigger? We could always store G on floppy disks (my computer doesn't have an optical drive or a USB port) and request more disks as we need them to perform the computation. Windows 3.1, which is what my machine at home is running, came on thirteen $5\frac{1}{4}$ inch floppy disks. The installation manager prompted for disks in no apparent order. "Insert disk 1. Insert Disk 13. Insert Disk 4. Insert Disk 2." We could do the same sort of thing when we write a program to solve the cycle detection problem.

Computer: "More memory is required to complete this job. Insert
             a new floppy and label it #2673873."

Computer: "Thank you."

Computer: "More memory is required to complete this job. Insert
             a new floppy and label it #2673874."

Me: "Wife, how long do we need to keep our tax informa-
             tion? I want to reuse another old floppy."

Computer:	"Thank you. Now insert floppy 25 for processing."
Computer:	"Thank you. Now insert floppy 2587687 for processing."
Computer:	"Thank you. Now insert a floppy with your tax information from 2005."
Me:	"Wife, have you been messing with my cycle detection program again?"

Assuming we can go out and buy more floppies as we need them, there is no limit to the amount of memory my computer can use. Therefore, my computer should be able to decide this language. But how would we *prove* that it can? We need an abstract definition of a computer that ignores all these issues of memory size, disk size, the price of floppies on eBay, etc. We need to define the word "computer", even though we already know what one is.

1.3   What is a computer?

We use computers all the time, but can we come up with a nice clean definition of a computer? How about this one:

> A computer takes input, processes it for some purpose, and produces output.

Under that definition, is your brain a computer? How about your digestive tract? As you might have guessed after seeing the trouble we went through to define "do", coming up with a definition of "computer" is not so easy. As with our definition of "do", it is best to start with a somewhat simplified definition. This will give us some practice constructing arguments about the properties of machines and languages.

Suppose you are working on a final project for a programming class the night before it is due (of course). You are trying to find a bug in your code. A huge thunderstorm has cut the power, so you can't use a debugger on your computer to help you. The professor is not one to put up with excuses, so you have decided (Heaven forbid) to trace through the execution of the program by hand. Unfortunately, every five minutes, you are interrupted by another one of your many friends inviting you to go out partying because their finals are over.

How much information would you have to record to make sure that after each interruption, you would be able to start over exactly where you left off?

Consider the program in Figure 1.2. (Obviously, this project was for an introductory course.)

SimpleProgram()

1   Initialize x to 0
2   Initialize i to 0
3   **while** $i < 10$
4   Set x to $x+i$
5   Increment i.
6   **end while**
7   **return** x

Figure 1.2: A simple program.

To trace the execution of this program under the described circumstances, you would need a candle or a flashlight. You would also need to keep track of the value of each variable and the number of the line you are about to execute. This is called the **state** of the program.

Definition 1.7 *The **state** of a program is a specification of the values for each of the variables and the line number that is about to be executed.*

For example, Figure 1.3 describes one possible state of the simple program above, while the subsequent sequence of states is shown in Figure 1.4.

line	i	x
3	7	21

Figure 1.3: A possible state of the simple program above.

This program can enter at most $(6)(11)(46)$ possible states because there are six lines of code, i can take on values from 0 to 10, and x is always in the range from 0 to 45, Actually, there are considerably fewer states since x is always the sum of the numbers from 1 to i or 1 to $i-1$, depending on which line number we are about to execute. The exact number of states, however, is

line	i	x
4	7	21
5	7	28
3	8	28
4	8	28
5	8	36
3	9	36
4	9	36
5	9	45
3	10	45
6	10	45

Figure 1.4: The sequence of states following the state described in Figure 1.3.

not important. The point is that the number of possible states is finite as long as the program uses a finite number of variables, the variables can take on only a finite number of values, and there are a finite number of lines in the program, which is the case in most final projects I have seen.

A machine with a finite and fixed amount of memory is called a **finite state machine**. We will use the finite state machine as our preliminary definition of computer. We still need to simplify things a little more, though, so we can practice reasoning about computation. Let's restrict the machine so that it reads one symbol from the input at a time and cannot go back to reread symbols that were already read once. This may at first seem entirely unrealistic, but when dealing with huge data files with petabytes worth of data like biological databases, internet search databases, etc., it is often desirable to make only one pass through the data. There are also some situations in which the data is transient, so we cannot make a second pass through the data. For example, if we were reading a continuous stream of X-ray data from deep space, we may not be able to store all of the data, so we would have to process it as we read it. The idea of severely limiting the number of passes an algorithm can make through the data forms the basis of what is called the **streaming model** of computation. The data in this case is referred to as a **data stream**.

If the machine is restricted to one pass through the data and it must keep track of information that appears in the input string, the machine needs to record the information in local variables – that is, as part of the state. For example, suppose we want to write a program to determine whether the number of 1's in the input string is even. Our program needs to solve the following decision problem:

GIVEN: A string of 0's and 1's.

QUESTION: Is the number of 1's in the string even?

In terms of languages, the language we want to decide is $L = \{x : x \in \{0,1\}^*$ and x contains an even number of 1's$\}$.
   Consider the algorithm in Figure 1.5. The algorithm certainly solves the

EvenOnesFirstTry()
1   Initialize *count* to 0
2   **while** input symbols remain to be read
3   Read the symbol
4   **if** the symbol read is a 1
5   **then** Increment *count* by 1
6   **end while**
7   **if** *count* is divisible by 2
8   **then return** YES
9   **else return** NO

Figure 1.5: An algorithm to decide the language $L = \{x : x \in \{0,1\}^*$ and x contains an even number of 1's$\}$.

problem and it makes a single pass through the data. Does it use a finite number of states? Actually, it does not. Because we have no limit on the number of 1's in the data stream, the variable *count* needs to be able to take on an infinite number of values for this algorithm to return the correct answer for every input. For suppose *count*'s maximum possible value is 2^{32} and the number of 1's in the data stream is $2^{32} + 1$. What is going to happen when *count* gets to 2^{32} and the algorithm tries to increment it? It depends on the particulars of the machine we are using and the programming language we have used to implement our algorithm. For example, the machine might set *count* back to 0, in which case *count* will be even while the number of 1's, $2^{32} + 1$, is odd (a bad thing). For a computer to solve the even number of 1's problem by executing this algorithm, it must be able to assign an infinite number of values to *count*. Therefore, it must be able to enter an infinite number of states – it is *not* a finite state machine.

Does that mean this problem cannot be solved by a finite state machine? If so, a finite state machine is a rather feeble machine indeed. What we have shown is that this particular algorithm requires an infinite number of states *not* that *every* algorithm to solve this problem requires an infinite number of states. For example, consider the algorithm in Figure 1.6.

EvenOnes-MoreEfficiently()
1   Initialize *isEven* to YES
2   **while** input symbols remain to be read
3   Read the next input symbol
4   **if** the symbol read is a 1
5   **then if** *isEven* is YES
6   **then** Set *isEven* to NO
7   **else** Set *isEven* to YES
8   **end while**
9   **return** *isEven*

Figure 1.6: Using a finite number of states, this algorithm decides the language $L = \{x : x \in \{0,1\}^*$ and x contains an even number of 1's$\}$.

Because this algorithm has a single variable and this variable can only take on two distinct values, a machine executing this algorithm can only enter a finite number of states. Therefore, the even number of 1's problem can be solved using a finite state machine.

1.4   Recap

The main question we set out to answer is, what is a computer and what can it do? We modified the second part of the question to be, what problems can computers solve? We then restricted ourselves to decision problems – problems that require a yes or no answer. We saw that we could encode decision problems as languages and changed the question once more to, what languages can computers decide? We also decided to start with a definition of a simple computer. As a first pass, we considered machines that have a finite and fixed amount of memory. These machines can enter a finite number of possible states. So our question has become, what languages can finite state machines decide? We begin to answer this question in the next chapter.

Chapter 2

Finite State Machines

2.1 Introduction

In Chapter 1 we saw one problem, the even number of 1's problem, that can be solved using a finite state machine. Can we come up with a simple problem that *cannot* be solved using a finite state machine? Recall that our initial algorithm for the even number of 1's problem in Figure 1.5 on page 11 required an infinite number of states because it counted the number of 1's in the data stream. Counting the number of 1's requires us to be able to count to an arbitrarily large number because the number of 1's in the data stream has no known upper bound. With a finite number of states, however, we have a limit on how high we can count.

Can we define a problem that requires us to count something that has no known upper bound? Suppose we want to test the data stream to see if it consists of some number of 0's followed by exactly the same number of 1's. For example, as part of your school's career development program, you go on a tour of a top-secret research lab. On the door to the lab, there is some sort of entry detection device that transmits a 0 for each person who enters. Once a person enters the lab, he or she cannot leave until the tour is over. When the tour is over, the exit door transmits a 1 for each person who leaves. The security system needs to read the transmissions from the door to make sure that the number of people who entered the room is the same as the number of people who exited the room. We have no idea how many people will enter the room, so there is no upper bound on the number of 0's in the data stream. OK, maybe it is a little unrealistic to say there is no upper bound on the number of

0's in the data stream since there is certainly an upper bound on the number of people on the planet. To make this more realistic, assume it is also possible for aliens from another dimension to enter the room. Since we do not know how many aliens there are, there is no known upper bound on the number of "people" entering the room at one time. The decision problem is defined formally as follows:

GIVEN: A binary string (i.e., a string over the alphabet $\{0, 1\}$).

QUESTION: Does the string consist of some number of 0's followed by the same number of 1's?

How would we write an algorithm to solve this problem? We could count the number of 0's and the number of 1's and test to see if they are equal, but we cannot do that with a finite number of states because the numbers have no upper limit. Perhaps we could keep track of all the 0's in memory and match them against the 1's as we read the 1's. We could even just put the 0's on a stack and pop them off as we read the 1's, making sure we reach the end of the stack at the same time that we reach the end of the data stream. Unfortunately, this would require a stack of infinite size because we do not know a limit on the number of 0's we will see.

Maybe we cannot solve this using a finite number of states. Let's think about how we would prove to ourselves that this problem cannot be decided by a finite state machine. As we saw with the even number of 1's problem, we cannot just come up with one algorithm to solve the problem and show that that particular algorithm requires an infinite number of states. We must show that all algorithms for this problem require an infinite number of states. That sounds hard. Maybe we should just stop here and forget all about figuring out what computers can and cannot do.

We could write a book about parrots instead. That would probably be pretty interesting. It could even be more useful, especially to people who have parrots as pets. We could spend an entire chapter on the difference between parakeets and parrots. Another chapter could talk about parrots as the pirate's best friend. Maybe we could include another chapter on parrot recipes: parrot soup, parrot cordon blue – wait, what? Animal rights activists would protest outside our houses; friends would avoid us; relatives would disown us.

We should stick to theoretical computer science. It is much less controversial and most people don't know what we are talking about, even if we include recipes. However, we need to do something to make things easier on ourselves. It often helps to draw a picture, so Figure 2.1 on page 18 shows a picture.

2.2 Focus on the states

Let's think about what is really essential in describing a finite state machine. Consider the structure of the efficient algorithm we designed in Chapter 1 for the even number of 1's problem, which we include again here:

EvenOnes-MoreEfficiently()
1 initialize *isEven* to YES
2 **while** input symbols remain to be read
3   read the next input symbol
4   **if** the symbol read is a 1
5   **then if** *isEven* is YES
6   **then** set *isEven* to NO
7   **else** set *isEven* to YES
8 **end while**
9 **return** *isEven*

This algorithm uses a finite number of states. Because of the way we have restricted access to the data, all of the algorithms that can be executed by a finite state machine are going to have this same general structure:

1 Initialize the internal variables
2 **while** input symbols remain to be read
3   change the internal variables based on the next input symbol
4 **end while**
5 **return** the result based on the values of the internal variables.

A finite state machine starts by initializing the internal variables. In other words, the machine starts by initializing the state. It then reads input symbols from the data stream one at a time. Each time it reads a symbol, the machine goes through some sort of processing to modify the internal variables. Depending on the problem, there may be a lot of processing or very little processing going on here. Regardless of the complexity of this processing, however, the net result is that the values of the internal variables and the line number have been changed – that is, the machine has changed states based on the input

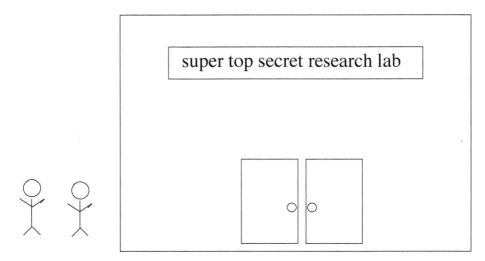

Figure 2.1: A picture.

symbol read. Finally, the return value is determined by the value of the internal variables. Therefore, we have a three step process:

1. Initialize the state;

2. While there are input symbols left in the data stream, change the state based on the next input symbol;

3. Return YES or NO based on the state in which we find the machine when the data stream ends.

In executing the EvenOnes-MoreEfficiently algorithm, the state of the machine is initialized by setting *isEven* to YES. When the machine processes an input symbol, it either leaves *isEven* alone because the input symbol is a 0, or it changes the value of *isEven* because the input symbol is a 1. At the end, the machine returns YES if *isEven* is YES and NO otherwise.

It really is sometimes easier to think about finite state machines if we have a picture, so Figure 2.2 shows a diagram describing the states of the machine and how they change based on the input. Each node in the diagram represents a state of the internal variables. In particular, node Y represents the state in which the value of *isEven* is YES. Node N represents the state in which the value of *isEven* is NO. The edges indicate how the machine moves from state

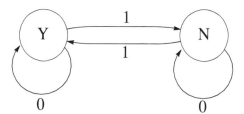

Figure 2.2: A simplified view of the states of a machine that decides the language $\{x : x \in \{0, 1\}^*, x$ has an even number of 1's$\}$.

to state based on the input. For example, the edge labeled 0 from Y to Y indicates that when a 0 is read in state Y, the machine stays in state Y. This reflects the fact that the value of *isEven* does not change when a 0 is read from the data stream. The edge labeled 1 from Y to N indicates that when a 1 is read from the data stream and *isEven* is YES, the value of *isEven* changes to NO.

For a diagram like this to be a complete representation of our machine, it needs to indicate two more things:

1. the state in which the machine starts;

2. at the end of the input, whether the machine returns YES or NO.

In the example above, the machine starts in state Y because *isEven* is initialized to YES in Line 1. If there is no more input to read and the machine is in state Y, the machine should return YES. Otherwise, the machine should return NO. We will call the state Y an **accepting state** since we can think of the machine as either accepting the input as a YES instance or rejecting the input as a NO instance.

We will denote the start state with an edge from nowhere labeled "START." A double circle on a state indicates that the state is an accepting state. Figure 2.3 describes the machine above with the start and accepting states indicated. This type of diagram is called a **state transition diagram** because it tells us how to get from one state to another based on the input. Note that state Y is both the start state and an accepting state. This implies, among other things, that the empty string is accepted by this machine.

The machine described in Figure 2.3 is called a **finite state automaton**.

Definition 2.1 *A* **finite state automaton** *is described by:*

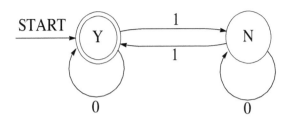

Figure 2.3: The state transition diagram for a machine that decides the language $\{x \in \{0,1\}^* : x$ has an even number of 1's$\}$.

1. *A set of states, one of which is designated as the unique start state;*

2. *A labeling of the states such that each state is labeled as either an accepting or a non-accepting state;*

3. *A transition rule that describes how the machine changes state based on the input symbols read.*

The automaton processes each input symbol one at a time. Once a particular input symbol has been read, the automaton cannot go back and read the symbol again. We say a finite state automaton, M, **accepts** *an input string if, after starting in the start state and processing the entire input string, M is in an accepting state. The* **language decided** *by M is $L(M) = \{x : M$ accepts $x\}$. A language that can be decided by a finite automaton is said to be* **regular**.

Before reading the next section, it is important to become more comfortable with finite state machines. Try the exercises below and read the solutions at the back of the book – in that order!!

Exercise 2.1 *Design finite automata for the following languages:*

a) *$L = \{x \in \{0,1\}^* :$ the length of x is a multiple of $4\}$.*

b) *$L = \{x \in \{0,1\}^* : x$ ends with a 1 followed by at least two 0's$\}$.*

c) *$L = \{x \in \{0,1\}^* : x$ does not contain two consecutive 0's$\}$.*

2.3 Deciding $\{0^n1^n : n \geq 0\}$ using a finite number of states... or not

Now that we have had a chance to design finite automata to decide a number of languages, let's think again about whether a finite state machine can decide the language $L = \{0^n1^n : n \geq 0\}$. Since there are an infinite number of possible strings of initial 0's and we are limited to a finite number of possible states, at least two strings of initial 0's must take the machine to the same state. This is known as the *pigeonhole principle*. If we have more pigeons than holes, at least two pigeons must be put in the same hole (assuming you are putting pigeons in holes in the first place, for which I am hard pressed to find a reason). For concreteness, let's suppose that after reading two 0's, the machine is in the same state as it would be after reading five 0's. Let's call this state Frisbee. Once the machine enters state Frisbee, it does not know how it got there. It could have gotten there by reading two 0's, or it could have gotten there by reading five 0's. What should the machine do if it reads two 1's after it enters state Frisbee? Figure 2.4 illustrates the situation we are considering.[1]

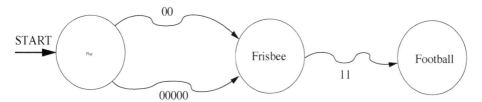

Figure 2.4: States in a hypothetical machine that decides the language $\{0^n1^n : n \geq 0\}$.

The squiggly line between the start state and Frisbee labeled 00 indicates that in reading 00 the machine follows some sequence of states that leads to state Frisbee. The squiggly line labeled 00000 indicates that in reading 00000 the machine follows a potentially different sequence of states that also leads to state Frisbee. The squiggly line labeled 11 indicates that after entering Frisbee and then reading two more 1's, the machine enters state Football.

Should the machine answer YES or NO if the data stream ends when the machine is in state Football? To get to state Football, the machine might have

---

[1]It is common knowledge among computer science professors that textbooks are full of subliminal messages. Whatever you do, do not read Cormen et al.'s Algorithms textbook backwards.

read 00 followed by 11, in which case the machine should answer YES because 0011 is in L. But the machine also might have read 00000 followed by 11, in which case the machine should answer NO because 0000011 is not in L. When the machine is in state Football, the machine has no idea how it got there. The decisions that the machine makes after entering state Football are independent of the symbols that were read before the machine entered state Football. The machine either has to answer YES every time it is in this state when the data stream ends, or the machine has to answer NO every time it is in this state when the data stream ends. Either way, the machine is going to answer the question incorrectly for at least one input. If the machine answers YES in state Football, then the machine will answer YES to 0000011. If the machine answers NO in state Football, then the machine will answer NO to 0011. This is a bad thing. What does it mean? If 00 and 00000 take the machine to the same state, the machine does not correctly decide the language $L = \{0^n 1^n : n \geq 0\}$.

Nothing in our argument depends on having two zeros and five zeros. We could have made the same argument for three zeros and 14,482 zeros. In other words, if we take an arbitrary pair of strings 0^m and 0^n with $m \neq n$, the two strings cannot possibly take the machine to the same state. If they do, the machine is going to answer incorrectly for at least one input. But that means each string in the set $\{0^n : n \geq 0\}$ takes the machine to a different state. Since this is an infinite set, the machine must be able to enter an infinite number of states.

What we have just argued is that no matter what algorithm we come up with to solve this problem, a machine executing this algorithm must be able to enter an infinite number of states. In other words, to be able to solve this problem, the machine cannot have a finite and fixed amount of memory at its disposal. It must have the ability to obtain more memory when it needs to – with a visit to eBay if necessary.

> Tour Guide: Ladies and Gentleman...and Aliens. We are experiencing technical difficulties with the exit door's security mechanism. It will not let anyone exit until we provide additional memory. A staff member is submitting a bid on eBay as we speak to get the equipment necessary to rectify this situation. In the mean time, relax and enjoy the donuts... uh... sorry... we ran out of donuts.

Chapter 3

Turing Machines

3.1 Introduction

We need a better definition of "computer" because the finite state automaton is not an adequate model for an in-depth study of computation. The problem of counting entries to and exits from a room seems like a problem we should be able to solve with a computer, yet it cannot be solved by a machine with a finite and fixed amount of memory. In our definition of computer, we need to make sure we have no fixed limit on the amount of memory the machine can use. You can think of the machine as having infinite memory, but it may be better to think of the machine as being able to request more memory as it needs it.

What kind of memory should this machine have? In the computers we use everyday, memory comes in many types: random access memory, hard disks, flash drives, floppy disks, DVDs, tapes, etc. Furthermore, each type of memory has its own access method. For example, with a random access memory, we can access any piece of memory directly without having to look at any other piece of memory. On the other hand, with a tape, we must move through the memory sequentially – to read the 10th piece of memory, we have to read through pieces 1 through 9 first. With a hard disk, we obtain chunks (or blocks) of memory at a time, but we can move around through the blocks in a semi-random order.

To make sure that our answer to the question "What is a computer and what can it do?" is not dependent on the storage media, let's assume we have a simple access method – sequential access like that of a tape. All of the other media mentioned above can simulate this type of access. This turns out not to be too big of a deal, but again, if we are careful in setting things up, our lives will be much easier in the long run (although our lives will often seem much more difficult initially).

To make sure our definition does not provide too much power, let's assume that we still have a very simple machine similar to that of a finite automaton in that the machine has a finite internal memory. However, we will augment this machine with an unlimited external memory in the form of a read-write tape.[1] The beginning of the tape will hold the input string. The remainder of the tape will be blank. The tape is divided into squares, with one symbol per square. The machine can only manipulate the contents of one tape square at a time. It will keep a pointer to the tape square with which it is currently working. This pointer is called the tape's **head**.

The machine we have described is called a **Turing machine** because it was introduced as a theoretical model of computation by Alan Turing in 1936. Figure 3.1 shows a picture.

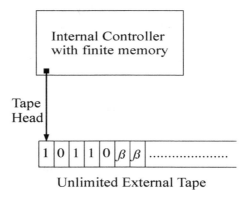

Unlimited External Tape

Figure 3.1: A Turing machine. β represents a blank tape square. The dots in the figure indicate that the blank tape squares go on forever.

The β in the sixth square of the tape in Figure 3.1 indicates that the square is blank. In other words, a square contains a special symbol, which we denote with β, if there is no input symbol in that square. If we move through the input

---

[1]During the first week of my first job after college, I worked with a tape drive that was about the size of a large refrigerator. I remember thinking that it cost about $100,000, but that can't be right. It was expensive, though, and I broke it.

starting at the first square, we know we are at the end of the input when we reach the first blank.

How do we program a Turing machine? Rather than talking about states like we did with finite automata, let's go back to dealing with computer programs the way we are used to dealing with computer programs: as sequences of instructions. However, there is one very important difference between the way we usually think about programs and the way we will think about Turing machine programs, at least initially. When we write regular computer programs, we take it for granted that we can store programs in our computer's memory and have the computer execute the program. This type of programming relies on some sort of underlying architecture that can read and execute programs. That Turing machines have this capability is too big an assumption to make in our initial definition. Until we convince ourselves that our simple Turing machine model is powerful enough to execute stored programs, we will think of each program we write as a description of a physical machine rather than a program to be given to a physical machine to execute. Therefore, unlike the computer programs that we are used to writing, each Turing machine program corresponds to a different machine. In such a world, labs for computer science courses would be very different. "Class, we have lab tomorrow, so bring your soldering tools ... and don't forget your infinite tapes." To emphasize that each program is a description of a particular machine, we will, for the moment, talk about designing Turing machines rather than writing programs for Turing machines.

To keep our Turing machines simple, the machine will support a small set of simple instructions. A description of a Turing machine will consist of a finite sequence of instructions from this set. In addition, each instruction in the sequence may have a label, which is optional.

The machine needs to be able to:

1. Read the tape and make decisions based on what is read;

2. Modify the contents of the tape;

3. Move left and right on the tape;

4. Indicate whether it accepts or rejects the input string.

To accomplish these tasks, the machine will have the following four instructions:

1. `if head is` *symbol* `then goto` *Label₁* `else goto` *Label₂*

   The `if-goto` instructions works as follows. If the tape square pointed to by the head contains the specified symbol, the machine will move to the line labeled *Label₁* in the program; otherwise, the machine will move to the line labeled *Label₂*.

2. `Write` *symbol*

   The `Write` instruction writes the specified symbol in the tape square pointed to by the head.

3. `Move` *direction*

   The `Move` instruction moves the tape head in the specified direction (either left or right). If the tape head is already at the leftmost tape square, the tape head does not move at all when a `Move Left` instruction is executed.

4. `Return` *result*:

   The `Return` instruction causes the machine to halt and return the specified result (either YES or NO).

The Turing machine executes its instructions sequentially unless the `if-goto` instruction specifies otherwise.

Notice that we have not provided this "programming language" with an assignment statement or any variables for that matter. This is intentional; it keeps us honest in terms of the amount of internal memory used by a machine. If we had variables, we might, without realizing it, get ourselves into a situation where our Turing machine required an unlimited amount of internal memory because one of the variables could take on an infinite number of possible values. We might, for example, do something completely unreasonable like maintain a counter.

We have also not provided any way for our programs to call subroutines. This too is intentional since subroutine calls require the machine to maintain a call stack. Recursive subroutines calls could be nested to an arbitrary depth, which would require a call stack that is not fixed in size. Keeping such a stack internally would violate our restriction that there is a fixed amount of internal memory. With a finite number of instructions, no variables, and no mechanism for invoking subroutines, each Turing machine is limited to a finite and fixed amount of internal memory.

Let's try to design some simple Turing machines. Suppose we want to decide the language $L = \{x : x \in \{0,1\}^*$ and x starts with $1\}$. All we need to do is look at the symbol pointed to by the head initially and accept if it is a 1. Here is a description of our machine:

```
        if head is 1 then goto ACCEPT else goto REJECT
REJECT: Return NO
ACCEPT: Return YES
```

OK, so that example was trivial. How about designing a Turing machine to decide the language: $L = \{x : x \in \{0,1\}^*$ and x starts and ends with the same symbol$\}$? For this problem, we could use the following general algorithm:

MatchFirstAndLast:
1   read the first symbol and remember it
2   move through the remaining input until we get to the last symbol
3   **if** the first symbol matches the last symbol
4   **then return** YES
5   **else return** NO

How can we translate this algorithm into a description of a Turing machine? The first issue we need to deal with is figuring out a way to remember the first symbol read. There are two types of memory available to us. We have a limited internal memory and we have an unlimited tape. Since we only need to remember one symbol, we should be able to use the internal memory. But we don't have variables. The only way to alter the internal memory of the machine is to move from one line in the program to another. Therefore, to remember the first input symbol, we need to create a separate section of our code for each of the two cases. We will have two sections of our code, READ-0 and READ-1, to indicate which symbol was read.

The first instruction in our Turing machine program is then:

```
if head is 1 then goto READ-1 else goto READ-0
```

Regardless of whether we have read a 0 or a 1, we need to get to the end of the input to find the last input symbol. The first blank on the tape is directly to the right of the last input symbol, so if we move to the right until we see the first blank, we can then move left one square to read the last input symbol.

```
          if head is 1 then goto READ-1 else goto READ-0
READ-1: Move Right
          if head is 0 then goto READ-1 else goto ELSE-1
ELSE-1: if head is 1 then goto READ-1 else goto END-1
END-1:  Move Left
          if head is 1 then goto ACCEPT else goto REJECT
READ-0: Move Right
          if head is 0 then goto READ-0 else goto ELSE-0
ELSE-0: if head is 1 then goto READ-0 else goto END-0
END-0:  Move Left
          if head is 0 then goto ACCEPT else goto REJECT
ACCEPT: return YES
REJECT: return NO
```

Figure 3.2: A Turing machine program to decide the language $L = \{x : x \in \{0,1\}^*$ and x starts and ends with the same symbol$\}$.

The Turing machine code in Figure 3.2 should do the trick. The line labeled READ-1 is used as the beginning of a loop that moves the tape head to the end of the input. The loop exits to the line labeled END-1 when we reach the first blank tape square.

Here are some exercises to give you a better feel for some of the issues involved in describing Turing machines:

Exercise 3.1 *How would the code in Figure 3.2 handle an empty input string?*

Exercise 3.2 *By expanding the code in Figure 3.2, describe a Turing machine that determines whether the input string is a palindrome, that is, the string reads the same forward as it does backward.*

Exercise 3.3 *As demonstrated by the code in Figure 3.2, we can find the last input symbol by moving right until we reach the first blank and then moving left one square. But what if we then needed to move back to the first input symbol? There is nothing to the left of the first input symbol, so we can't move beyond it to the left and then move back one tape square to the right analogous to what we do with the last input symbol. The way our Turing machine is defined, when the head is at the position of the first input symbol, a* Move Left *does nothing* *at all and provides no indication that we are already at the left end of the tape. How can we design a Turing machine program capable of determining that it has reached the leftmost input symbol?*

Making our lives easier.

Certainly this is not the easiest language for implementing algorithms, but it has a certain amount of expressive power. For example, we are using the `if-goto` to implement repeat-until loops (also known as do-while loops) starting on the lines labeled READ-1 and READ-0. This is similar to the way people used to code before the constructs of structured programming made their way into high level programming languages. If we had repeat-until loops and standard if-then-else statements that executed blocks of code, the code in Figure 3.2 could be written like the code below:

```
1   if head is 1
2      then begin
3              repeat
4                 Move Right
5              until the head is β
6              Move Left
7              if head is 1
8                 then return YES
9                 else return NO.
10          end
11     else begin
12              repeat
13                 Move Right
14              until the head is β
15              Move Left
16              if head is 0
17                 then return YES
18                 else return NO.
19          end
```

Why not add these constructs to our language so we don't have to deal with all the goto's and labels, which can make things pretty confusing? In other words, we will add the following three structured programming constructs to our Turing machine programming language:

1. if-then-else

> **if** head is x
> **then begin**
>   ⟨execute some block of code⟩
> **end**
> **else begin**
>   ⟨execute a different block of code⟩
> **end**

As with many programming languages, we will dispense with the **begin** and **end** when only a single line of code is to be executed. In that case, the if-then-else construct will be:

> **if** head is x
> **then** ⟨execute some line of code⟩
> **else** ⟨execute some line of code⟩

2. while loop

> **while** head is x
>   ⟨execute some block of code⟩
> **end while**

3. repeat-until loop

> **repeat**
>   ⟨execute some block of code⟩
> **until** head is x

It shouldn't be hard to see that for any Turing machine description written with the loop and if-then-else constructs above, there is an equivalent Turing machine description that uses only the four basic instructions. In other words, these additional constructs are purely for notational convenience. They do not add any power to the Turing machine model. When describing Turing machines using these constructs, however, we need to be careful that the conditions on the if statements and loops depend only on the current contents of the tape square pointed to by the head.

Exercise 3.4 *For each of the structured programming constructs above, write equivalent code using the four basic instructions.*

3.2 Turing machines can count!

Do Turing machines have more power than finite automata? We saw that one of the crucial limitations of finite automata is their inability to count to an arbitrarily large number. Can a Turing machine count? If a Turing machine is going to count without a limit on the size of the counter, it is going to have to use the tape to keep track of the counter.

Let's write a small portion of the code for a Turing machine to increment a counter, ignoring the input for the moment. We'll keep track of the counter in binary using a # to mark the beginning of the counter. In other words, we will have a new symbol that is not part of the input alphabet but that the machine can write to the tape. We'll call the set of symbols that the machine can read from and write to the tape the **tape alphabet**. The tape alphabet must be fixed and finite for each machine.

First, we need to initialize the counter. This is done by writing # to mark the beginning of the counter, moving right to write 0, and then moving left to get back to the beginning of the counter. Here is the code:

    Write #
    Move Right
    Write 0
    Move Left

Notice that as we add bits, new bits will appear on the right side of the counter. Why in the world is that important you ask? Because, we need to decide whether we want the high order bit to be on the left or on the right. When we normally write numbers, our numbers grow to the left, the newest digit is put to the left of the other digits. On the tape, however, the counter is going to grow the other way, so our counter will be backwards. In other words, 10011 will represent $25 = 1 \cdot 2^0 + 1 \cdot 2^3 + 1 \cdot 2^4$ rather than $19 = 1 \cdot 2^4 + 1 \cdot 2^1 + 1 \cdot 2^0$.

Below is the code to increment the counter, assuming we start at the # delineating the beginning of the counter. Note that we use code highlighting to emphasize that our description uses the structured programming constructs rather than sticking to the four basic instructions. The double slashes denote comments just as in C++ and Java.

```
1   Move Right
    // change all 1's to 0's until first 0 is found
2   while head is 1
3       Write 0
4       Move Right
5   end while
    // change the first 0 to a 1
6   Write 1
    // get back to the beginning of the counter
7   repeat
8       Move Left
9   until head is #
```

The first while loop increments the counter by turning each 1 at the beginning of the counter to 0. It stops when the machine reaches the first 0 in the counter or the machine reaches a blank, which indicates the end of the counter. A 1 is then written over the 0 or the blank to increment the counter. The second loop moves back to the # that signifies the beginning of the counter.

Exercise 3.5 *Design a Turing machine to increment the counter using only the four basic instructions.*

Exercise 3.6 *Design a Turing machine to decrement the counter. (You can choose whether to use only the four basic instructions or the structured programming constructs.)*

How could we use the code above to count the number of 0's in the input string? We could keep the counter on the tape after the input. Each time the machine sees a 0 in the input string, the machine would have to move to the counter portion of the tape, increment the counter, and then move back to where it was in the input string. All of this moving back and forth on the input tape is really tedious and annoying and I have a very strong aversion to tedious and annoying programming.[2] What would make our lives much easier is to have a second tape to keep track of the counter. If we have one external tape of potentially unlimited length, why not have two?

---

[2]That is why I quit that job at the company where I broke the tape drive.

So, instead of just having a single tape, let's say we have an input tape, which initially holds the input, and a work tape, which is initially blank, for storing things like counters and other stuff we need to keep track of. The instruction set needs to be altered slightly to deal with multiple tapes. In particular, any time we look at the contents of one of the tapes, write a symbol on one of the tapes, or move the head on one of the tapes, we have to specify which tape we are talking about. Here is a complete description of our Turing machine to count the number of 0's in the input string:

```
   // initialize the counter on the work tape
 1 Write # on work tape
 2 Move Right on work tape
 3 Write 0 on work tape
 4 Move Left on work tape

   // read and count symbols until the first blank
 5 while the head on input tape is not β
 6    if the head on input tape is 0
 7      then begin
                // increment the counter on the work tape
 8         Move Right
 9         while the head on work tape is 1
10             Write 0 on work tape
11             Move Right on work tape
12         end while
13         Write 1 on work tape
14         repeat
15             Move Left on work tape
16         until the head on work tape is #
17      end
18    Move Right on input tape
19 end while
```

Now that we know how to count, we can design a Turing machine to decide the language $L = \{0^n 1^n : n \geq 0\}$. Let's keep a counter on the work tape. As the machine reads the 0's, it increments the counter. As the machine reads the 1's, it decrements the counter. If the counter is 0 when all of the input has been read, then the input string is in the language. (Of course, we also need to verify that the input has the correct format – that is, all of the 0's come before any of the 1's.)

Exercise 3.7 *Write the complete description of a Turing machine that decides the language $L = \{0^n 1^n : n \geq 0\}$ using a second tape as a work tape to keep track of the counter.*

While having more than one tape simplified our Turing machine description, we could have solved this problem even if our machine had only one tape. In fact, any Turing machine with multiple tapes can be simulated by a machine with a single tape, so having more than one tape does not allow a machine to solve problems that could not be solved with a one-tape Turing machine.

Exercise 3.8 *Show how a Turing machine with one tape can simulate a Turing machine with k tapes, for any fixed number k. Remember the set of symbols that can be written to the tape is not restricted to the input alphabet. As long as we have a finite number of tape symbols, we can write whatever symbols we like to the tape. We could even have symbols in our tape alphabet to represent k other symbols. For example, in a single tape square we could write a compound symbol, $(0, 1, 1, 1, 0, \beta, 1)$, to represent the contents of the tape squares of seven different tapes. Though I typed 15 symbols to write this compound symbol, to a Turing machine this will be a single symbol. (Imagine a civilization of aliens who use only one symbol, a straight line. Residents of that civilization would think that H requires three symbols, yet we think of H as a single symbol.) As long as there are a finite number of tapes on the machine with multiple tapes, there are a finite number of different symbols in the tape alphabet of the one-tape machine.*

Exercise 3.9 *Suppose we allow a Turing machine with k tapes to work with all k tapes simultaneously. This modified Turing machine is called a* **multi-tape Turing machine***. Show how a Turing machine with k tapes that is restricted to working with one tape at a time can simulate a multi-tape Turing machine that has k tapes. From this exercise and the last exercise, we can conclude that any multi-tape Turing machine can be simulated by a one-tape Turing machine. Therefore, the multi-tape Turing machine does not solve any decision problems beyond those that can be solved by a one-tape Turing machine.*

3.3   The Church-Turing Thesis

We have a machine with four instructions, a finite internal memory, and an unlimited external tape. Is this a pretty good definition of a computer? Does it adequately capture the true power of the computers we use? In other words, are there any decision problems that can be solved using a computer that cannot be solved using a Turing machine? No! There is no purely mechanical computing device that is more powerful than a Turing machine. This statement is referred to as the **Church-Turing Thesis**.

The Church-Turing Thesis: Any problem that can be solved by a purely mechanical computing device can be solved by a Turing machine.[3]

Are you kidding me? This machine with four primitive instructions is as powerful as a the most powerful computer in the world? Well, it depends a bit on what we mean by "as powerful." For our purposes, the answer is yes. It might take a little longer for a Turing machine to solve a problem, but if a computer can solve the problem, then so can a Turing machine. We've already seen that Turing machines can count. If they can count, they can add. If they can add, they can multiply. If they can multiply, they can control NASA's Deep Space One spacecraft. OK, so moving from multiplication to controlling a spacecraft is a giant leap. There is a lot more than just multiplication going on in a spacecraft. But when you think about it, any computer has a relatively small instruction set and some kind of memory, which may come in various forms. The individual instructions that a computer can execute are fairly simple. All they do is move bits around in memory in some systematic way. These instructions could certainly be performed by a finite sequence of Turing machine instructions. It would not necessarily be easy to translate the source code written in our favorite programming language to Turing machine code, but it can be done. Still, there are a couple of things about programming Turing machines that seem very different from programming regular computers. First, we don't allow variables or subroutines. Second, we have to use a soldering iron instead of a keyboard to "write" programs because we need to create a separate physical machine for each problem we wish to solve.

The variable issue can be resolved easily with multiple tapes. Multiple tapes, of course, are not required to support variables since anything we can do

---

[3]There is some controversy over the best way to state the Church-Turing Thesis and its implications. See the notes at the end of the book for references.

with multiple tapes can be done with one tape. Having multiple tapes, however, makes it easier. For each variable in our program, we could have a different tape. To assign a value to a variable, we just need to change the contents of that variable's tape. As long as there are a finite number of variables, we will have a finite number of tapes.

The soldering problem is a little stickier. To retire our soldering tools once and for all, we need to design a Turing machine that can read and execute any other Turing machine program. A Turing machine with this capability is called a **universal Turing machine**. Once we have a universal Turing machine, we can go back to our luxurious life hammering out code on keyboards and having surgery for carpel tunnel syndrome.

Let's create a universal Turing machine that has three tapes. On the input tape will be a program P and an input string w to give to P. Since any k-tape Turing machine can be simulated by a one-tape Turing machine, let's assume that P is a description of a one-tape machine. The first thing our universal machine will do is copy P to the second tape, leaving only the input string w on the input tape. Then the universal machine needs to walk through the instructions in P on the second tape, manipulating the input tape based on the current instruction in P. After one of P's instructions is executed, the universal machine moves to the instruction in P that should be executed next. In the case of a `Move` or `Write` instruction, that means moving to the next instruction on the tape. In the case of an `if-goto` instruction, the universal machine needs to find the instruction with the correct label. The label can be written to the third tape and the universal machine can walk through P comparing this label with the label of each instruction in P. In the case of a `Return` instruction, the universal machine should itself return the value indicated by P's `Return` instruction. Let's leave the details for the exercises.

Exercise 3.10 *Write a complete description of a universal Turing machine.*

Our construction of a universal Turing machine demonstrates that Turing machines have the power that we have come to expect from computers, namely that the computer can execute programs that are stored in memory. The construction could even be modified to allow calls to subroutines with parameter passing using an additional tape to maintain a call stack. Thus, a seemingly complex programming structure can be built on top of a very simple machine model. Once we accept this, we no longer have to confine ourselves to the tedium of programming Turing machines. We are free to talk about algorithms informally, knowing that the formal underpinnings provide us with a solid theoretical foundation. In other words, we aren't cheating when we write algorithms in pseudocode.

3.4 So what exactly is a computer anyway?

Let's briefly summarize the above discussion and define some terminology that we will need in the remainder of the book. We have defined a Turing machine as follows:

Definition 3.1 *A* **Turing machine** *consists of an internal memory that has a finite and fixed size and an external memory in the form of an unlimited tape. Each machine can be described by a program consisting of a sequence of labeled instructions. The machine supports four instructions:*

1. `if head is` *symbol* `then goto` *Label$_1$* `else goto` *Label$_2$*

2. `Write` *symbol*

3. `Move` *direction*

4. `Return` *result*

The input string to the Turing machine is provided on the beginning of the tape. Any tape square beyond the input string contains a special symbol, β, to represent a blank. The Turing machine begins at the first instruction and executes instructions in sequential order unless otherwise directed by an `if-goto` *instruction. The machine halts after executing a* `Return` *instruction, returning the value specified.*

Definition 3.2 *The set of possible symbols from which the input string is created is called the machine's* **input alphabet**. *The set of symbols that can be read from and written to the tape is called the* **tape alphabet**. *The tape alphabet includes but is not restricted to the input alphabet. Both the input and tape alphabets are fixed and finite for each machine.*

Definition 3.3 *A* **universal Turing machine** *is a Turing machine that, given an input string w and a description of a Turing machine program P, can execute P with w as P's input string.*

As with finite automata, we will talk about the set of strings that are accepted by the Turing machine. However, since a Turing machine may not halt for all inputs, we will not say the Turing machines *decides* this language. Instead, we use the term **recognizes**, reserving "decides" for the case of a Turing machine that always halts. This is consistent with our original definition of "decides" (Definition 1.6).

Definition 3.4 *The language* **recognized** *by a Turing machine M, denoted $L(M)$, is the set of strings for which the Turing machine returns* YES. *We say a language L and its corresponding decision problem are* **recognizable** *if $L = L(M)$ for some Turing machine M. We say a language L and its corresponding decision problem are* **decidable** *if $L = L(M)$ for some Turing machine M that halts for all inputs. (Note that any decidable language is also recognizable.)*

The Church-Turing Thesis states that any problem that can be solved by a purely mechanical computing device can be solved by a Turing machine. Therefore, when we use the term "computer", we mean any mechanical device with power equivalent to that of a Turing machine. If we want to answer the question "What can a computer do?", we need only determine what problems can be solved by Turing machines. Since we are initially restricting ourselves to decision problems, our task becomes one of determining which problems can be decided by Turing machines.

We finally have a good definition of "computer". Now we have to find out what one can do.

Chapter 4

Unsolvable Problems

4.1 Introduction

So what kinds of problems can Turing machines solve? Maybe a better question would be, are there any problems that Turing machines cannot solve? Consider the following decision problem, which is called the **ACCEPTANCE PROBLEM**.

GIVEN: Two strings, P and w.

QUESTION: Is P the source code for a program that accepts input string w?

How could we design an algorithm to solve this problem? First, let's make sure we understand the problem. We need to design an algorithm that takes two inputs. The first input should be the source code for a program P. If it is not valid source code, our algorithm should return NO. (We will assume it is straightforward to determine if a string is valid source code.) The second input is any string w. Our program must return YES if P returns YES whenever P is given w as input. It must return NO if P returns NO or if P runs forever when given w as input. For example, suppose our program is given the string 0001 and the source code for the following program called `AcceptSomething`:

```
AcceptSomething(x):
  if x ends in 0
    then return YES
    else return NO
```

39

Our program should return NO because AcceptSomething does not accept 0001. On the other hand, if our program is given the source code for AcceptSomething and the string 001111110, it should return YES.

How are we going to design a program to solve the ACCEPTANCE PROBLEM? Remember, we have a universal machine, so we can execute any program we are given. Why don't we execute the program we are given with the string we are given and look at the answer returned? For example, if we are given the source code for AcceptSomething and the string 0001, we can just run AcceptSomething with input 0001 and see what happens.

To make it clear when our programs are using the universal Turing machine capabilities, let's assume we have a subroutine called Execute(P, w) that given the source code for a program P along with a string w, executes P with w as the input string. Execute(P, w) returns whatever P returns and runs forever whenever P runs forever.

Using Execute(P, w), we can write our program to solve the ACCEPTANCE PROBLEM as follows:

```
Accepts(P,w):
  if Execute(P,w) returns YES
    then return YES
    else return NO
```

That was simple wasn't it. Let's try it on an example:

```
Encomium(x):
  while x ≠ 0101
      Move Right
  end while
  return YES
```

What does Encomium do? When it gets down to the return statement, it returns YES regardless of what it was given as input, so it looks like it accepts everything. Does it ever get down to the return statement? Not unless x is 0101. In other words, this program returns YES when given 0101, but it runs forever otherwise. What should our algorithm do when given the source code for Encomium and input string 0? It should return NO because Encomium does not accept 0. However, our algorithm is actually going to *run* Encomium with input string 0. Encomium will run forever, so our algorithm will run forever. Does our algorithm solve the ACCEPTANCE PROBLEM? No. To solve a decision problem, we have to return the correct answer for every possible instance of the problem. Here we have an instance of the problem for which our algorithm doesn't return any answer at all. Recall our definition of *solves* (Definition 1.2):

> A computer **solves** a decision problem if it *halts* and returns the correct answer for every instance of the problem.

Maybe there is no program to solve the ACCEPTANCE PROBLEM. After all, we have tried for at least five minutes to come up with a program and we have failed. What more evidence do we need? Perhaps we should try to *prove* that the ACCEPTANCE PROBLEM is unsolvable.

If we had a program that solved the ACCEPTANCE PROBLEM, then we could certainly write other programs that use this program as a subroutine. Let's do that. Assume we have a subroutine $\texttt{Accepts}(P, w)$ that halts and returns the correct answer for every instance of the ACCEPTANCE PROB-LEM. If P is the source code for a program that accepts input string w, then $\texttt{Accepts}(P, w)$ returns YES; otherwise, $\texttt{Accepts}(P, w)$ returns NO.

What is the difference between $\texttt{Execute}(P, w)$ and $\texttt{Accepts}(P, w)$? Like $\texttt{Accepts}$, $\texttt{Execute}(P, w)$ returns YES if P is the source code for a program that returns YES when given w. However, it may not return NO otherwise. If P runs forever when given w as input, $\texttt{Execute}(P, w)$ will run forever. $\texttt{Accepts}(P, w)$, on the other hand, can never run forever because we have assumed that it *solves* the ACCEPTANCE PROBLEM.

That $\texttt{Accepts}(P, w)$ halts for all inputs implies that the following program halts for all inputs.

```
Weird(Source):
   if Accepts(Source,Source) returns YES
      then return NO
      else return YES
```

What is Weird really doing? It takes a string, Source, as input and passes it to Accepts as both the source code for the program and the input string. If Weird is given the source code for Encomium as input, it is going to test to see if Encomium accepts the string:

```
"Encomium(x):
   while x ≠ 0101
       set x to 01
   end while
   return YES"
```

Assuming `Accepts` works correctly, `Weird` is going to return YES since `Encomium` only accepts when given 0101, and even if the source code for `Encomium` is converted to binary, it is safe to assume it will not be encoded as 0101.

Let's consider another example. What would happen if the input we give to `Weird` is the source code for `Weird` itself? It may seem strange at first to think of the source code for a program being passed into the program itself, but there is nothing that prevents us from doing that. The source code for a program is just a string like any other string passed in as input. For example, suppose we had a program called `myZip` that compresses files. Assuming `myZip` takes the name of the file to compress as an argument and that the source code for the program is in a file named `myZip.c`, the command `myZip myZip.c` instructs `myZip` to compress its own source code.

Suppose `Weird` returns YES when given the source code for `Weird`. Then in the if statement on the first line of `Weird`, `Accepts(Source,Source)` must have returned NO. Since we assume `Accepts` works correctly, this means the program represented by `Source` rejects the input string `Source`. But `Source` is the source code for `Weird`. If `Accepts` correctly solves the ACCEPTANCE PROBLEM, then `Accepts(Source,Source)` returning NO implies that `Weird` must return NO when `Weird` is given its own source code as input. But we just supposed that `Weird` returned YES when given its own source code – just go back and read the first sentence of this paragraph. This is a contradiction. Since making the assumption that `Weird` returns YES when given its own source code as input leads to a contradiction, the assumption is not valid.

As we stated earlier, because `Accepts` halts on every input, `Weird` must halt on every input. So, if `Weird` does not return YES when given its own source code as input, the only other possibility is that `Weird` returns NO when given its own source code as input. But for `Weird` to return NO, the condition on the if statement must be true, so `Accepts(Source,Source)` must return YES when `Source` is the source code for `Weird`. If `Accepts` correctly solves the ACCEPTANCE PROBLEM, `Accepts(Source,Source)` returning YES implies that `Weird` must return YES when `Weird` is given its own source code as input. But we just supposed that `Weird` returned NO when given its own source code. Again we have a contradiction.

Figure 4.1 summarizes the above discussion. Since either return value for `Weird` results in a contradiction, we must have made some other assumption

if Weird(Source) returns	then Accepts(Source,Source) returns	but then Weird(Source) returns
YES	NO	NO
NO	YES	YES

Figure 4.1: Weird outputs and implications when Source is the source code for Weird. The entries in the third column contradict the entries in the first column.

that is invalid. The only other assumption we made, however, is that Accepts works correctly. Therefore, this assumption is invalid. But we chose Accepts to be *any* algorithm that solves the ACCEPTANCE PROBLEM, so there can be no algorithm that solves the ACCEPTANCE PROBLEM. The ACCEPTANCE PROBLEM is, therefore, unsolvable.

When talking about decision problems, we generally use the term **undecidable** rather than unsolvable.

Definition 4.1 *A decision problem is said to be* **undecidable** *if there is no algorithm that solves it.*

4.2 Reductions

Suppose you take a work-study job as a grader for your favorite computer science professor's intro class. The work itself is not terribly challenging, but there are 500 students in the course and if you do not get all of the programs graded within a week of the due date, your pay will be reduced by 50%. (Your favorite computer science professor is pretty tough.) To make your life easier and more interesting, you write a script to run the programs on the set of test cases provided by the professor. Your code runs so well on the first assignment that you have all of the students' programs graded in an hour. This job is going to be easy. You wait until the night of the sixth day to grade the second assignment. After all, a college student has an active social life. An hour after you start the script, you check the output file. There is only one line! "Running test for student: G. Cantor." You go to run the script again but realize that the first run has not yet finished. Judging by the output, the script appears to be stuck running the first student's program! You only have a couple of hours left to grade and it looks like you are going to have to grade all 500 programs by hand. You start up Cantor's program on the first test case and wait, and wait, and wait. This is going to take forever. That's it!! Cantor's program has an infinite loop. This Cantor guy is going to pay. You remove Cantor from the student file and start your scripts again, watching the output carefully. Several more students have infinite loops. Are these kids morons? How hard is it to figure out if your program contains an infinite loop? Don't they test their code? Hey, maybe you could write a script to make sure each student's program will terminate on each test case before running the grading scripts.

We have seen that it is impossible to write a program to decide, given the source code for a program P and an input string w, whether P accepts w. Is it possible to write a program to decide whether P halts when given w? This problem is known as the **HALTING PROBLEM**. The ACCEPTANCE PROBLEM and the HALTING PROBLEM seem very similar, so it would not be unreasonable to suspect that the HALTING PROBLEM is also undecidable. To prove this, let's assume otherwise and see if we can derive a contradiction just as we did with the ACCEPTANCE PROBLEM. Recall that the only difference between the subroutine $\texttt{Execute}(P, w)$, which we know exists, and our hypothetical subroutine $\texttt{Accepts}(P, w)$, which we now know does not exist, is in the return value (or lack thereof) for the case where P runs forever when given w as input. Figure 4.2 summarizes the three cases we encounter in trying to solve the ACCEPTANCE PROBLEM.

	Given w, P returns	$\texttt{Execute}(P, w)$ returns	$\texttt{Accepts}(P, w)$ should return
1.	YES	YES	YES
2.	NO	NO	NO
3.	nothing; it runs forever	nothing; it runs forever	NO

Figure 4.2: Cases for the ACCEPTANCE PROBLEM

The difficulty we face in deciding the ACCEPTANCE PROBLEM is in differentiating between being in one of the first two cases and being in the third case. If we are in the third case, our program should return NO. If we are in one of the first two cases, our program can just run $\texttt{Execute}(P, w)$ and return the result. Since $\texttt{Execute}(P, w)$ is guaranteed to halt in the first two cases, our program would always halt. Therefore, if we could differentiate between being in one of the first two cases and being in the third case, which is exactly what a program that solves the HALTING PROBLEM does, we could solve the ACCEPTANCE PROBLEM.

So, suppose the HALTING PROBLEM is decidable and let $Halts(P, w)$ be any subroutine that decides it. Using Halts, create a program that solves the ACCEPTANCE PROBLEM as follows:

```
AcceptsUsingHalts(P,w):
    if Halts(P,w) returns YES
    then return Execute(P,w)
    else return NO
```

Since we know the ACCEPTANCE PROBLEM is undecidable, this provides the desired contradiction, and we can conclude that the HALTING PROBLEM is undecidable.

Let's try another problem. What if we want to determine whether a given program decides the language consisting of the single string 01. In other words, the program accepts 01 but rejects everything else. We'll call this problem the **USELESS LANGUAGE PROBLEM**:

GIVEN: A string Source.

QUESTION: Is Source the source code for a program that accepts the
            string 01 and nothing else?

This seems like it might be easier than the HALTING PROBLEM, but let's try to prove it is undecidable anyway by creating a program to decide the ACCEPTANCE PROBLEM given a hypothetical subroutine to decide the USELESS LANGUAGE PROBLEM.

Let Useless(Source) be a hypothetical subroutine that solves the USELESS LANGUAGE PROBLEM. Create the following program to solve the ACCEPTANCE PROBLEM:

```
AcceptsUsingUseless(P,w):
    Let Source = "DoNotRunThis(x):
                        if x is 01
                            then return Execute(P,w)
                            else return No"
    return Useless(Source)
```

Note that Source is the source code for a program, DoNotRunThis, that operates as follows. If x, the string passed in to DoNotRunThis as input, is not

01, `DoNotRunThis` returns NO. If x is 01, then `DoNotRunThis` returns YES *if* P accepts w; otherwise `DoNotRunThis` either runs forever or returns No. So if P accepts w, then `DoNotRunThis` accepts only 01. If P rejects w or runs forever when given w, then `DoNotRunThis` accepts nothing. It is important to realize that `AcceptsUsingUseless` is simply creating the source code for the program `DoNotRunThis`. `AcceptsUsingUseless` is not actually executing the programs represented by `DoNotRunThis` or P (unless `Useless()` does). It is also important to understand that from the perspective of `DoNotRunThis`, P and w are constants. Each instance (P, w) generates different source code for `DoNotRunThis`.

Suppose P returns YES when given w. Then `DoNotRunThis` returns YES for 01 and rejects everything else. Consequently, `Useless(Source)` returns YES. On the other hand, if P returns NO or runs forever when given w, then `DoNotRunThis` accepts nothing and `Useless(Source)` returns NO. Our hypothetical program for the USELESS LANGUAGE PROBLEM, therefore, can be used to solve the ACCEPTANCE PROBLEM because P accepts w if and only if `Useless(Source)` returns YES. Since the ACCEPTANCE PROBLEM is undecidable, the USELESS LANGUAGE PROBLEM must also be undecidable.

Take note of what we have done here. We have taken an instance (P, w) of the ACCEPTANCE PROBLEM and created an instance `Source` of the USELESS LANGUAGE PROBLEM such that (P, w) is a YES instance of the ACCEPTANCE PROBLEM if and only if `Source` is a YES instance of the USELESS LANGUAGE PROBLEM. We'll refer to this type of transformation from instances of one problem to instances of another problem as an **instance mapping reduction**.[1]

Definition 4.2 *An* **instance mapping reduction** *from a problem A to a problem B is an algorithm that takes an instance x of A and creates an instance y of B such that x is a* YES *instance of A if and only if y is a* YES *instance of B. We use the notation* $A \leq_m B$ *to indicate that there is an instance mapping reduction from A to B.*

---

[1]Computer scientists generally refer to this type of reduction as a **many-one reduction**. Sipser (2006) is the exception, referring to this type of reduction as a "mapping reduction". The term "instance mapping reduction" is used here to emphasize that we are converting an instance of one problem into an instance of another problem. The term "many-one" is used by others because the reduction may convert many instances of the first problem into the same instance of the second problem. This latter fact, however, does not play any role in the material covered by this book.

Did we use an instance mapping reduction in our proof that the HALTING PROBLEM is undecidable? In that case, we did not actually transform an instance of the ACCEPTANCE PROBLEM into an instance of the HALTING PROBLEM, so we did not use an *instance mapping* reduction in that argument. However, anytime we use a hypothetical subroutine for one problem to create a program to solve another problem, we are using a more general type of reduction called a **Turing reduction**.

Definition 4.3 *A* **Turing reduction** *from a problem A to a problem B is a program that solves A using a hypothetical subroutine for solving B. We use the notation $A \leq_T B$ to indicate that there is a Turing reduction from A to B.*

An instance mapping reduction is a special case of a Turing reduction. One way to tell that a Turing reduction is in fact an instance mapping reduction is to look at the return statement. The `AcceptsUsingUseless` program simply creates an input `Source` for the hypothetical `Useless` program and returns the result of `Useless(Source)`. It is a simple transformation of a ACCEPTANCE PROBLEM instance to an USELESS LANGUAGE PROBLEM instance. The `AcceptsUsingHalts` program, on the other hand, uses the return value for the hypothetical subroutine `Halts` to make a decision about how to proceed; it does not simply use the return value of `Halts` as its own return value.

We can use either type of reduction to prove problems are undecidable.

Theorem 4.4 *If problem A is undecidable and there is a reduction from problem A to problem B, then problem B is also undecidable.*

Let's try to reduce the ACCEPTANCE PROBLEM to another problem called the **NON-REGULARITY TESTING PROBLEM**:

GIVEN: A string `Source`.

QUESTION: Is `Source` the source code for a program that recognizes a language that is not regular? In other words, is it impossible to design a finite automaton, M, such that M recognizes the same language as the program represented by `Source`?

To develop an instance mapping reduction from the ACCEPTANCE PROBLEM to the NON-REGULARITY TESTING PROBLEM, we need to take an instance (P, w) of the ACCEPTANCE PROBLEM and create an instance

Source of the NON-REGULARITY TESTING PROBLEM such that (P, w) is a YES instance of the ACCEPTANCE PROBLEM if and only if Source is a YES instance of the NON-REGULARITY TESTING PROBLEM. Here is our reduction:

1. Given the input string (P, w)

2. Let AlienCounter(x) be a program that decides $\{0^n 1^n : n \geq 0\}$. We developed such a program in Exercise 3.7.

3. Create the source code for a new program as follows:

```
Source = "DoNotRunThisEither(x):
            If Execute(P,w) returns YES
                then return Execute(AlienCounter,x)
                else return NO"
```

Notice that instance mapping reductions are themselves algorithms and it will become important for us to think of them that way later when we discuss computational complexity in Chapter 6. For example, we could write the reduction above as:

Reduce(P, w)

1   Let *Source* = "DoNotRunThisEither(x):
```
            If Execute(P,w) returns YES
                then return Execute(AlienCounter,x)
                else return NO"
```
2   **return** *Source*

Now consider the language recognized by DoNotRunThisEither. If P returns YES when given w, then DoNotRunThisEither accepts every string in $\{0^n 1^n : n \geq 0\}$, which we proved is not a regular language in Section 2.3. If P returns NO or runs forever when given w, then DoNotRunThisEither accepts nothing – that is, the set of strings accepted by DoNotRunThisEither is the empty set, which we know is a regular language. Thus, P accepts w if and only if the language recognized by DoNotRunThisEither is non-regular, which is exactly what we need for a reduction: (P, w) is a YES instance of the ACCEPTANCE PROBLEM if and only if Source is a YES instance of the NON-REGULARITY TESTING PROBLEM.

Since the ACCEPTANCE PROBLEM is undecidable and the ACCEP-
TANCE PROBLEM can be reduced to the NON-REGULARITY TESTING
PROBLEM, the NON-REGULARITY TESTING PROBLEM is also unde-
cidable.

4.3 Rice's Theorem

We have just seen that the problem of testing whether the language recognized
by a given Turing machine satisfies a particular property is undecidable for
two different properties. The first property was the property of including only
the string 01, while the second property was the property of being non-regular.
It seems like we may be able to use the same kind of proof to show that the
problem of testing whether a recognizable language satisfies *any* particular
property is undecidable. We can, as long as the property is not trivial. A **trivial
property** of languages is one that holds for all recognizable languages or holds
for no recognizable language. For example, the property of a recognizable
language being recognized by a Turing machine is trivial since all recognizable
languages are recognized by a Turing machine.

Theorem 4.5 (Rice's Theorem) *For any property of recognizable languages
that is non-trivial, the following problem is undecidable:*

GIVEN: *A string* Source.

QUESTION: *Is* Source *the source code for a program such that the
                language recognized by the program has the property?*

To prove this theorem, we will assume the empty language does not have
the property. Exercise 4.1 asks you to prove the theorem when the empty
language does have the property. Let M be a program such that $L(M)$ has the
property. (Since the property is non-trivial, we know such a program exists.)
We can reduce the ACCEPTANCE PROBLEM to the generic property testing
problem as follows:

1. Given an instance (P, w) of the ACCEPTANCE PROBLEM

2. Create the source code for a program as follows:

```
Source = "DoNotRunThis(x):
            if Execute(P,w) returns YES
              then return Execute(M,x)
              else return NO"
```

Consider the language recognized by DoNotRunThis. From the point of view of DoNotRunThis, P and w are constants. DoNotRunThis takes only one input, x. If P returns YES when given w, then DoNotRunThis will always execute the then part of the if statement regardless of the input, x. In that case, DoNotRunThis will accept x if and only if M accepts x. In other words, the language recognized by DoNotRunThis is $L(M)$. If P returns NO or runs forever when given w, then DoNotRunThis will always execute the else part of the if statement or run forever, in which case the language recognized by DoNotRunThis is the empty language. Since we assumed that $L(M)$ has the property and the empty language does not have the property, (P, w) is a YES instance of the ACCEPTANCE PROBLEM if and only if Source is a YES instance of the property testing problem. Therefore, we have reduced the ACCEPTANCE PROBLEM to the problem of testing this property and we can conclude that the property testing problem is undecidable for any non-trivial property.

Exercise 4.1 *In the proof of Rice's Theorem, we assumed that the empty language does not have the property. How can we make such an assumption? Prove that Rice's Theorem holds when the empty language has the property in question.*

The implications of Rice's Theorem are somewhat troubling for people who would like to develop programs that automatically test software for correctness. Even if our software simply provides YES or NO answers to queries, there is no algorithm that can read the software and verify that it provides the correct answer for all queries.

4.4 Exercises

Exercise 4.2 *We have seen problems that are undecidable. Is it possible there are problems that are* **unrecognizable***, by which we mean there is no algorithm that returns YES for each YES instance and returns NO or runs forever* *for each* NO *instance? Let's consider a problem called the* **REJECTION PROBLEM**:

GIVEN: *Two strings, P and w.*

QUESTION: *Is P either not the source code for any program or the source code for a program that rejects input string w?*

Prove that the REJECTION PROBLEM is unrecognizable.

Exercise 4.3 *The result of the previous exercise shouldn't be all that surprising. The set of* YES *instances of the REJECTION PROBLEM is the set of* NO *instances of the ACCEPTANCE PROBLEM. Being able to recognize both* YES *and* NO *instances of a problem implies that we are able to decide the problem. We already have* Execute(P,w) *to recognize the* YES *instances of the AC-CEPTANCE PROBLEM. If we had* RecognizeRejection(P,w) *to recognize* NO *instances of the ACCEPTANCE PROBLEM, we could decide the ACCEP-TANCE PROBLEM.*

This specific argument can be generalized to any problem.

Theorem 4.6 *Let L be the set of* YES *instances for a given problem. Let $\overline{L}$ be the set of* NO *instances for the problem. (Note: $\overline{L}$ is simply the complement of L.) Then L is decidable if and only if $\overline{L}$ is decidable.*

Prove this theorem formally.

Exercise 4.4 *We have developed a theory of computation based on decision problems – our machines are given inputs and must respond by saying* YES *or* NO. *More formally, we have defined computation as determining whether a given string is in a particular language. Maybe this way of viewing computation is all wrong. Great time to think of that, isn't it? Suppose we have a machine that simply generates information without any input whatsoever. For example, what if a machine generates all of the digits of π or all prime numbers – just for fun or perhaps to transmit into space to attract aliens who like donuts.[2] Such a machine would never even halt. Is that machine computing? It seems like it is. Does our theory give us any information about this type of computation? Modify the Turing machine model so that a Turing machine generates a language rather than decides a language. Relate the set languages generated by your model to the decidable and recognizable languages.*

---

[2]You should read the book *Contact* by Karl Sagan.

Chapter 5

Nondeterminism

5.1 Introduction

In Chapter 4, we saw problems that cannot be solved by any mechanical computing device (assuming we believe the Church-Turing Thesis). Can a person "solve" these undecidable problems? Is a person a mechanical computing device? Certainly a Turing machine looks nothing like a brain. In fact, a brain has finite memory. Huh? Then human brains can only enter a finite number of states, so humans can only solve problems that can be solved using a finite automaton, unless we can ask for more memory when we need it? Hey, we *can* ask for more memory because we can write things down on a piece of paper that, holy crow, looks just like a Turing machine tape!

```
I am a Turing machine.
```

Obviously people are not just Turing machines. We are free to make choices that are not predetermined. Our decisions are not fixed at the time we are created. We have free will. At least, we think we do. Can we extend the Turing machine definition to account for free will so we can use it to model people as well as computers?

What instruction does the Turing machine have for decision making? The if-goto makes decisions. The other instructions just write, move, and return. Let's modify the if-goto to give the Turing machine the power to make choices that are not determined at the time the machine is created. For example, suppose we want to allow a Turing machine to reject all strings that start with 0 but to decide for itself whether to accept or reject any given string that begins with 1. We would like to do something like this:

```
      if head is 1 then goto ACC or REJ else goto REJ
ACC:  Return YES
REJ:  Return NO
```

It looks like we can simply modify the if-goto instruction to specify a set of possible labels rather than just one label. The Turing machine is then free to "choose" any one of these labels as the label of the next line to execute. In other words, our if-goto becomes:

```
if head is symbol
   then goto one of  {Label₁,..., Labelₖ}
   else goto one of  {Label₁,..., Labelₜ}
```

where k and t are both at least 1. We'll call the Turing machine with this modified if-goto a **nondeterministic Turing machine**.

Is a nondeterministic Turing machine really a good model of free will? It seems kind of lame. What if we asked a Turing machine to pick a number? The machine would have an infinite set of numbers to choose from. However, the nondeterministic if-goto can only make a finite number of choices because there are only a finite number of lines in a program. Can we write a nondeterministic Turing machine program to pick a number? Suppose on the tape, the program keeps a counter that is initialized to 0. After initializing the counter, the program enters a loop that repeatedly increments the counter. We'll use nondeterminism to allow the program to decide which iteration of the loop is the last one. In other words, after each iteration, the program nondeterministically decides whether to end or continue the loop. Here's the code:

```
       Set counter to 0
LOOP:  Increment the counter
       if any symbol then goto {LOOP, EXIT}
EXIT:  Return the value of the counter.
```

Maybe this is really not such a bad model of free will. After all, what more could we ask of our model than to be able to pick a number?

Now that we have a new computational model, let's see what languages it can decide that cannot be decided by our previous model, which we'll refer to as a **deterministic Turing machine** to avoid ambiguity. First, we need to be clear about what we mean for a nondeterministic Turing machine to decide a

language. To do that, it is helpful to consider nondeterminism in the context of
search algorithms.

5.2 Nondeterminstic search algorithms

Consider using a **breadth-first search** to search from a start node to a goal
node in a directed graph, such as the graph in Figure 5.1. Breadth-first search

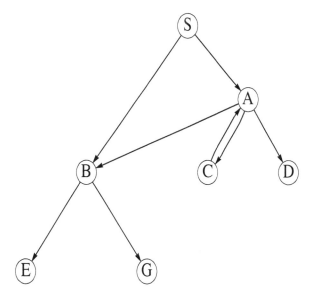

Figure 5.1: A graph to search. S is the start node. G is the goal node.

begins at the start node, S. It expands this node, by which we mean that it takes
all of the nodes adjacent to the start node and adds them to a list of "open"
nodes called the OPEN list. The OPEN list consists of nodes that have been
encountered but not yet expanded. Breadth-first search repeatedly removes
and expands nodes from the OPEN list until the goal is found or the OPEN list
becomes empty. Breadth-first search maintains the OPEN list as a queue so
that the nodes are expanded in the order they are encountered. The algorithm
appears in Figure 5.2.

    Depth-first search operates exactly like breadth-first search except that it
maintains the OPEN list as a stack. This means that in depth-first search the
most recent node found is the next node expanded.

Breadth-first search$(V, E, startNode)$:

1   let *OPEN* be a queue that is initially empty
2   add *startNode* to *OPEN*
3   initialize *GoalFound* to No
4   **while** *OPEN* is not empty and *GoalFound* is No
5   remove a node x from the front of *OPEN*
6   **if** x is a goal node
7   **then** set *GoalFound* to YES
8   **else** append all of the nodes adjacent to x to *OPEN*
9   **end while**
10   **return** *GoalFound*

Figure 5.2: Breadth-first search.

The order in which nodes are expanded by a search algorithm defines a **search tree**. For example, consider searching the graph in Figure 5.1 for goal node G starting at node S. A breadth-first tree is shown in Figure 5.3a, while a possible depth-first tree is shown in Figure 5.3b.

In the depth-first tree, we assumed that B was the first child of A that was expanded. If C had been the first child expanded, depth-first search would have continued to go around the cycle $A \rightarrow C \rightarrow A$ forever. Breadth-first search also has the potential to run forever, but only if there is no goal node in the graph and the graph has cycles. At the cost of additional memory, we could avoid this behavior in both algorithms by keeping track of the nodes that have been visited and preventing previously visited nodes from being added to the OPEN list a second time.[1]

A **nondeterministic search algorithm**, described in Figure 5.4, begins by expanding the start node as in the deterministic search algorithms above. However, rather than adding all of the nodes adjacent to the start node to an OPEN list, the nondeterministic search algorithm nondeterministically chooses a single adjacent node, which we will refer to as the open node. If the open node is not a goal node, the algorithm nondeterministically chooses a node adjacent to the open node to become the new open node. This process of non-

---

[1]The cost of keeping track of visited nodes may be prohibitive, as in artificial intelligence applications for example. (See Russell and Norvig (2010) and Nilsson (1998).)

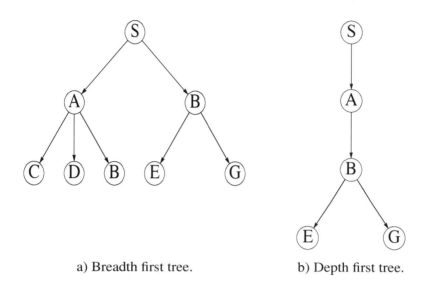

a) Breadth first tree.   b) Depth first tree.

Figure 5.3: Breadth-first and depth-first trees for the graph in Figure 5.1.

Nondeterministic Search($V, E, startNode$):

1 initialize *openNode* to *startNode*
2 initialize *GoalFound* to No
3 **while** there are nodes adjacent to *openNode* and *GoalFound* is No
4   nondeterministically choose a node adjacent to *openNode*
5   set *openNode* to the node chosen
6   **if** *openNode* is a goal node
7   **then** set *GoalFound* to YES
8 **end while**
9 **return** *GoalFound*

Figure 5.4: A nondeterministic search algorithm.

deterministically traversing a path from the start node continues until a goal is found or until we reach a node that has no nodes adjacent to it. Reaching such a dead end does not imply that the graph is without a goal node. Rather, it implies only that the path chosen by the nondeterministic search algorithm did not include the goal.

The search "tree" for a nondeterminstic search algorithm is a single path through the graph. Figure 5.5 shows a successful and an unsuccessful nondeterministic search of the graph in Figure 5.1.

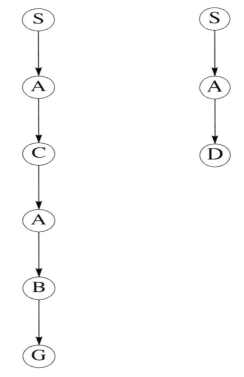

a) Successful search.   b) Unsuccessful search.

Figure 5.5: A successful and an unsuccessful nondeterministic sequence of choices for the graph in Figure 5.1. Tremendously illuminating, isn't it?

Now consider the decision problem of determining whether a goal node is reachable from the start node in a given graph. Breadth-first search is guaranteed to find the goal node if it exists because it examines all nodes k edges away from the start node before examining nodes $k+1$ edges away. However, since breadth-first search may run forever if the goal is not in the graph, it does not solve the problem unless we include the check to make sure it does not add the same node to the OPEN list twice. Without a check to make sure it is not going around a cycle, depth-first search does not even guarantee it will *find* the goal node when the goal node is in the graph. So, as written above, breadth-first and depth-first search do not solve the reachability problem.

Since the nondeterministic search algorithm above also has the potential to run forever, we would not say that it solves this decision problem either. For a nondeterministic algorithm to solve a decision problem, all sequences of nondeterministic choices must lead to eventual termination for every instance. Furthermore, the nondeterministic algorithm cannot answer YES for any NO instance, and for every YES instance, there must be some sequence of nondeterministic choices that leads the algorithm to return YES.

Definition 5.1 *A nondeterministic algorithm* **solves a decision problem** *if all of the following conditions are met:*

1. **TERMINATION:** *for every instance of the problem, all possible sequences of nondeterministic choices lead to eventual termination;*

2. **NO FALSE POSITIVES:** *for every* NO *instance, all possible sequences of nondeterministic choices lead to the algorithm returning* NO;

3. **CORRECT ANSWER IS POSSIBLE:** *for every* YES *instance, there is at least one possible sequence of nondeterministic choices that leads the algorithm to return* YES.

Notice that we treat YES instances and NO instances differently in this definition. For a NO instance, the algorithm can never answer incorrectly. However, the machine can sometimes provide the wrong answer for YES instances as long as there is some possible sequence of nondeterministic choices after which the algorithm returns YES for that instance.

Exercise 5.1 *You may be wondering why we allow some possible sequences of nondeterministic choices to return* NO *when given* YES *instances yet still consider the algorithm to solve the decision problem. Suppose we required all possible sequences of choices to return the correct answer for every instance* *of the problem. Show that with these requirements nondeterminism would not provide any additional power by providing a simple way to convert any such nondeterministic algorithm to a deterministic one.*

Does Definition 5.1 give nondeterministic Turing machines the ability to decide languages that deterministic Turing machines cannot decide? Before we answer that question, it might be useful to look at the question in terms of finite automata rather than Turing machines. This could give us some insight into the question regarding Turing machines.

5.3   Nondeterministic finite automata

How can we add free will (a.k.a. nondeterminism) to a finite automaton? Recall that a finite automaton includes a transition rule that specifies for each state and input symbol, which state the machine will enter next. The transition rule is the decision making component of a finite automaton, just like the if-goto is the decision making component of the Turing machine. To allow a finite automaton to make decisions nondeterministically, we could allow the machine to make a choice among a number of states rather than forcing it to go to one particular state when it reads an input symbol. The resulting machine is called a **nondeterministic finite automaton**. (We'll refer to the deterministic version of the finite automaton as a **deterministic finite automaton (DFA)**.)

For example, suppose we had a machine described by the transition diagram in Figure 5.6. If the machine starts in state *Start* and reads a 0, to which state does the machine go? It can choose to go to either *Nirvana* or *Hades*.

The nondeterministic finite state automaton is defined formally as follows:

Definition 5.2 *A* **nondeterministic finite state automaton (NFA)** *is specified by:*

1. *A set of states, one of which is designated as the unique start state;*

2. *A labeling of the states such that each state is labeled as either an accepting or a non-accepting state;*

3. *A transition rule that describes for each state and input symbol a set of possible next states.*

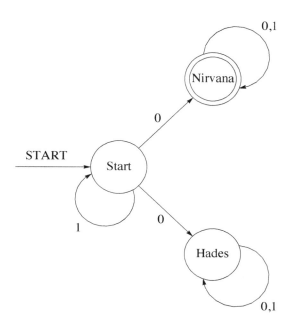

Figure 5.6: A nondeterministic finite automaton.

The automaton begins at the start state and processes each input symbol one at a time without going back to look at previous input symbols. At each state, the automaton reads the next input symbol, nondeterministically chooses a state from the set of possible next states specified by the transition rule, and moves to that state.

As with the nondeterministic Turing machine, we consider a string to be in the language decided by a nondeterministic finite automaton if and only if some sequence of nondeterministic choices leads the machine to accept the string.

Definition 5.3 *We say a nondeterministic finite state automaton M **accepts** an input string if after starting in the start state and processing the entire input string, it is possible for M to be in an accepting state. In other words, there is some sequence of nondeterministic choices that leads the machine to an accepting state. The language decided by a nondeterministic finite automaton M is the set of strings accepted by M.*

Consider the following two languages:

$$L_1 = \{x : x \text{ contains an even number of 1's}\}$$
$$L_2 = \{x : x \text{ does not contain two consecutive 0's}\}$$

We know from Chapter 2 that both of these languages can be decided by deterministic finite automata. We would like to design a nondeterministic finite automaton to decide the **concatenation** of L_1 and L_2. The concatenation of L_1 and L_2, written as $L_1 \cdot L_2$, is defined to be the language consisting of strings that can be broken into two parts such that the first part, x_1, is in L_1, while the second part, x_2, is in L_2. For example, the string $w = 1101010$ is in $L_1 \cdot L_2$ because w can broken into $x_1 = 11$ and $x_2 = 01010$. Since x_1 contains an even number of 1's, x_1 is in L_1, and since x_2 does not contain two consecutive 0's, x_2 is in L_2. We can split w in other ways as well: x_1 could be the whole string and x_2 could be the empty string, for example. As long as there is at least one way to split w appropriately, w is in the concatenation of the two languages. The string 01000, for example, is not in $L_1 \cdot L_2$ because no matter how we split 01000 either the first part will have an odd number of 1's or the second part will contain two consecutive 0's.

Chapter 2 provides deterministic finite automata to decide L_1 and L_2 individually. (See Figure 5.7.) Is there a way to concatenate these two machines to create a larger machine that decides $L_1 \cdot L_2$? One problem with this approach is that we don't know where to break the string. How will our machine determine the correct time to switch from the first machine to the second machine? This is where nondeterminism is helpful in our design – our machine can just guess that it is the right time to switch. Any time our machine has seen an even number of 1's, the machine can guess that it is has read the first part of the string. At that point, it should switch to checking to make sure the remainder of the string does not have two consecutive 0's. To accomplish this, the nondeterministic machine can transition from the state Even to the second machine. If it reads a 1 in Even, it should transition to Last=1. If it reads a 0 in Even, it should transition to Last=0. Figure 5.8 shows the transition diagram.

Consider the input string $w = 0010101$. Is this string accepted by the NFA? It should be, but let's make sure. The machine starts in state Even. When the machine reads the 0 at the beginning of the input string, the machine could decide to stay in state Even or it could move to state Last=0. When the machine reads the next input symbol, a 0 in this case, the machine could be in one of three states: if it had been in Even, it could decide to stay in Even or move to

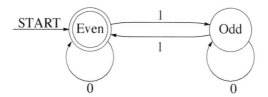

(a) A finite automaton that decides $L_1 = \{x \in \{0,1\}^* : x \text{ contains an even number of 1's}\}$.

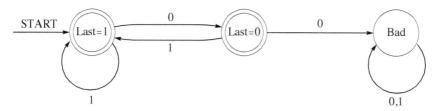

(b) A finite automaton that decides $L_2 = \{x \in \{0,1\}^* : \text{at least every other symbol in } x \text{ is a 1}\}$.

Figure 5.7: Two deterministic finite automata that we would like to concatenate.

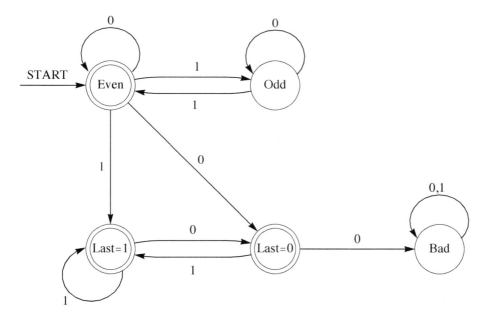

Figure 5.8: An nondeterministic finite automaton to decide the concatenation of L_1 and L_2 above.

Last=0; if it had been in Last=0, it must now move to state Bad. Let's keep track of the states in which the machine could find itself using the table in Figure 5.9.

Symbol Read	Possible States
0	{Even, Last=0}
0	{Even, Last=0, Bad}
1	{Odd, Last=1, Bad}
0	{Odd, Last=0, Bad}
1	{Even, Last=1, Bad}
0	{Even, Last=0, Bad}
1	{Odd, Last=1, Bad}

Figure 5.9: A trace of the possible states encountered by the NFA from Figure 5.8 on input string 0010101.

The first two lines of the table in Figure 5.9 reflect the discussion in the previous paragraph. After reading the third symbol, a 1, the machine could again be in one of three states. If it had been in state Even before reading the 1, the machine must have moved to state Odd; if it had been in state Last=0, the machine must have moved to state Last=1; and if it had been in state Bad, the machine must have stayed in state Bad. The rest of the lines in the table follow similarly.

Can we tell from the table whether the string 0010101 is in the language decided by this machine? One of the states in which the machine could find itself after it has read the entire input string, Last=1, is an accepting state, so 0010101 is in the language.

Are there languages that can be decided using a nondeterministic finite automaton that cannot be decided by a deterministic finite automaton? We could prove that there aren't by showing that the execution of any nondeterministic finite automaton can be simulated by a deterministic algorithm that uses a finite and fixed amount of memory. A deterministic simulation of an NFA would need to keep track of all of the states in which the NFA could find itself at any given time and check that this set includes an accepting state when the input is finished. This is exactly what we did in Figure 5.9 above.

In the formal description of our algorithm in Figure 5.10, $NEXT(s, a)$ is the set of possible next states specified by the transition rule for state s and input *a*. Notice that *CurrentStateSet* and *NextStateSet* can only take on a

Simulate-NFA

```
1   initialize CurrentStateSet to the set containing only the start state.
2   while input remains to be read
3       read input a
4       initialize NextStateSet to empty
5       for each state s in CurrentStateSet
6           add the states in NEXT(s, a) to NextStateSet
7       end for
8       set CurrentStateSet to NextStateSet
9   end while
10  if there is an accepting state in CurrentStateSet
11      then return YES
12      else return NO
```

Figure 5.10: A deterministic simulation of a NFA. *CurrentStateSet* is the set of states in which the NFA could currently be.

finite number of values since each maintains a subset of the *finite* set of states in the nondeterministic machine. The only other variables are *s* and *a*. Since *s* is one of the states and *a* is one of the input symbols, these two variables are also limited to a finite number of possible values. Because we have a program with a finite number of lines and a finite number of variables that each can take on a finite number of values, we have a finite state machine. Furthermore, it is deterministic. Thus, we have simulated a nondeterministic finite automaton with a deterministic finite automaton.

We can convert this program into a state transition diagram by focusing on the variable *CurrentStateSet*. The other variables are just temporary variables that are used to update *CurrentStateSet*. For example, consider simulating the NFA from Figure 5.8. The value of *CurrentStateSet* will be initialized to include the state Even. If the simulation program reads a 0, then *CurrentStateSet* changes to {Even, Last=0}. If it reads a 1, then *CurrentStateSet* changes to {Odd, Last=1}. Figure 5.11 describes the changes that could take place.

The table specifies the transition rule for the DFA, where the states of the DFA are the possible values that *CurrentStateSet* can take on. The states of the DFA, therefore, represent subsets of the NFA's states. The corresponding

	0	1
{Even}	{Even, Last=0}	{Odd, Last=1}
{Even, Last=0}	{Even, Last=0, Bad}	{Odd, Last=1}
{Odd, Last=1}	{Odd, Last=0}	{Even, Last=1}
{Even, Last=0, Bad}	{Even, Last=0, Bad}	{Odd, Last=1, Bad}
{Odd, Last=0}	{Odd, Bad}	{Even, Last=1}
{Even, Last=1}	{Even, Last=0}	{Odd, Last=1}
{Odd, Last=1, Bad}	{Odd, Last=0, Bad}	{Even, Last=1, Bad}
{Odd, Last=0, Bad}	{Odd, Bad}	{Even, Last=1, Bad}
{Odd, Bad}	{Odd, Bad}	{Even, Bad}
{Even, Last=1, Bad}	{Even, Last=0, Bad}	{Odd, Last=1, Bad}
{Even, Bad}	{Even, Last=0, Bad}	{Odd, Last=1, Bad}

Figure 5.11: State transition table for the DFA corresponding to algorithm Simulate-NFA from Figure 5.10.

transition diagram appears with abbreviated state names in Figure 5.12.

Because it is possible to have a state in the DFA for every subset of states in the original NFA, the DFA could have exponentially more states than the NFA. Nondeterminism, therefore, may allow for more efficient use of resources. However, we are not yet concerned with efficiency. Our goal was simply to show that the sets of problems solvable in the two models are the same.

5.4   Free will is useless

Given that we can simulate a nondeterministic finite automaton with a deterministic finite automaton, we might suspect that we could do the same sort of thing to simulate a nondeterministic Turing machine with a deterministic one. This would show that any decision problem that can be solved by a nondeterministic Turing machine can also be solved by a deterministic Turing machine. In the NFA simulation, the DFA needed to keep track of the set of possible states in which the NFA could be at any point in time. This information was stored in the DFA's states. To simulate a nondeterministic Turing machine program with a deterministic one, we'll need to keep track of the line number that is about to execute and the contents of the tape. We'll refer to this as a

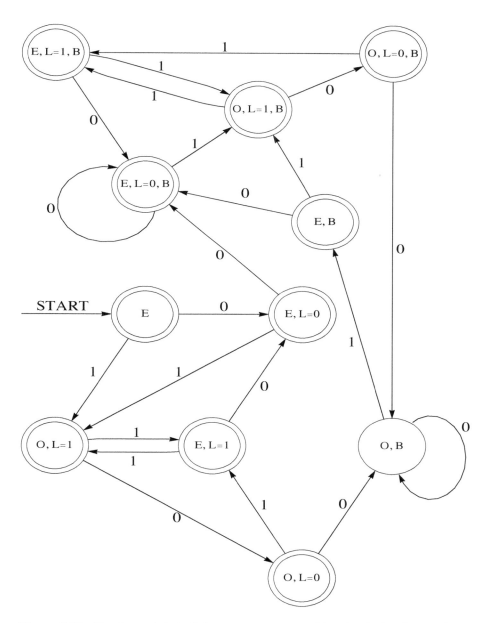

Figure 5.12: The deterministic finite automaton created by simulating the nondeterministic finite automaton from Figure 5.8 as described in Figure 5.11. The NFA's state names have been abbreviated with E for Even, O for Odd, L=0 for Last=0, L=1 for Last=1, and B for Bad.

configuration to avoid confusing it with the states of a finite automaton.

Consider the simple nondeterministic program in Figure 5.13. Regardless

```
 1. LOOP:         if head is 1
                      then goto {THEN1,THEN2}
                      else goto {ELSE}
 2. ELSE:         Move right
 3.               if head is any symbol
                      then goto LOOP
                      else goto {THEN1}
 4. THEN1:        if head is 0
                      then goto {THEN2, CHECK-LAST}
                      else goto {END1}
 5. END1:         Move right
 6.               if head is any symbol
                      then goto THEN1
                      else goto THEN2
 7. THEN2:        Move right
 8. CHECK-LAST:   if head is 1
                      then goto {ACCEPT}
                      else goto {REJECT, THEN2}
 9. ACCEPT:       Return YES
10. REJECT:       Return NO
```

Figure 5.13: A nondeterministic program that does nothing useful at all. (Unlike our previous descriptions of Turing machine programs, the line numbers are included so that we can refer to them when describing different configurations.)

of what this program actually does, can we write a deterministic Turing machine program such that the language decided by the deterministic program is exactly the same as the language decided by this nondeterministic program? To simulate the nondeterministic program with a deterministic program, the deterministic program will initialize the set of possible nondeterministic configurations with the initial configuration, which indicates that:

1. the input string is on the tape;

2. the head is pointing to the first tape square;

3. the first line in the program is about to be executed.

For the program in Figure 5.13 and the input 101, the initial configuration would be:

Line number about to execute	Tape contents
1	[1]01

where the square brackets indicate the position of the tape head.

Since the symbol at the head is a 1, the nondeterministic program will choose to go to either THEN1 or THEN2. The deterministic program is going to need to keep track of the fact that the nondeterministic program could be in either one of two configurations after making this choice. The two possible configurations are:

Configuration Number	Line number about to execute	Tape contents
1	4	[1]01
2	7	[1]01

The deterministic program then needs to determine which set of configurations follow in one step from each of these two configurations. This process continues until a configuration that returns YES is encountered or all possible configurations return NO.

We can view the possible computation paths of the nondeterministic program for a particular input as forming a graph, which we call the **configuration graph,** in which there is one vertex for each of the possible configurations that can be reached. For example, Figure 5.14 shows the configuration graph for the nondeterministic program listed in Figure 5.13 with input 101.

This procedure of starting from the initial configuration, investigating all possible configurations that are one step away from the initial configuration, and then all possible configurations that are two steps away, and so on, until we find a configuration that returns YES or all possible configurations return NO is equivalent to doing breadth-first search on the configuration graph. The "goal" we are looking for is the vertex that corresponds to the nondeterministic program returning YES.

The deterministic program, of course, does not have access to the nondeterministic program's configuration graph for every possible input. The deterministic program must compute the configuration graph on the fly. This is not difficult, however, since each time the deterministic program expands a node

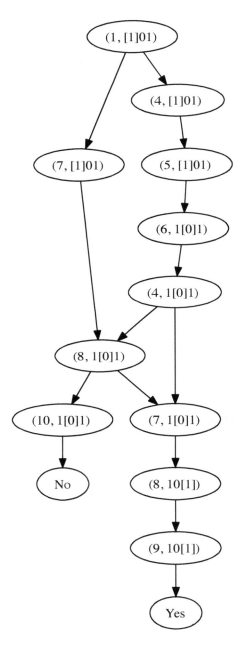

Figure 5.14: The configuration graph for the nondeterministic program in Figure 5.13 with input 101.

from the OPEN list, it need only compute the set of configurations that follow in one step from the configuration represented by the node.

For a configuration graph corresponding to a YES instance, the goal is in the graph, so breadth-first search will find the goal and return YES. Configuration graphs corresponding to NO instances will not include the goal node. As long as the configuration graph is finite, however, the deterministic machine will halt and return NO after it has searched the entire graph. The configuration graph *will be finite* for any nondeterministic machine that always halts. Consequently, for any language that is decided by a nondeterministic Turing machine, there is a corresponding deterministic Turing machine that decides that same language.

Theorem 5.4 *If there is a nondeterministic Turing machine that decides a language L, then there is a deterministic Turing machine that decides L.*

Nondeterminism, therefore, provides no additional power to the Turing machine in terms of the languages that can be decided. We can say the same thing for the languages that can be recognized by the two models.

Theorem 5.5 *If there is a nondeterministic Turing machine that recognizes a language L, then there is a deterministic Turing machine that recognizes L.*

Exercise 5.2 *Modify the argument preceeding Theorem 5.4 to prove Theorem 5.5*

Contrary to the title of this section, we will see that the concept of nondeterminism is far from useless. Oddly enough, nondeterminism plays a crucial role in determining the types of problems that can be solved in practice – and it has nothing at all to do with modeling free will.

Chapter 6

Computational Complexity

6.1 Introduction

So, what is a computer and what can it do? We have a good definition of a computer, we have seen some problems that computers can solve, and we have seen some problems that computers cannot solve. Is a partition of decision problems into those that are decidable and those that are undecidable a satisfactory explanation of what a computer can do?

Consider the following problem. There are two roommates, Tim and Francine, deciding on their dinner plans. Being recent college graduates, they have limited choices. They can eat one of two things: pig's tongue or spaghetti.[1] Tim and Francine have to decide on what to eat and who is going to cook. Tim loves the taste of pig's tongue but can't stand to cook it. Francine hates when Tim cooks spaghetti because he throws it at the wall to see if it is done, making the wall all sticky and inviting cockroaches into the kitchen. We would like to determine if it is possible for the outcome to satisfy both people (without either one of them changing their cooking habits). Since there are two possible outcomes for each choice to be made, we can model the choices using Boolean variables. Let x be the variable for the dinner choice, with $x =$ TRUE meaning they eat pig's tongue. Let y be the variable for the cook, with $y =$ TRUE meaning that Tim cooks dinner. Tim's preference can be stated as the Boolean formula $(\overline{x} \vee \overline{y})$. (Either they don't eat pig's tongue or Tim doesn't cook.)

---

[1] My cousins went to visit my mother's aunt once. She served them pig's tongue, which is apparently a delicacy in some parts of the world. No one ever went to visit my mother's aunt again.

Francine's preference can be stated as $(x \lor \bar{y})$. (Either they eat pig's tongue or Tim doesn't cook.) Obviously, we can satisfy both of them if Tim doesn't cook – that is, by setting $y =$ FALSE.

This isn't a terribly interesting problem from a computational viewpoint. But what if Tim and Francine are the stars of a new reality TV show where the viewers' preferences determine the outcome? Each viewer submits his or her preference as a simple "OR" of the two Boolean variables x and y or their negations, just as Tim and Francine's preferences were stated above. Tim and Francine, with the aid of a computer, have to choose an outcome that satisfies as many of the viewers as possible.

This problem of maximizing the number of satisfied viewers isn't all that difficult. There are only two Boolean variables, so there are only four possible outcomes. Even if this was the most watched show on the planet with a billion viewers, we could test all four of the outcomes in under a minute. The producers, however, are always making things more complicated to keep the viewers' interest. They add more and more variables for things like who cleans, who shops, who calls the exterminator, etc. Expecting that their audience may not be comprised of the most sophisticated viewers, the producers still require the viewers to express their preferences using a simple OR of any two of the Boolean variables or their negations. From now on, we'll refer to a Boolean variable or it's negation as a **literal** so we don't have to keep saying "a Boolean variable or its negation." We'll refer to an OR of any number of literals as a **clause**. In the case of *The Tim and Francine Show*, a clause represents a single viewer's stated preference.

Now we have a real computational problem on our hands:

GIVEN: 1.   a set of Boolean variables,
              2.   a collection of clauses, each containing exactly two
                   literals constructed from two different variables.

OBJECTIVE: Find an assignment of values to the Boolean variables
                   such that the number of satisfied clauses (i.e., clauses
                   that evaluate to TRUE) is maximized.

Unfortunately, this isn't a decision problem; it is an optimization problem because we are trying to find an outcome that maximizes something rather than simply answering YES or NO. Since we have so far restricted our discussion to decision problems, let's consider a related decision problem known as **2-SATISFIABILITY (2SAT)**.

GIVEN: 1.   a set of Boolean variables,
              2.   a collection of clauses, each containing exactly two
                    literals constructed from two different variables.

QUESTION: Is there an assignment of values to the Boolean variables
            such that every clause is satisfied (i.e., such that every
            clause evaluates to TRUE)?

In 2SAT, rather than maximizing the number of satisfied clauses, we must determine if it is possible to satisfy every clause. We'll come back to the optimization problem, known as **MAX2SAT**, after we have more of a theory with which to work. Note, however, that MAX2SAT must be at least as "hard" as 2SAT since if we had a truth assignment that satisfied the maximum number of clauses, we could simply check to see if that truth assignment satisfied all of the clauses.

Exercise 6.1 *What type of reduction did we just use to argue that MAX2SAT is at least as hard as 2SAT?*

Can we come up with an algorithm that solves 2SAT?
Hm...
hmm...
hmmmm...
hmmmmmmmm...
What if we just try all the possible outcomes? This algorithm certainly solves the problem, but the show is only 60 minutes long. Will the algorithm be able to come up with a solution quickly enough? Consider how much time the algorithm takes to solve an instance of 2SAT that includes n variables. There are 2^n possible outcomes. When the viewers cannot all be satisfied, the algorithm needs to check every possible outcome. This requires at least 2^n clause evaluations. Suppose we can evaluate 250 trillion clauses in a second with our super fast computer and the producers include 100 variables in a show. How long will it take to determine that the audience cannot be satisfied using this algorithm? At least 1,607,877 centuries.

Does it matter that 2SAT is decidable if "decidable" doesn't take into account any practical limitations on computing power? If every algorithm that solves a particular problem is going to take a million centuries to return a result, that problem certainly cannot be considered decidable in practice. But how do we determine what is decidable in practice? We need some way of measuring how complex a problem is in terms of the resources an algorithm requires to solve the problem. The first resource we consider is time.

6.2   Time

In the discussion of 2SAT above, we measured the running time of our algorithm as a function of a particular characteristic of the problem instance, namely the number of variables, n. The running time of that algorithm is $\Omega(2^n)$ in the worst case. The number of variables seemed like a natural parameter – the more variables we have, the more time we require. This measure of running time gives us the ability to see how well our algorithm scales up to bigger problem instances. (In the case of our 2SAT algorithm, not well.) We would like find a general characteristic of problem instances that indicates how "big" the problem instances are. Since we are using the Turing machine as our machine model, the parameter we will use is the number of symbols required to encode the problem instance as an input to a Turing machine. It seems intuitive that, in general, bigger problem instances will require longer encodings than smaller problem instances.

Definition 6.1 *We say the **running time** of a Turing machine is $O(T(n))$ if for each $n \geq 0$, the maximum number of steps the machine takes before halting on any input string of length n is $O(T(n))$. A problem can be **solved in $O(T(n))$ time** if it can be solved by a Turing machine whose running time is $O(T(n))$.*

In the above definition, we tacitly assume the problem instance is encoded using some "natural" encoding scheme. "Natural" is not a particularly technical term, but we will not go into a more detailed discussion of what "natural" really means in this context because encoding schemes are necessarily problem specific... and this book is supposed to be short. We simply assume the encoding scheme is easy to compute and does not create inputs that are unnecessarily large. For example, a scheme that encodes each YES instance as a 1 and each NO instance as a 0 is clearly out of bounds because it would require the encoder to solve the problem and pass the solution to the machine as input, leaving nothing for the machine to compute. It would also not be permissible to pad the end of the input with an exponential number of 1's since this would create an unnecessarily large input.

Given this definition of the time required to solve a problem, what problems should we consider solvable in practice? Our analysis of the brute force algorithm above for 2SAT demonstrates that problems requiring 2^n time should not be considered solvable in practice. What does that leave us with? We consider a problem to be a candidate for being solvable in practice if it can be solved in $O(n^k)$ for some constant k. Such a problem is said to be solvable in **polynomial time** because n^k is a polynomial in n, the size of the problem instance. We denote the set of all polynomial time solvable decision problems as P.

Definition 6.2 P *is the set of decision problems that can be solved in polynomial time on a Turing machine.*

It is important to realize that n^k could be large depending on k, so not all problems in P are solvable in practice. Consider the data in Figure 6.1.

			Running Time		
Input Size	n	n^3	n^{10}	1.1^n	2^n
10	$4 \cdot 10^{-14}$ s	$4 \cdot 10^{-12}$ s	$4 \cdot 10^{-5}$ s	10^{-14} s	$4 \cdot 10^{-12}$ s
100	$4 \cdot 10^{-13}$ s	$4 \cdot 10^{-9}$ s	11.6 d	$6 \cdot 10^{-11}$ s	10^6 c
1000	$4 \cdot 10^{-12}$ s	$4 \cdot 10^{-6}$ s	10^6 c	$3 \cdot 10^{17}$ c	10^{277} c
10000	$4 \cdot 10^{-11}$ s	$4 \cdot 10^{-3}$ s	10^{16} c	∞	∞
100000	$4 \cdot 10^{-10}$ s	4 s	10^{26} c	∞	∞
1000000	$4 \cdot 10^{-9}$ s	1 h	10^{36} c	∞	∞

Figure 6.1: The time required by an algorithm of the specified running time on various input sizes. The running time is assumed to represent the actual number of instructions executed by the algorithm, while the machine is assumed to be capable of executing 250 trillion instructions per second. Note: s represents seconds; h represents hours; d represents days; c represents centuries; ∞ is a really long time.

When $n = 10$, all of the machines have reasonable times. When $n = 100$, however, the 2^n time machine is no longer useful. The 1.1^n time machine takes well under a second when $n = 100$, but the $n = 1000$ line shows that the 1.1^n time machine is not useful even for moderately large inputs. Problems that require exponential time, therefore, cannot be considered solvable in practice even when the base is smaller than 2. (That was a big fat lie. See Exercise 6.4.) This is one motivation for considering P to be the set of problems that are candidates for being solvable in practice. Exponential time is just way too long.

Notice, however, that the n^{10} time machine takes over a million centuries when $n = 1000$. Why not restrict ourselves to problems solvable by polynomial time machines where the largest exponent in the polynomial (its *degree*) is small? One reason is that although we measure time with respect to the Turing machine, we would like our results on the complexity of problems to be independent of the particular type of machine used to solve the problem. Our results on undecidability in Chapter 4 are machine independent because of the Church-Turing Thesis. Recall that the Church-Turing Thesis states that there is no computational device more powerful than a Turing machine in terms of the set of decision problems that can be solved. All computational models that have as much power as a Turing machine are equivalent. However, the Turing machine is a model of a very simple machine. This simplicity makes the Church-Turing Thesis more plausible but it may make our analysis of time less generally applicable. For example, a machine with random access to memory rather than sequential access may be able to solve some problems much more quickly than a Turing machine.

Fortunately, the set of decision problems that are solvable in polynomial time on all reasonable machine models is the same as the set of decision problems that are solvable in polynomial time on a Turing machine. This statement is sometimes referred to as the **strong form of the Church-Turing Thesis**.[2] For a particular problem, there might be an n^2 time random access algorithm but no better than a n^6 time Turing machine algorithm. However, there is no problem that can be solved in polynomial time on a machine with random access to memory that cannot be solved in polynomial time on a Turing machine. This is true not just for machines with random access to memory but for all reasonable machine models that people have come up with so far, where "reasonable" is somewhat ill-defined. One requirement for a machine model to be considered reasonable is that the machine must not be able to access more than a constant amount of memory in any single time step. This implies that the memory required by an algorithm is at most a constant multiplied by the time required.

Since Turing machine programs look very different from the computer programs that we typically write, we usually measure the running time of algorithms using a machine model more like the standard computer architecture we are accustomed to. In this model, called a **Random Access Machine (RAM)**, we have variables of various types; arrays; simple arithmetic instructions such

---

[2]It is also referred to as the **Extended Church-Turing Thesis**.

as addition, subtraction, multiplication, and division; comparison instructions; control flow instructions; and an assignment operator. Rather than going into a great deal of detail on the technicalities involved in defining a RAM and showing that the set of problems solvable in polynomial time on a RAM is the same as that on a Turing machine, we will assume that the underlying machine provides the simple instructions available in a typical programming language and that the time taken by each of these instruction is constant. We do need to be careful not to allow the numbers computed during the execution of our algorithms to get too large. As demonstrated by the following exercise, this would violate the restriction that a reasonable machine can access only a constant amount of memory in any single time step.

Exercise 6.2 *Show that if the RAM described above includes multiplication in its instruction set and we measure the memory consumed by the machine as the number of bits needed to write down the largest number created at any point in the computation, the RAM would not obey our restriction on the relationship between time and memory.*

Multiplication gives us the ability to quickly create extremely large numbers, so we need to be careful when we make claims about the running times of our algorithms. In particular, it is possible to create numbers that are 2^n bits long in $O(n)$ steps. For the algorithms described in the rest of this book, multiplication is not a big issue.

Exercise 6.3 *Show that 2SAT is in* P.

Exercise 6.4 *Compute the times for an algorithm with running time $2^{n^{1/(100)}}$ as we did in Figure 6.1. You should see fairly reasonable running times unless n is impracticably large. Algorithms with exponential running times but where the exponent is much smaller than n would certainly be practical. On the other hand, try to design an algorithm that does something useful and has running time $2^{n^{1/(100)}}$.*

6.3 Combinatorial explosions

Let's consider another problem. Suppose, right out of college, you take a job for a mining company. The company has tried to automate the mining process

as much as possible on a very tight budget. They have a robot to deliver explosives to drop-off points near the ends of tunnels that need to be expanded. At
each of these drop-off points, there is another robot that detonates the explosives. Neither type of robot is very sophisticated. The delivery robot is given
a route and a bunch of explosives. It travels along the route, and at each drop-
off point, leaves the same amount of explosives. Unfortunately, if the robot
reaches a drop-off point a second time in its route, it will drop-off a second
batch of explosives. Even more unfortunately, the robots that actually detonate
the explosives use all of the explosives they are given. Using twice the amount
of explosives required at any one expansion point could bring down the whole
mine.

This operation is explained to you on your first day of work because you
are being put in charge of monitoring the delivery robots. In particular, your
job is to ensure that the route chosen for the delivery robot reaches each drop-
off point exactly once. After spending the morning calling your college friends
to tell them how much money you are making for talking on the company
phone (cell phones don't work in caves), you head to the lunch cave with your
copy of *The Dialogues of Plato* under your arm. Your manager stops you
to let you know one more thing. You get very little time to verify that the
route is satisfactory before the robot takes off, and in an odd coincidence, your
office/cave is right above the part of the mine that is being expanded. At this
point, you wonder why you ever listened to that strange college admission's
officer with the talking laptop who convinced you not to major in Philosophy.

The mine is too big and the tunnels changing too quickly for you to verify
each route by hand, so you'll need to design and implement an efficient algorithm to solve the problem in general. You quickly realize that you can model
the problem using a graph in which the vertices represent the drop-off points
and the edges represent the tunnels. For example, Figure 6.2 shows a robot in
trouble.

Modeled with a graph, the robot route verification problem becomes:

GIVEN: 1.   A graph $G(V, E)$, where V is the set of vertices and
                E is the set of edges;
           2.   a sequence of vertices $\langle v_1, \ldots, v_k \rangle$.

QUESTION: Is the sequence of vertices a valid route through the graph?
           In other words, does the sequence of vertices satisfy the
           following two conditions?

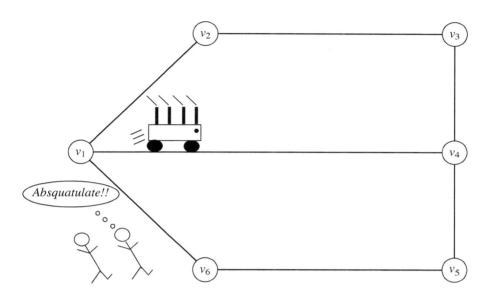

Figure 6.2: A robot running through the mine starting at v_1. Aliens from Chapter 2 running away.

    1. Each vertex appears exactly once;

    2. The sequence of vertices forms a cycle – that is, $(v_i, v_{i+1}) \in E$ for each $i, 0 \le i < k$, and $(v_k, v_1) \in E$.

A path satisfying the conditions in the problem definition above is called a **Hamiltonian cycle**. For example, the sequence $\langle v_1, v_2, v_3, v_4, v_5, v_6 \rangle$ defines a Hamiltonian cycle in the graph from Figure 6.2.

Lucky for you, this problem is easy to solve. Your algorithm can simply trace through the route verifying the three conditions above. You write your program and go back to your book. The program works so efficiently that within a week, your boss is impressed and you are promoted. In your new position, you will be designing the routes for the robots rather than just verifying that the routes won't blow the place up. Your spirits are so high that the first thing you do in your new position is call your friends to tell them that you really don't have time to talk anymore because you are now extremely busy and therefore extremely important. You approach your new job as you did your old one. You try to design an efficient algorithm to solve the problem, which is now:

GIVEN: A graph $G(V,E)$.

OBJECTIVE: Find a valid route through the graph. In other words, find
            a Hamiltonian cycle.

This looks like it might be a little trickier than just verifying that a path is a Hamiltonian cycle. Being well-trained in the design of algorithms, you decide to look at a couple of small examples. First you consider the case in which there are separate tunnels connecting each drop-off point to every other drop-off point. This is the case in which the graph is *complete*. (See Figure 6.3.) In

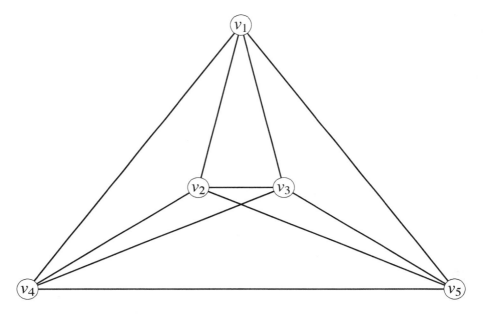

Figure 6.3: Any simple cycle including all the vertices in a complete graph is a Hamiltonian cycle.

this case, the problem is easy. In a complete graph with n vertices, every cycle of n distinct vertices is a Hamiltonian cycle.

Next you consider the graph in Figure 6.4 in which it is impossible to cycle from drop-off point v_4 through drop-off point v_5 and back again without going through drop-off point v_1 twice. Notice that this graph does not even have a Hamiltonian cycle. Wow, when the tunnel layout is such that there is no Hamiltonian cycle, no matter what route you choose, the whole mine is going to collapse. You decide that the first thing you need to do is to solve the

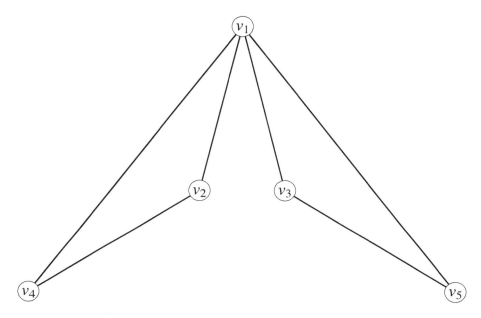

Figure 6.4: A graph without any Hamiltonian cycle.

problem of determining whether a graph has a Hamiltonian cycle so you can get out of there if the answer is no. You now have a decision problem, which is called the **HAMILTONIAN CYCLE** problem:

GIVEN: A graph $G(V,E)$.

QUESTION: Is there a Hamiltonian cycle in the graph?

After months of trying to find something better than an exponential time algorithm for solving this problem, your manager comes into your office with a security guard and a phone bill. It seems your inability to quickly come up with routes for the robot has caused huge delays in the mining process. Your services are no longer needed. You move back into your parents' house with time on your hands. You can't stop thinking about the HAMILTONIAN CYCLE problem. Why was it so easy to verify that a proposed solution to the HAMILTONIAN CYCLE problem is indeed a solution but so hard to determine if a graph has a Hamiltonian cycle?

The HAMILTONIAN CYCLE problem is said to have a *polynomial time verifier*. A **verifier** is an algorithm that takes two inputs. The first input is an instance of the problem. In the HAMILTONIAN CYCLE case, this would be the graph. The second input is a **certificate**, which is intended to certify that the first input is indeed a YES instance. For HAMILTONIAN CYCLE, the sequence of vertices making up the Hamiltonian cycle constitutes a certificate. It is straightforward to determine whether or not a sequence of vertices is a Hamiltonian cycle. If it is, the verifier answers YES. If it is not, the verifier answers NO. In general, a problem is **verifiable** if there is a verifier for the problem that satisfies the following properties:

1. For each YES instance x, there is a certificate c such that the verifier answers YES when given x and c.

2. For each NO instance y and every certificate c, the verifier answers NO when given y and c.

A problem is **verifiable in polynomial time** if there is a verifier for the problem with running time that is polynomial in the size of the first input, the first input being the instance of the problem. Since we called the set of decision problems with polynomial time algorithms P, let's call the set of decision problems with polynomial time verifiers NP (of course). NP stands for **Nondeterministic Polynomial time**. We call this set NP because there is a polynomial time verifier for a decision problem if and only if there is a nondeterministic Turing machine that solves the problem in polynomial time, where we say the running time of a nondeterministic Turing machine is the length of the longest possible computation path.

Definition 6.3 *The **running time** of a nondeterministic machine is $O(T(n))$ if for each $n \geq 0$, the maximum number of steps the machine takes before halting in any sequence of nondeterministic choices on any input string of length n is $O(T(n))$. A problem can be **solved nondeterministically in $O(T(n))$ time** if it can be solved by a nondeterministic Turing machine with running time that is $O(T(n))$.*

Definition 6.4 NP *is the set of decision problems that are solvable in polynomial time on a nondeterministic Turing machine.*

Let's develop a nondeterministic algorithm for HAMILTONIAN CYCLE that simply walks around the vertices of the graph in a nondeterministic order until it has crossed $|V|$ edges, where $|V|$ is the number of vertices in the graph.

If the algorithm gets back to the start before seeing any vertex twice, it has found a Hamiltonian cycle. Here is a complete description of the algorithm:

NondeterministicHamiltonianCycle(V, E)

```
1    Let start be any vertex in V.
2    Initialize v to start.
3    for i = 1 to |V|        // |V| is the number of vertices in the graph
4        Nondeterministically choose a vertex u adjacent to v.
5        if u has been marked as seen
6          then return No
7          else begin
8                  Mark u as having been seen.
9                  Set v to u
10               end
11   end for
12   if u is start
13     then return YES
14     else return No
```

Because of the nondeterministic choices made by the algorithm, there are many possible computation paths. However, no matter what sequence of choices is made, the loop iterates $O(|V|)$ times. Therefore, the nondeterministic running time of the algorithm is $O(|V|)$. This implies that HAMILTONIAN CYCLE is in NP.

Exercise 6.5 *Argue that the nondeterministic algorithm described above correctly solves the HAMILTONIAN CYCLE problem.*

Exercise 6.6 *Show that a decision problem is in NP if and only if the problem has a polynomial time verifier.*

As you lay on your parents' couch between less and less frequent phone conversations with your employed friends, you wonder why were you able to design a polynomial time verifier but not a polynomial time algorithm for the HAMILTONIAN CYCLE problem. If it is possible to verify a solution to a problem in polynomial time, shouldn't it be possible to tell whether a solution exists in polynomial time? In other words, shouldn't P = NP? Maybe not. Verifying a proposed solution is indeed a solution seems easier than finding a solution, so maybe P ≠ NP.

No one knows whether $P = NP$ and plenty of people have been trying to figure it out since the early 1970's. The Clay Mathematics Institute listed the P vs NP problem as one of their "Millenium problems" in 2000. The prize for solving the problem is $1,000,000. It is perhaps the most important open question in computer science and now that you are unemployed you have become obsessed with answering it. Unfortunately, you get a job offer – in sales.

6.4 Polynomial time reductions

You are offered a job traveling the country selling robots. Each month you are given a list of cities that you must visit. You don't mind traveling, but you have to pay for your own travel expenses, so this job is not ideal. Since you enjoy designing algorithms more than working on your sales pitch, you immediately begin designing an algorithm to minimize your travel expenses. The first thing you need to do when given a list of destinations is to collect information on the cost of travel between each pair of cities on your list. Given that cost information, you would like to compute the cheapest possible tour through all of the cities. In other words, you want to solve the following problem:

GIVEN: A set of cities and a cost for traveling between each pair of cities.

OBJECTIVE: Find a tour through the cities with minimum cost.

After a few moments of thought, you realize that you could pay out more than you earn in this job. You estimate your expected revenue from sales. If the cost of the best possible tour exceeds this expected revenue, you are better off sitting on your parents' couch thinking about the P vs NP problem. Your problem has become a decision problem known as the **TRAVELING SALESMAN PROBLEM (TSP)**:

GIVEN: A set of cities, a cost for traveling between each pair of cities, and a target cost T.

QUESTION: Is there a tour through the cities such that the total cost of the tour is at most T?

If you are given a tour, you can easily determine if the cost of the tour is at most T. In other words, you can design a polynomial time verifier for

TSP in which the proposed tour serves as the certificate. This means TSP is in NP. You are stumped, though, in trying to design a polynomial time algorithm to solve the problem in general, and the more you think about the problem, the more you think about your experience with the HAMILTONIAN CYCLE problem. Don't these problems seem eerily similar? (Well, maybe not "eerily".)

If we think of the cities in a TSP instance as vertices in a complete graph and the costs between cities as the weights of the corresponding edges in the graph, then in both problems we are looking for simple cycles through the graph that contain every vertex. In other words, both problems require us to output a permutation of the vertices. The difference between the two problems arises in the way the output permutation is restricted. In HAMILTONIAN CY-CLE, the permutation is restricted by the existence or non-existence of edges. In TSP, the permutation is restricted by the cost of the edges and the target cost T. Perhaps there is a way to develop a correspondence between the existence of an edge in the graph given in the HAMILTONIAN CYCLE instance and the cost of the corresponding edge in the TSP instance.

Let H be the graph in the HAMILTONIAN CYCLE instance. Let's create a complete graph G on the same set of vertices as H and assign costs to each edge in G in a way that indicates whether or not the edge corresponds to an edge in H. In TSP, higher cost edges are less likely to be usable in a tour, so when two vertices do not have an edge between them in H, we want the cost between them to be high. When two vertices do have an edge between them in H, we want the cost between them to be low. Let's try something simple. Let the cost of an edge in G be 1 if the edge is in H and 2 otherwise. Consider the two example graphs we looked at in our discussion of the HAMILTONIAN CYCLE problem. Figure 6.5 shows what happens when we have a complete graph as the HAMILTONIAN CYCLE instance. Obviously no edges need to be added and each edge is assigned cost 1. Any Hamiltonian cycle in H corresponds to a TSP tour in G of cost $|V|$, where V is the set of vertices.

Now consider the example in Figure 6.6, a graph that does not contain a Hamiltonian cycle. Edges of cost 1 in G correspond to edges from H, while edges of cost 2 connect vertices that are not adjacent in H. Because H does not contain a Hamiltonian cycle, any Hamiltonian cycle in G must contain an edge that does not appear in H. Since a TSP tour is a Hamiltonian cycle, any TSP tour in G must include an edge of cost 2. Consequently, the cost of any TSP tour must be at least $|V| + 1$.

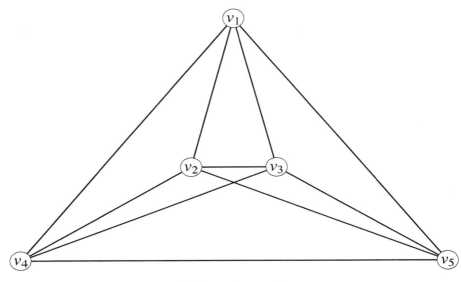

(a) A complete graph.

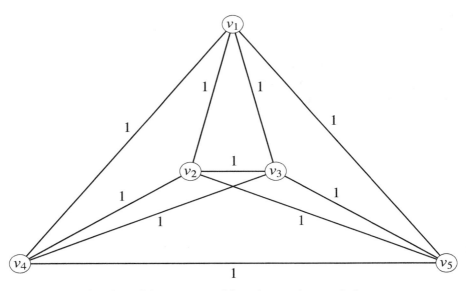

(b) The TSP instance created from the complete graph above.

Figure 6.5: A complete graph transformed into a TSP instance.

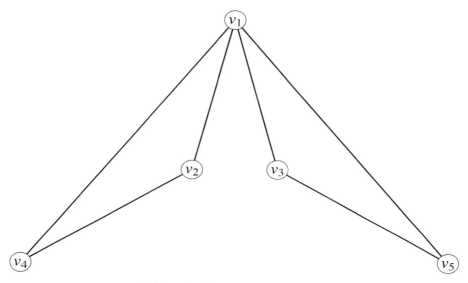

(a) A graph without a Hamiltonian cycle.

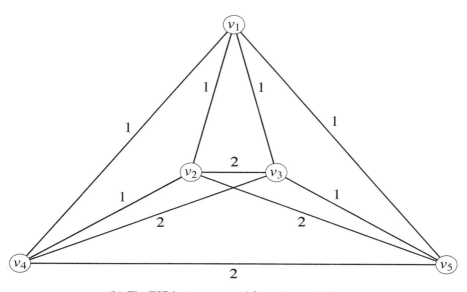

(b) The TSP instance created from the graph above.

Figure 6.6: A graph with no Hamiltonian cycle transformed into a TSP instance.

It looks like a Hamiltonian cycle in H is a TSP tour in G of cost $|V|$. Furthermore, any TSP tour in G of cost $|V|$ is a Hamiltonian cycle in H. What we have here is an instance mapping reduction from HAMILTONIAN CYCLE to TSP. Recall from Definition 4.2 that an instance mapping reduction from a problem A to a problem B takes an instance x of A and creates an instance y of B such that x is a YES instance of A if and only if y is a YES instance of B.

Let's recap our reduction from HAMILTONIAN CYCLE to TSP and formally prove it is correct. Given an instance of the HAMILTONIAN CYCLE problem (i.e., a graph $H(V,E)$), create an instance of the TSP problem as follows:

1. Let the set of cities be the vertices from H.

2. For each pair of cities, u and v, set $cost(u,v) = \begin{cases} 1 & \text{if } (u,v) \in E \\ 2 & \text{otherwise} \end{cases}$

3. Set the target value $T = |V|$.

Let G be the graph corresponding to the TSP instance created by this reduction. Suppose there is a Hamiltonian cycle in H. This cycle is a TSP tour of cost $|V|$ in G. Now suppose there is a TSP tour with cost at most T in G. Since there must be $|V|$ edges in this tour and $T = |V|$, each edge in the tour must have cost 1. This tour, then, must consist entirely of edges from H. Therefore, the TSP tour is a Hamiltonian cycle in H. We can conclude that there is a Hamiltonian cycle in H if and only if there is a TSP tour with cost at most T in G.

This reduction is very easy to compute. We could easily take an instance of HAMILTONIAN CYCLE and create the specified instance of TSP in time that is polynomial in the size of the graph. What does this tell us? If we had a polynomial time algorithm for TSP, we could create a polynomial time algorithm for the HAMILTONIAN CYCLE problem as follows:

1. Given an instance of HAMILTONIAN CYCLE, transform it into an instance of TSP as specified above in polynomial time.

2. Run the hypothetical polynomial time algorithm for TSP and return the result.

If the algorithm returns YES, indicating that there is a TSP tour with cost at most T, then the HAMILTONIAN CYCLE instance is a YES instance. If the algorithm returns No, indicating that there is no TSP tour with cost at most T, then there is no Hamiltonian cycle in the given graph. Therefore, the algorithm returns the correct answer for each instance of the HAMILTONIAN CYCLE problem.

If the size of the HAMILTONIAN CYCLE instance is n, the time taken by Step 1 of this algorithm is $O(n^k)$, for some constant $k > 0$. Step 2 runs in time that is polynomial in the size of the TSP instance. The size of the TSP instance created will also be $O(n^k)$ since as part of our assumption that we have a reasonable model of computation, we limit the machine to use no more than a constant amount of memory in any single time step. If the size of the TSP instance created is at most cn^k, for some constant c, then the running time of Step 2 is $O\left(\left(cn^k\right)^b\right) = O\left(c^b n^{bk}\right)$ for some contant $b > 0$. Since b, c, and k are constants, this is polynomial in n, the size of the original HAMILTO-NIAN CYCLE instance. The algorithm above is therefore a polynomial time algorithm for HAMILTONIAN CYCLE.

We have just shown that a polynomial time algorithm for TSP can be used to create a polynomial time algorithm for HAMILTONIAN CYCLE. Consequently, TSP must be at least as hard to solve as HAMILTONIAN CYCLE, with respect to polynomial time. Polynomial time reductions, like the one above, are an indispensable tool for relating the complexities of different problems.

Theorem 6.5 *Let A and B be two decision problems. If there is a polynomial time instance mapping reduction from A to B, written $A \leq_m^p B$, then if B is in P, A must be in P.*

Exercise 6.7 *Prove Theorem 6.5.*

6.5 NP-complete problems.

Still sitting on your parents' couch, you begin to wonder whether other problems in NP might be related in the same way that HAMILTONIAN CYCLE and TSP are related. Too much thinking for one day. You call your best friend, who works for an insurance company and who still has time to talk to you. Unfortunately, today he is out of the office. There has been an explosion at a mine and he is assessing the damage. You lay back on the couch and watch your favorite TV show, *The Tim and Francine Show*.

Host: "So Tim, how did you and Francine meet?"

Tim   "Well, I took a bus home from the airport one morn-
             ing a long time ago. I had a choice of sitting next to
             this guy who looked like a pot head in the front or
             this woman in the back who was reading a book. The
             choice was obvious. I struck up a conversation and
             the rest is history. That bus ride changed my life."

Host   "Wow, lucky that seat wasn't taken. What do you do
             for a living Tim?"

Tim   "I am a professor of English literature."

Host   "English lit huh? Who is your favorite author?"

Tim   "Well, my specialty is Chaucer but my personal fa-
             vorite author has always been E. B. White."

Host   "OK, let's get on with the show. In the past, the
             viewers have been restricted to specifying their pref-
             erences as an OR of two literals. However, we have
             recently purchased a new super fast computer system,
             so today we are allowing viewers to specify an OR of
             as many literals as they want!"

You are thrilled. However, because of your recent obsession with algorithms, you begin to wonder about the algorithm used to determine the outcome based on the viewers' preferences. If it is possible to satisfy all of the
viewers, will Tim and Francine be able to find the satisfying outcome? In other
words, can they solve the following problem quickly enough for the show to
flow smoothly?

GIVEN: 1.   a set of Boolean variables;
             2.   a collection of clauses, each consisting of an OR of
                  any number of distinct literals formed using these
                  variables.

QUESTION: Is there an assignment of values to the Boolean vari-
             ables such that every clause is satisfied (i.e., evaluates
             to TRUE?

The problem is referred to as the **SATISFIABILITY** problem or just **SAT**. In 1971, Stephen Cook proved that SAT has a very interesting property: every problem in NP can be reduced to SAT in polynomial time. By Theorem 6.5, this implies that if there is a polynomial time algorithm for SAT, then there is a polynomial time algorithm for every problem in NP. In other words, if SAT is in P, then P = NP. SAT, then, is as hard as any other problem in NP with respect to polynomial time and is said to be NP-**complete**.

Definition 6.6 *A problem B is* NP-**complete** *if B is in* NP, *and for every problem A in* NP, *there is a polynomial time instance mapping reduction from A to B.*

Theorem 6.7 (Cook-Levin Theorem) *SAT is* NP-*complete.*

The proof of this theorem is rather long. However, it is worthwhile to work through it so that we can see how nondeterministic computation can be efficiently encoded in a Boolean formula.

6.6 Proof of the Cook-Levin Theorem

Consider any problem A in NP. We need to show that A can be reduced to SAT in polynomial time. Since A is an arbitrary problem in NP, we don't really know much about it. The only thing we do know is that there is a nondeterministic Turing machine N_A that decides A and whose running time is $O(n^k)$ time, for some constant k. Therefore, we can restate the problem as:

GIVEN: A string x.

QUESTION: Does N_A accept x?

Since N_A accepts x if and only if there is some path from the starting configuration to an accepting configuration in the configuration graph for N_A on input x, we can restate the problem again as:

GIVEN: A string x.

QUESTION: Is there a path from the starting configuration to an accepting configuration in the configuration graph for N_A on input x?

It is this problem that we will reduce to SAT. For each input string x, we need to create a set of clauses that can be satisfied simultaneously if and only if there is a path through the configuration graph leading from the starting configuration to an accepting configuration. Recall from Chapter 5 that each node in the configuration graph for N_A on input string x represents a particular configuration for the machine consisting of:

1. the line number about to be executed;

2. the contents of the tape;

3. the position of the head.

First, we need to define the variables over which our clauses will be created. These variables need to be expressive enough to represent N_A being in a particular configuration at a particular time step in the computation. We need three types of Boolean variables, one for each part of the configuration:

1. LINE$[t, l]$ for each possible time step t and line number l;

2. HEAD$[t, i]$ for each time step t and each tape square i;

3. SYMBOL$[t, i, \alpha]$ for each time step t, each tape square i, and each symbol α.

We interpret LINE$[t, l]$ = TRUE to mean that line l of the program will be executed at time step t. We interpret HEAD$[t, i]$ = TRUE to mean the head is at square i on the tape at time t. We interpret SYMBOL$[t, i, \alpha]$ = TRUE to mean that at time t the symbol at square i on the tape is α.

We can use these variables to represent any configuration at any time step. For example, the formula:

LINE$[1, 1] \wedge$ HEAD$[1, 1]$
$$\wedge \text{SYMBOL}[1, 1, 0] \wedge \text{SYMBOL}[1, 2, 1] \wedge \text{SYMBOL}[1, 3, 1]$$

represents an initial configuration with 011 as the input string. In other words, if we assign TRUE to each of the variables in this formula, we interpret that to mean that at time 1, line 1 is about to be executed, the head is at the first tape square, and the symbols on the tape are 011.

Next we need to combine these variables into a set of clauses that can be satisfied simultaneously if and only if there is a path from the starting configuration to an accepting configuration in the configuration graph. Since we must be able to transform the input string into our formula in polynomial time, we need to be careful that the computation we perform is not too complex. The computation needed to create each clause below is minimal, so as long as the size of the formula created is polynomial in the size of the input string, the reduction can be done in polynomial time.

First we should check to make sure that the number of variables we need is polynomial in the size of the input string. Since the running time of N_A is $O(n^k)$ for some constant k, we know the maximum length of any path beginning at the starting configuration is at most $cn^k + 2$ for some constant c and any input of size n. Therefore, there are at most $cn^k + 2$ time steps to consider. Furthermore, since a Turing machine can access only one new square on a tape in each time step, the maximum number of squares used by N_A on the tape is also $cn^k + 2$. Finally, we know that the number of lines in the program for N_A does not changed based on the input. If we let l be the number of lines in the program and a be the number of symbols in the tape alphabet, we need to create $l(cn^k + 2)$ LINE variables, $(cn^k + 2)(cn^k + 2)$ HEAD variables, and $a(cn^k + 2)(cn^k + 2)$ SYMBOL variables. The total number of variables is, therefore, polynomial in n.

Exercise 6.8 *Why did we need to use $cn^k + 2$ instead of cn^k?*

We are now prepared to develop the complete set of clauses defined over these variables. We need three types of clauses:

1. clauses that force any satisfying truth assignment to assign values to variables that are consistent with our interpretation of the variables;

2. clauses that ensure any satisfying truth assignment corresponds to a valid sequence of line numbers executed in the program;

3. clauses that ensure the contents of the tape are updated properly.

Again, to ensure this reduction takes no more than polynomial time, we need to make sure we do not create too many clauses. To simplify the exposition, counting the clauses created is left as an exercise.

Exercise 6.9 *Verify that the number of clauses created in the proof of the Cook-Levin Theorem is polynomial in n.*

Clauses to ensure consistent interpretation

We need to ensure that any satisfying truth assignment assigns values to variables in a way that is consistent with our interpretation. In particular, in any configuration occurring along a single computation path, N_A cannot be at two different line numbers, cannot have the head at two different tape squares, and cannot have two different symbols in the same tape square. To ensure consistency at each possible individual time step t, therefore, we need to add clauses to our formula for each time step t as follows:

For all line numbers l and k such that $l \neq k$, add the clause:

$$\overline{\text{LINE}[t,l]} \vee \overline{\text{LINE}[t,k]}.$$

For all tape squares i and j such that $i \neq j$, add the clause:

$$\overline{\text{HEAD}[t,i]} \vee \overline{\text{HEAD}[t,j]}.$$

For all tape squares i and all symbols α and γ such that $\alpha \neq \gamma$, add the clause:

$$\overline{\text{SYMBOL}[t,i,\alpha]} \vee \overline{\text{SYMBOL}[t,i,\gamma]}.$$

To see how these clauses work, consider a truth assignment that sets two different LINE variables to TRUE for the same time step. For example, suppose a truth assignment sets both LINE$[10,1]$ and LINE$[10,2]$ to TRUE. That truth assignment will not satisfy the clause $\left(\overline{\text{LINE}[10,1]} \vee \overline{\text{LINE}[10,2]} \right)$. Any truth assignment that satisfies all of the clauses above cannot set more than one of the LINE variables to TRUE, more than one of the HEAD variables to TRUE, nor more than one of the SYMBOL variables for a single tape square to TRUE for any particular time step.

Clauses to ensure consistent progression through the program

We must also ensure consistency between time steps. If the instruction to be executed at time t is Move or Write, for example, then the line at time $t+1$ is simply the next line in the program. In other words, for each line l such that the instruction at line l is either Move or Write, we have for each time step t:

$$\text{LINE}[t,l] \implies \text{LINE}[t+1,l+1].$$

Our deep knowledge of Boolean logic tells us that $p \Rightarrow q$ is equivalent to $\overline{p} \vee q$, so we can convert this implication into the clause:

$$\overline{\text{LINE}[t,l]} \vee \text{LINE}[t+1, l+1].$$

If the instruction to be executed at time t is Return, then the program halts, so the line number should not change from that time step onward. Therefore, for each line l such that the instruction at line l is Return, we have for each time step t:

$$\text{LINE}[t,l] \Rightarrow \text{LINE}[t+1, l]$$

which is equivalent to the clause:

$$\overline{\text{LINE}[t,l]} \vee \text{LINE}[t+1, l].$$

An if-goto instruction is slightly more complicated, of course, since the next line to be executed will depend on the symbol at the head's current position on the tape. Furthermore, since this is a nondeterministic program, there could be a choice of a number of different lines to go to. For each line l, such that the instruction at line l is:

```
if head is α
   then goto {then₁,...,thenᵣ}
   else goto {else₁,...,elseₛ}
```

we have two implications for each time step t and each tape square i:

$$\text{LINE}[t,l] \wedge \text{HEAD}[t,i] \wedge \text{SYMBOL}[t,i,\alpha]$$
$$\Rightarrow \text{LINE}[t+1, then_1] \vee, \dots, \vee \text{LINE}[t+1, then_r]$$

$$\text{LINE}[t,l] \wedge \text{HEAD}[t,i] \wedge \overline{\text{SYMBOL}[t,i,\alpha]}$$
$$\Rightarrow \text{LINE}[t+1, else_1] \vee, \dots, \vee \text{LINE}[t+1, else_r]$$

Using De Morgan's laws and the equivalence of $p \Rightarrow q$ and $\overline{p} \vee q$, we can see that these two implications are equivalent to the following two clauses:

$$\overline{\text{LINE}[t,l]} \vee \overline{\text{HEAD}[t,i]} \vee \overline{\text{SYMBOL}[t,i,\alpha]}$$
$$\vee \text{LINE}[t+1, then_1] \vee, \dots, \vee \text{LINE}[t+1, then_r]$$

$$\overline{\text{LINE}[t,l]} \vee \overline{\text{HEAD}[t,i]} \vee \text{SYMBOL}[t,i,\alpha]$$
$$\vee \text{LINE}[t+1, else_1] \vee, \dots, \vee \text{LINE}[t+1, else_r]$$

Clauses to ensure the consistency of the tape contents

We have clauses to ensure consistency at an individual time step and clauses to ensure that each line follows from the previous line according to the instructions in the program. We must also ensure that the position of the head and the symbols written to the tape are consistent with the program's instructions. If you have gotten this far, you should be able to convince yourself that the following implications converted into clauses suffice.

First, we need to ensure that the head moves correctly. For each line l such that the instruction at line l is Move Right, we have for each time step t and tape square i:

$$\text{LINE}[t,l] \wedge \text{HEAD}[t,i] \;\Rightarrow\; \text{HEAD}[t+1,i+1].$$

For each line l such that the instruction at line l is Move Left, we have for each time step t and tape square $i > 1$:

$$\text{LINE}[t,l] \wedge \text{HEAD}[t,i] \;\Rightarrow\; \text{HEAD}[t+1,i-1].$$

We need a different clause for tape square 1 since the machine does not move if the instruction is Move Left from the first tape square:

$$\text{LINE}[t,l] \wedge \text{HEAD}[t,1] \;\Rightarrow\; \text{HEAD}[t+1,1].$$

Since no other instruction changes the head position, for each line l such that the instruction at line l is not a Move instruction, we have for each time step t and each tape square i:

$$\text{LINE}[t,l] \wedge \text{HEAD}[t,i] \;\Rightarrow\; \text{HEAD}[t+1,i].$$

Next, we need to ensure that the symbols are written to the tape correctly. For each line l such that the instruction at line l is Write α, we have for each time step t and tape square i:

$$\text{LINE}[t,l] \wedge \text{HEAD}[t,i] \;\Rightarrow\; \text{SYMBOL}[t+1,i,\alpha].$$

To ensure that we only change the symbol at the head position, we need the following set of clauses. For each tape square i, we have for each time step t:

$$\overline{\text{HEAD}[t,i]} \wedge \text{SYMBOL}[t,i,\alpha] \;\Rightarrow\; \text{SYMBOL}[t+1,i,\alpha].$$

In addition, to ensure that no instruction other than a `Write` changes the contents of the tape, for each line l such that the instruction at line l is not a `Write` instruction, we have for each time step t, each tape square i, and each tape symbol α:

$$\text{LINE}[t,l] \wedge \text{HEAD}[t,i] \wedge \text{SYMBOL}[t,i,\alpha] \Rightarrow \text{SYMBOL}[t+1,i,\alpha].$$

Finally, we need clauses to ensure that the computation begins at the starting configuration and ends at an accepting configuration. To represent the starting configuration for an input string $x = \alpha_1 \alpha_2 \ldots \alpha_n$, create a clause:

$$\text{LINE}[1,1] \wedge \text{HEAD}[1,1]$$
$$\wedge \text{SYMBOL}[1,1,\alpha_1] \wedge \text{SYMBOL}[1,2,\alpha_2] \wedge \ldots \wedge \text{SYMBOL}[1,n,\alpha_n]$$
$$\wedge \text{SYMBOL}[1,n+1,\beta] \wedge \ldots \wedge \text{SYMBOL}[1,cn^k+2,\beta]$$

If $l_1, l_2, \ldots, l_k$ are lines in the program that return YES, we have the following clause to ensure that the machine reaches an accepting configuration:

$$\text{LINE}[cn^k+2,l_1] \vee \text{LINE}[cn^k+2,l_2] \vee \ldots \vee \text{LINE}[cn^k+2,l_k]$$

For this clause to be satisfied, we must be at one of the accepting configurations at the last time step.

Our complete formula consists of:

1. clauses forcing any satisfying truth assignment to assign values to variables that are consistent with our interpretation of the variables;

2. clauses ensuring that any satisfying truth assignment corresponds to a valid sequence of line numbers executed in the program;

3. clauses ensuring the contents of the tape are updated properly;

4. a clause ensuring that the machine starts in the starting configuration;

5. a clause ensuring that the machine ends in an accepting configuration.

N_A accepts x if and only if this formula is satisfiable. Since this formula can be created in time that is polynomial in the length of x, any language A in NP can be reduced to SAT in polynomial time. Therefore, SAT is NP-complete.

Chapter 7

Reduce, Reuse, Recycle!

We watched way too much *Bob the Builder* in my house.

7.1 Introduction

By Theorem 6.5, the existence of a polynomial time algorithm for an NP-complete problem would imply that any problem in NP could be solved in polynomial time. In other words, finding a polynomial time algorithm for an NP-complete problem would prove that P = NP. Since it is widely believed that P $\neq$ NP, proving that a problem is NP-complete provides pretty good evidence that there is no polynomial time algorithm to solve the problem.

We know that SAT is NP-complete, but what about the other problems, HAMILTONIAN CYCLE and TSP, that we considered in Chapter 6? To prove that HAMILTONIAN CYCLE is NP-complete, we would have to show that there is a polynomial time instance mapping reduction from every problem in NP to HAMILTONIAN CYCLE. To do that, we could do something similar to what we did for SAT: show how to encode an accepting nondeterministic computation for an arbitrary problem in NP as a graph with an Hamiltonian cycle. That seems like it might be a little harder than encoding computation as a Boolean formula. What if instead we could reduce SAT to HAMILTONIAN CYCLE in polynomial time? Then, for each problem A in NP, we could reduce A to HAMILTONIAN CYCLE in polynomial time as follows:

1. Given an instance of problem A.

2. Convert the instance to an equivalent instance of SAT in polynomial time as described in Chapter 6.

3. Convert the SAT instance into an equivalent instance of HAMILTO-NIAN CYCLE using our hypothetical polynomial time reduction.

Any YES instance of A would be transformed into a YES instance of SAT, which would then be transformed into a YES instance of HAMILTONIAN CYCLE. Any NO instance of A would be transformed into a NO instance of SAT, which would then be transformed into a NO instance of HAMILTONIAN CYCLE. Therefore, this is an instance mapping reduction of A to HAMILTO-NIAN CYCLE. Furthermore, the reduction runs in time that is polynomial in the size of the instance of A because the composition of polynomials is a polynomial. For example, suppose we can reduce a problem A to SAT in n^3 time. Because of our restriction that a machine can only use a constant amount of memory in a single time step, the size of the SAT instance created for an instance x of A would be $O(|x|^3)$, where $|x|$ is the size of x. If our reduction of SAT to HAMILTONIAN CYCLE takes n^2 time, then the reduction from A to HAMILTONIAN CYCLE takes $O(|x|^6)$ time overall. The existence of a polynomial time reduction from SAT to HAMILTONIAN CYCLE would therefore imply that HAMILTONIAN CYCLE is NP-complete. (Remember, we already know that HAMILTONIAN CYCLE is in NP). In general, we have the following extremely useful result:

Theorem 7.1 *Let B and C be decision problems such that B is* NP*-complete and C is in* NP. *If there is a polynomial time instance mapping reduction from B to C, then C is also* NP*-complete.*

Exercise 7.1 *Prove Theorem 7.1.*

7.2 Three is a crowd.

Before trying to reduce SAT to HAMILTONIAN CYCLE, let's try a couple of simpler reductions. First, consider a restricted version of SAT in which every clause has exactly three distinct literals. This problem, called **3SAT**, is often easier to use than SAT in reductions and is defined formally as follows:

GIVEN: 1.   a set of Boolean variables,

2. a collection of clauses over the variables containing three distinct literals each.

QUESTION: Is there an assignment of values to the Boolean variables such that every clause is satisfied.

To prove that 3SAT is NP-complete, we first need to prove that 3SAT is in NP by constructing a polynomial time verifier. What could serve as a certificate that tells us it is possible to satisfy all of the clauses at once? How about the truth assignment that satisfies them? In other words, given an instance of 3SAT and a particular assignment of truth values to the Boolean variables, verify that this truth assignment satisfies all of the clauses. We can certainly do that in polynomial time, so 3SAT is in NP.

The next thing we need to do is to show how to take an instance of SAT and create an instance of 3SAT such that the answers for the two instances are the same. Furthermore, we need to show that this can be done in polynomial time. So, let $X = \{x_1, x_2, \ldots, x_n\}$ be the set of variables and $C = \{c_1, c_2, \ldots, c_m\}$ be the set of clauses in an arbitrary instance of SAT. We need to create a set of variables and a set of clauses for the 3SAT instance. There is nothing that says we have to use the variables from our SAT instance in the 3SAT instance we create. We could use an entirely different set of variables, but it seems reasonable to start with the same set of variables and see how far we can get.

To create a set of clauses, it may be easier to work with one of the SAT clauses at a time rather than trying to work with the entire set of clauses at once. First, suppose we have a 2-literal clause, $(x_1 \lor x_2)$, in the SAT instance. Let's see if we can replace this clause with one or more 3-literal clauses in such a way that the entire resulting set of 3SAT clauses is equivalent to this single clause. To turn a 2-literal clause into a 3-literal clause, we need to add another literal to the clause. We could add a literal for an existing variable like x_3, but since we would prefer to have the changes we make to one clause not affect other clauses, let's create a new variable called w. That way we won't have to worry too much about where x_3 appears in the other SAT clauses. If we were to simply replace $(x_1 \lor x_2)$ with $(x_1 \lor x_2 \lor w)$, then we would no longer be required to set either of x_1 or x_2 to TRUE to satisfy the clause. Instead, we need to replace $(x_1 \lor x_2)$ with two clauses: $(x_1 \lor x_2 \lor w)$ and $(x_1 \lor x_2 \lor \overline{w})$. If x_1 and x_2 are both FALSE, we can only satisfy one of the two clauses. On the other hand if either x_1 or x_2 are TRUE, we satisfy both clauses. Therefore, replacing every 2-literal clause with a pair of 3-literal clauses in this way gives us an equivalent set of clauses.

Can we do the same sort of thing with clauses that have only a single literal, say (x_1)? We are going to need to add two more variables; name them y and z. The following set of 3-literal clauses is equivalent to (x_1):

$$(x_1 \lor y \lor z) \land (x_1 \lor y \lor \bar{z}) \land (x_1 \lor \bar{y} \lor z) \land (x_1 \lor \bar{y} \lor \bar{z})$$

(You should verify this equivalence, perhaps with a truth table.)

It looks like we've got something here. Let's try a clause that has four literals, say $(x_1 \lor x_2 \lor x_3 \lor x_4)$. We can't just break the clause up into $(x_1 \lor x_2 \lor x_3)$ and (x_4) and then replace the (x_4) clause with four 3-literal clauses as described above because the connection between x_4 and the other variables would be lost. Setting x_4 to TRUE would satisfy the original clause but would not be sufficient to satisfy the two 3SAT clauses because one of x_1, x_2, or x_3 would also have to be TRUE to satisfy $(x_1 \lor x_2 \lor x_3)$.

For two clauses to have some kind of connection without depending on the other clauses in the formula, the two clauses need to have at least one variable in common. So let's add another variable, call it u, and split the clause into two clauses, with u being represented by a literal in both. Let's say we have $(x_1 \lor x_2 \lor u)$ as the first clause. If x_1 and x_2 are both FALSE, then for $(x_1 \lor x_2 \lor u)$ to be satisfied, u must be TRUE. So we want u being TRUE to force either x_3 or x_4 to be TRUE in any satisfying truth assignment. In other words, we want our second clause to be equivalent to $u \Rightarrow x_3 \lor x_4$. As everyone knows from kindergarten (or from the Stuff You Need To Know section of this book), $u \Rightarrow x_3 \lor x_4$ is equivalent to $(\bar{u} \lor x_3 \lor x_4)$ because if p and q are Boolean formulas, $p \Rightarrow q$ is equivalent to $\bar{p} \lor q$. The 4-literal clause, then, can be replaced by two 3-literal clauses $(x_1 \lor x_2 \lor u)$ and $(\bar{u} \lor x_3 \lor x_4)$.

Let's see if we can do the same sort of thing for 5-literal clauses and come up with a general approach for everything bigger than that. Assume our clause is $(x_1 \lor x_2 \lor x_3 \lor x_4 \lor x_5)$. As in the 4-literal case, we want to break this up and add variables to connect the clauses. We are going to have three clauses in this case since otherwise we would have three of the original literals in one clause, leaving no room for a connecting variable. So the clauses are going to look something like $(x_1 \lor x_2 \lor \_\_\_)$, $(\_\_\_ \lor x_3 \lor \_\_\_)$, and $(\_\_\_ \lor x_4 \lor x_5)$. We just need to fill in the blanks. To connect the first two clauses, we can add a variable u^1 and have it appear positively in the first clause and negatively in the second, as we did for the 4-literal case. To connect the second two clauses, we can add a variable u^2 and do the same thing, giving us:

$$(x_1 \lor x_2 \lor u^1), \left(\overline{u^1} \lor x_3 \lor u^2 \right), \text{ and } \left(\overline{u^2} \lor x_4 \lor x_5 \right).$$

These three clauses are equivalent to the original 5-literal clause. (Again, you should verify this.)

If we had six literals, we could add yet another variable, u^3, and one more clause giving us:

$$\left(x_1 \vee x_2 \vee u^1\right), \left(\overline{u^1} \vee x_3 \vee u^2\right), \left(\overline{u^2} \vee x_4 \vee u^3\right), \text{ and } \left(\overline{u^3} \vee x_5 \vee x_6\right).$$

Now we can see a general approach to use when there are more than three literals. If the j-th clause has $k > 3$ literals, then we add $k - 3$ new variables, $u_j^1, u_j^2, \ldots, u_j^{k-3}$, and create $k - 2$ clauses:

$$\left(x_1 \vee x_2 \vee u_j^1\right),$$
$$\left(\overline{u_j^k} \vee x_{k-1} \vee x_k\right),$$
$$\text{and } \left(\overline{u^i} \vee x_{i+2} \vee u^{i+1}\right) \text{ for each } i, 1 \leq i < k - 3$$

Since each clause in the SAT instance has been replaced by an equivalent set of 3SAT clauses in such a way that no interference with any of the other SAT clauses is introduced, the 3SAT instance is satisfiable if and only if the SAT instance is satisfiable. Therefore, we have a valid reduction.

We still need to argue that the reduction can be computed in polynomial time. To make things more concrete, the entire algorithm to perform the reduction is listed in Figure 7.1. The algorithm is not terribly complex. There is one main loop that walks through the list of clauses. Inside the loop, there is some simple list manipulation. Only in the last else is there any need for an inner loop and this loop iterates $k - 4$ times, where k is the number of literals that occur in the clause. The total running time, therefore, is proportional to sum of the sizes of the clauses. Since it is reasonable to assume that the encoding will require at least 1 bit for each literal in each clause, the number of bits needed to encode a SAT instance is at least as large as the sum of the clause sizes. Therefore, the running time of the reduction is polynomial in the size of the SAT instance and we can conclude that 3SAT is NP-complete.

Exercise 7.2 *In the reduction from SAT to 3SAT, we created many new variables. Show that other variables from the SAT instance could be used instead of new variables when the number of literals in the SAT clause is 1 or 2. Also show that new variables are necessary (at least for this particular reduction) for a SAT clause in which the number of literals is 4.*

Reduce SAT to 3SAT$(\{x_1,\ldots,x_n\},\{c_1,\ldots,c_m\})$

1   Initialize $3SATClauses$ to be empty

2   Initialize $3SATVariables$ to be $\{x_1,\ldots,x_n\}$.

3   **for** $j=1$ to m // m is the number clauses

4   Let k be the number of literals in c_j

5   Let $l^1,\ldots,l^k$ be the k literals in c_j.

6   **switch**

7   **case** $k=1$:

8   Add two new variables, y_j and z_j, to $3SATVariables$

9   Add the following clauses to $3SATClauses$:
$$\left(l^1 \vee y_j \vee z_j\right),\ \left(l^1 \vee \overline{y_j} \vee z_j\right),\ \left(l^1 \vee y_j \vee \overline{z_j}\right),\text{ and } \left(l^1 \vee \overline{y_j} \vee \overline{z_j}\right)$$

10   **break**

11   **case** $k=2$:

12   Add a new variable w_j to $3SATVariables$.

13   Add $\left(l^1 \vee l^2 \vee w_j\right)$ and $\left(l^1 \vee l^2 \vee \overline{w_j}\right)$ to $3SATClauses$.

14   **break**

15   **case** $k=3$:

16   Add c_j to $3SATClauses$

17   **break**

18   **case** $k>3$:

19   Add $k-3$ new variables $u_j^1,\ldots,u_j^{k-3}$ to $3SATVariables$

20   Add $\left(l^1 \vee l^2 \vee u_j^1\right)$ and $\left(\overline{u_j^{k-3}} \vee l^{k-1} \vee l^k\right)$ to $3SATClauses$.

21   **for** $i=1$ to $k-4$

22   Add $\left(\overline{u_j^i} \vee l^{i+2} \vee u_j^{i+1}\right)$ to $3SATClauses$.

23   **end for**

24   **break**

25   **end switch**

26   **end for**

27   **return** $(3SATVariables, 3SATClauses)$

Figure 7.1: A polynomial time reduction from SAT to 3SAT.

7.3 First grade math.

Your parents convince you to go back to babysitting to earn some money since you are less than fully employed. Your first job is to watch a first grader named Crystal while her parents go out for a Valentine's Day dinner. Crystal spends most of her time playing educational games on the computer, so this is a pretty easy task. Tonight she is playing a math game on the Public Broadcasting System's website, www.pbskids.org. The game consists of a ferris wheel and a number of people waiting in line to ride the ferris wheel. Each bucket[1] on the ferris wheel has a different number of seats. The goal is to put people on the ferris wheel and watch them ride. The trick is that for the ferris wheel to turn on, each bucket has to be completely empty or completely full and all of the people have to be on board. In the example portrayed so exquisitely by Figure 7.2, there are 3 "people" in line, so the solution is to use the buckets with capacities 1 and 2. (I hope you were able to figure that out for yourself. Crystal did.)

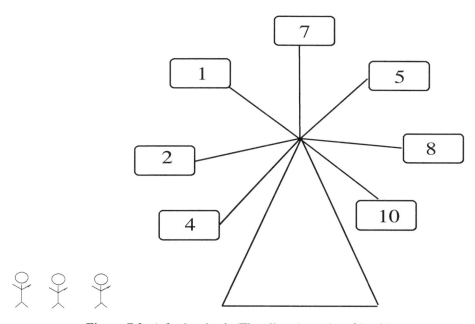

Figure 7.2: A ferris wheel. (The aliens brought a friend.)

---

[1] What do you call the things on a ferris wheel that people sit in?

Since you have nothing else to do while Crystal plays, you decide to amuse yourself by quickly sketching out an efficient algorithm to solve the general ferris wheel problem. You formulate the problem as a decision problem:

GIVEN: A finite set of positive integers A (the bucket capacities) and a positive target sum T (the number of people in line).

QUESTION: Is there a subset, S, of the integers such that $\sum_{a \in S} a = T$?

This is first grade math, so it should be easy, right? After hours of trying, you are no closer to a finding a polynomial time algorithm. At midnight, Crystal's parents walk in to find you on the couch under a ream of paper and Crystal asleep on the kitchen floor in a puddle of chocolate syrup and ice cream. You must have been a little distracted when Crystal asked if she could get herself a snack at 8:00pm. Oh well, another job lost.

The first grade math problem above is called **SUBSET-SUM**. It is NP-complete. To prove this, we first need to show that SUBSET-SUM is in NP. In designing a polynomial time verifier for SUBSET-SUM, what should we use as a certificate? Well, how about a subset S? Given an instance of the problem and a subset S, the verifier can simply sum the numbers in S and verify the sum is equal to the given target. Certainly, we can do this in polynomial time.

Showing that SUBSET-SUM is NP-complete looks like it might be a little tricky because this doesn't look like a satisfiability problem at all. It has nothing to do with Boolean formulas, but let's see if we can relate it to 3SAT in some way.

In 3SAT, we either set a literal to TRUE or we set it to FALSE. In SUBSET-SUM, we either choose a number or we don't. Each of these is a binary choice. Given the similarity between assigning a truth value to a literal and choosing an element, it might seem reasonable to create some kind of a correspondence between literals and numbers such that a literal being TRUE corresponds to choosing a number and a literal being FALSE corresponds to not choosing a number or perhaps choosing a different number.

For each variable x_i, we'll create two numbers, v_i and v'_i, where choosing v_i corresponds to setting x_i to TRUE and choosing v'_i corresponds to setting $\overline{x_i}$ to TRUE, which is equivalent to setting x_i to FALSE. For this type of correspondence to work, we'll need to ensure that v_i and v'_i can never appear together in a valid SUBSET-SUM solution. The only way to restrict the contents of the subsets allowed as valid SUBSET-SUM solutions is by specifying the target value, T. Before we start trying to figure out how to set up T to ensure that any SUBSET-SUM solution corresponds to a well-defined truth assignment, let's consider what other roles T might be asked to play.

If we think of a truth assignment as a solution for a 3SAT instance and a subset as a solution for a SUBSET-SUM instance, then the collection of clauses in 3SAT and the target value in SUBSET-SUM each restrict the set of possible solutions. Because the clauses and the target value play similar roles in their respective problems, another possible role for our target value to play is to ensure that any subset that is a solution for the SUBSET-SUM instance corresponds to a *satisfying* truth assignment in the 3SAT instance. The target value, then, has two roles:

1. ensure that a solution to the SUBSET-SUM instance corresponds to a *well-defined* truth assignment for the 3SAT instance (i.e., ensure that exactly one of v_i and v_i' are included in the subset);

2. ensure that a solution to the SUBSET-SUM instance corresponds to a *satisfying* truth assignment for the 3SAT instance.

Unfortunately, a set of variables and a set of clauses each look very different from a target number. After all, a set is a whole bunch of things and a number is only one thing. We need a way to think of the target number as a collection of things, so let's think of the target number as a collection of digits, one for each variable and one for each clause.

How can we set up the digits in the target value to ensure that exactly one of v_i and v_i' are included in the subset? If v_i and v_i' both had a 1 in the x_i digit and the target value also had a 1 in that digit, we would have to have exactly one of v_i and v_i' in any solution to SUBSET-SUM. This is assuming, of course, that we don't have to worry about any other number interfering with the x_i digit in the sum, so we need to remember to make sure we do not have any carries when we add up all the numbers.

Here is what we have so far: Given an instance of 3SAT consisting of n variables and m clauses, create elements of the set S that are $n + m$ digit numbers and create the target value T as an $n + m$ digit number. Label the first n digits x_1 through x_n and the remaining digits c_1 through c_m. For each variable x_i, create two numbers v_i and v_i' for the SUBSET-SUM instance. Each will have a 1 in the x_i digit and a 0 in the remaining "variable" digits. T will have a 1 in each of the variable digits. We don't yet know what to do with the "clause" digits.

Consider an instance of 3SAT consisting of four variables and two clauses, $(x_1 \vee \overline{x_3} \vee x_4)$ and $(\overline{x_1} \vee x_2 \vee \overline{x_4})$. Our instance of SUBSET-SUM is going to look something like this:

	x_1	x_2	x_3	x_4	c_1	c_2
v_1:	1	0	0	0	?	?
v_1':	1	0	0	0	?	?
v_2:	0	1	0	0	?	?
v_2':	0	1	0	0	?	?
v_3:	0	0	1	0	?	?
v_3':	0	0	1	0	?	?
v_4:	0	0	0	1	?	?
v_4':	0	0	0	1	?	?
T:	1	1	1	1	?	?

Any subset of the numbers whose sum is T will include exactly one of v_i and v_i' for each i. Therefore, we have successfully set up the target value to ensure that any solution to SUBSET-SUM corresponds to a well-defined truth assignment. Next, we need to ensure that any solution to SUBSET-SUM corresponds to a *satisfying* truth assignment.

In the example above, choosing v_1 corresponds to setting x_1 to TRUE. Setting x_1 to TRUE satisfies the first clause but not the second. We need some way of expressing that the truth assignment corresponding to a subset that includes v_1 satisfies clause c_1 but not clause c_2. The obvious thing to do would be to set up v_1 to have a 1 in the c_1 digit and a 0 in the c_2 digit. Taking v_1 would then give us a partial sum of:

	x_1	x_2	x_3	x_4	c_1	c_2
v_1:	1	0	0	0	1	0

The 1 in the c_1 digit indicates that by choosing v_1, we have satisfied clause c_1. If we set up the other numbers in the same way, with a 1 in the clause digit if the corresponding literal is in the clause and a 0 otherwise, it would sort of make sense to set T up with a 1 in every clause digit.[2] This reflects the fact

---

[2] Eery music, portending doom.

that for each clause, we need to choose a number corresponding to a literal contained in that clause.

For the 3SAT instance consisting of $(x_1 \vee \overline{x_3} \vee x_4)$, and $(\overline{x_1} \vee x_2 \vee \overline{x_4})$, the SUBSET-SUM instance would be:

	x_1	x_2	x_3	x_4	c_1	c_2
v_1:	1	0	0	0	1	0
v_1':	1	0	0	0	0	1
v_2:	0	1	0	0	0	1
v_2':	0	1	0	0	0	0
v_3:	0	0	1	0	0	0
v_3':	0	0	1	0	1	0
v_4:	0	0	0	1	1	0
v_4':	0	0	0	1	0	1
T:	1	1	1	1	1	1

Taking v_1 and v_4' would give us the following partial sum:

	x_1	x_2	x_3	x_4	c_1	c_2
v_1+v_4':	1	0	0	1	1	1

Both clause digits are set to 1, so we just need to choose one of v_2 and v_2' and one of v_3 and v_3' to get the x_2 and x_3 digits set. The subset $\{v_1, v_2', v_3, v_4'\}$ is a solution for this SUBSET-SUM instance. The corresponding truth assignment, $x_1 = \text{TRUE}$, $x_2 = \text{FALSE}$, $x_3 = \text{TRUE}$, $x_4 = \text{FALSE}$, is a satisfying truth assignment for the 3SAT instance.

This appears to be an instance mapping reduction from 3SAT to SUBSET-SUM. Let's look at a bigger example before writing out a formal proof. Suppose the instance of 3SAT consists of the following 10 clauses over 4 variables:

1. $(x_1 \vee \overline{x_3} \vee x_4)$

2. $(x_1 \vee \overline{x_3} \vee \overline{x_4})$

3. $(x_1 \vee x_3 \vee x_4)$

4. $(x_1 \vee x_3 \vee \overline{x_4})$

5. $(x_2 \vee \overline{x_3} \vee x_4)$

6. $(x_2 \vee \overline{x_3} \vee \overline{x_4})$

7. $(x_2 \vee x_3 \vee x_4)$

8. $(x_2 \vee x_3 \vee \overline{x_4})$

9. $(x_1 \vee x_2 \vee x_4)$

10. $(x_1 \vee x_2 \vee \overline{x_4})$

Figure 7.3 shows the corresponding SUBSET-SUM instance.

	x_1	x_2	x_3	x_4	c_1	c_2	c_3	c_4	c_5	c_6	c_7	c_8	c_9	c_{10}
v_1:	1	0	0	0	1	1	1	1	0	0	0	0	1	1
v_1':	1	0	0	0	0	0	0	0	0	0	0	0	0	0
v_2:	0	1	0	0	0	0	0	0	1	1	1	1	1	1
v_2':	0	1	0	0	0	0	0	0	0	0	0	0	0	0
v_3:	0	0	1	0	0	0	1	1	0	0	1	1	0	0
v_3':	0	0	1	0	1	1	0	0	1	1	0	0	0	0
v_4:	0	0	0	1	1	0	1	0	1	0	1	0	1	0
v_4':	0	0	0	1	0	1	0	1	0	1	0	1	0	1
T:	1	1	1	1	1	1	1	1	1	1	1	1	1	1

Figure 7.3: The SUBSET-SUM instance created for the ten clauses listed above: $(x_1 \vee \overline{x_3} \vee x_4)$, $(x_1 \vee \overline{x_3} \vee \overline{x_4})$, $(x_1 \vee x_3 \vee x_4)$, $(x_1 \vee x_3 \vee \overline{x_4})$, $(x_2 \vee \overline{x_3} \vee x_4)$, $(x_2 \vee \overline{x_3} \vee \overline{x_4})$, $(x_2 \vee x_3 \vee x_4)$, $(x_2 \vee x_3 \vee \overline{x_4})$, $(x_1 \vee x_2 \vee x_4)$, and $(x_1 \vee x_2 \vee \overline{x_4})$.

It is easy to verify that any truth assignment that sets both x_1 and x_2 to TRUE is a satisfying truth assignment. In fact, there is no way to satisfy this particular 3SAT instance without setting both x_1 and x_2 to TRUE. Choosing v_1 and v_2 gives us the partial sum:

	x_1	x_2	x_3	x_4	c_1	c_2	c_3	c_4	c_5	c_6	c_7	c_8	c_9	c_{10}
$v_1 + v_2$:	1	1	0	0	1	1	1	1	1	1	1	1	2	2

Uhh... we have clause digits that sum to 2. That is not good. This reduction doesn't work!! When the 3SAT instance is such that any satisfying truth assignment sets two literals in some clause to TRUE, there will be no way to find a solution to the SUBSET-SUM instance created. In other words, for a YES instance of 3SAT, our reduction has created a NO instance of SUBSET-SUM.

It would be a lot nicer if the 3SAT problem required exactly one of the literals in each clause to be set to TRUE, but it doesn't, so we will have to modify the reduction – or maybe not. What if 3SAT with the restriction that exactly one literal in each clause be set to TRUE is also NP-complete. That would be nice since it looks like our reduction works when the 3SAT problem has this restriction. In other words, the reduction above looks like a valid instance mapping reduction to SUBSET-SUM from the following problem, which we'll call **1in3SAT**:

GIVEN: 1.   a set of Boolean variables,

                 2.   a collection of clauses over the variables containing three distinct literals each.

QUESTION: Is there an assignment of values to the Boolean variables such that exactly one literal in every clause is TRUE?

1in3SAT is indeed NP-complete, so we don't have to modify our reduction other than to say that we are reducing from 1in3SAT instead of 3SAT.

Exercise 7.3 *Prove that 1in3SAT is NP-complete.*

A complete description of the reduction from 1in3SAT to SUBSET-SUM appears in Figure 7.4. To show that this is a valid reduction, we need to prove

Reduce1in3SATtoSubsetSum($\{x_1,\ldots,x_n\},\{c_1,\ldots,c_m\}$):

1   **for** each variable x_i in the 1in3SAT instance,
2   Create two elements v_i and v_i', initially 0, for the set A
3   Set the x_i digit of both v_i and v_i' to 1.
4   **for** each clause c_j
5   **if** x_i is in c_j
6   **then** Set the c_j digit of v_i to 1
7   **else if** $\overline{x_i}$ is in c_j
8   **then** Set the c_j digit of v_i' to 1
9   **end for**
10 **end for**
11 Let T be a $n+m$ digit number with a 1 in each digit.
12 **return** A and T.

Figure 7.4: The reduction from 1in3SAT to SUBSET-SUM

that the clauses are satisfiable according to the 1in3SAT restrictions if and only if there is a subset of the numbers that sums to T. To simplify things a little, we will assume that x_i and $\overline{x_i}$ never appear in the same clause. If they do, that clause is satisfied by every truth assignment and can be ignored. If necessary, we can preprocess the 1in3SAT instance to remove such clauses. Let's also assume that each variable is represented as either a positive literal or a negative literal in at least one clause. If some variable doesn't appear, just drop that variable from the 1in3SAT instance. All of the v_i's and v_i''s will be distinct under these assumptions. That is a good thing. Also, note that there can be no carries since the sum of all of the numbers has 3 as its largest digit without carries.

Suppose there is a satisfying truth assignment t for the 1in3SAT instance. Remember, for 1in3SAT, the truth assignment satisfies a clause if exactly one of the literals in the clause is set to TRUE. Construct a subset S by choosing v_i if $t(x_i) = $ TRUE and choosing v_i' otherwise, for each i. This ensures that the variable digits of the sum are all 1. Now, for each clause c_j, the truth assignment sets exactly one of the three literals in c_j to TRUE. For concreteness, let $\overline{x_i}$ be the literal from c_j that is set to TRUE by the truth assignment. A nearly identical argument applies when the literal in questions is x_i. Since $t(\overline{x_i})$ is TRUE, v_i' is in S. Furthermore, since $\overline{x_i}$ is in c_j, v_i' has a 1 in the c_j digit. No other literal in c_j is set to TRUE by t, so no other member of S has the c_j digit set to 1. Therefore, the c_j digit in the sum is 1. Since this is true for each c_j, the sum of the numbers in the subset is exactly T.

Next, suppose there is a subset S that sums to T. Create the following truth assignment:

$$t(x_i) = \begin{cases} \text{TRUE} & \text{if } v_i \in S \\ \text{FALSE} & \text{if } v_i' \in S \end{cases}$$

First note that for each i, exactly one of v_i or v_i' must be in S if the numbers in S sum to T. This means t is well-defined. Now, for an arbitrary j, consider the c_j digit in the sum, which must be 1. There must be exactly one number in S such that the c_j digit of that number is 1. Suppose that number is v_i, for some i. Then $t(x_i) = $ TRUE, and because of the way our reduction created v_i, x_i must be in c_j, so c_j is satisfied by t. Similarly, suppose that number is v_i', for some i. Then $t(x_i) = $ FALSE, and because of the way our reduction created v_i', $\overline{x_i}$ must be in c_j, so again c_j is satisfied by t. Therefore, for each clause c_j, t satisfies c_j. Furthermore, t must set exactly one literal in c_j to TRUE. If t set two literals in c_j to TRUE, then both of the numbers corresponding to those two literals must be in the subset. Since both of these numbers have a 1 in the c_j digit, the sum of the numbers in the subset would have a 2 in the c_j digit. Contrary to our assumption, the sum would not be equal to the target value in that case.

We have argued that this reduction maps every YES instance of 1in3SAT to a YES instance of SUBSET-SUM and maps every NO instance of 1in3SAT to a NO instance of SUBSET-SUM. We still need to argue that the reduction can be computed in polynomial time.

The way the reduction is written on page 113, it looks like the running time is $\Theta(nm)$, depending on how we do the digit manipulations. This can certainly be optimized further, but we only care about whether this is polynomial in the size of the 1in3SAT instance, so $\Theta(nm)$ should be sufficient. We do need be careful, however, to make sure we understand exactly what the size of the 1in3SAT instance is. It would be reasonable to encode the 1in3SAT instance by indicating the number of variables, n, followed by the list of m clauses. For example, the instance $\langle\{x_1,x_2,x_3,x_4\},\{(x_1 \vee x_2 \vee \overline{x_3}),(x_1 \vee \overline{x_2} \vee \overline{x_4})\}\rangle$, which has four variables and two clauses, could be encoded as $\langle 4,[1,2,-3],[1,-2,-4]\rangle$, where negative numbers indicated negated literals. It takes $\Theta(\log_2 n)$ bits to encode n in binary and $\Theta(\log_2 n)$ bits to write down each literal in a clause. Since there are 3 literals in each of the m clauses, we have $\Theta(m\log_2 n)$ bits total. We may have a problem here because $\Theta(mn)$ is not polynomial in $m\log_2 n$ since n is exponential in $\log_2 n$. Figure 7.5 illustrates the exponential difference in size between n and $\log_2 n$.

Let's look more closely at the relationship between $\Theta(mn)$, which is the running time, and $\Theta(m\log_2 n)$, which is the size of the problem instance. If m were about as large as n, say $\Theta(n)$, then the size of the problem instance would be $\Theta(n\log n)$, while the running time would be $O(n^2)$. In that case, the running time would be polynomial because n^2 is polynomial in $n\log n$.

The trouble arises when m is small in relation to n. For example, when $m = \log_2 n$, the running time is $\Theta(n\log_2 n)$, while the size of the problem instance is $\Theta((\log_2 n)^2)$. This is an exponential difference. Luckily, n is guaranteed to be $O(m)$ because each clause has exactly 3 literals, giving us $3m$ literals total. Consequently, there can be at most $3m$ variables because we assume every variable is represented by a literal in some clause. Therefore, $O(nm) = O(m^2)$, which is polynomial in $m\log_2 n$. Phew.

We have proven that 1in3SAT can be reduced to SUBSET-SUM in polynomial time and that SUBSET-SUM is in NP. Since 1in3SAT is NP-complete, we can conclude that SUBSET-SUM is NP-complete ... and Crystal shouldn't feel bad if she has trouble with the ferris wheel game.

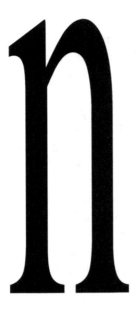

Figure 7.5: Compared to $\log n$, n is really, really big, as you can see.

Exercise 7.4 *Like 1in3SAT, other variants of 3SAT can also be useful in reductions. For example, in* **Not-All-Equal-3SAT** *(**NAE3SAT***), satisfying truth assignments are restricted from setting all three literals in any clause to* TRUE. *Prove that NAE3SAT, defined formally below, is* NP-complete.

GIVEN: 1. *a set of Boolean variables,*

2. *a collection of clauses formed from these variables and containing three distinct literals each.*

QUESTION: *Is there an assignment of values to the variables that satisfies every clause but does not set all of the literals in any clause to* TRUE*?*

7.4 HAMILTONIAN CYCLE is NP-complete

Now that we have a couple of reductions under our belts, we should have no trouble reducing SAT to other problems. Let's try reducing SAT to HAMILTO-NIAN CYCLE. To make life a little easier, we are instead going to reduce SAT to **DIRECTED HAMILTONIAN CYCLE**, which is the HAMILTONIAN CYCLE problem in a directed graph.

In both SAT and DIRECTED HAMILTONIAN CYCLE, as in all of our problems, finding a solution involves making choices subject to constraints. In SAT, we choose values for Boolean variables. In DIRECTED HAMILTO-NIAN CYCLE, for each edge, we choose whether or not to include the edge in the cycle. Luckily, these are both binary choices. Our reduction needs to develop some sort of correspondence between assigning a value to a Boolean variable and including an edge or leaving it out. For example, our reduction could create two vertices, L and R, connected to each other with two directed edges as part of a larger graph, as shown in Figure 7.6. We cannot use both

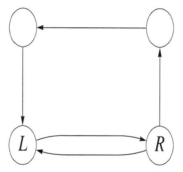

Figure 7.6: An example of a correspondence between assigning a value to a variable and including an edge in a Hamiltonian cycle. A Hamiltonian cycle that traverses the directed edge (L, R) corresponds to a truth assignment that sets the corresponding variable to TRUE. A Hamiltonian cycle that traverses the directed edge (R, L) corresponds to a truth assignment that sets the corresponding variable to FALSE.

edges between L and R in any Hamiltonian cycle because taking both edges would create a cycle inside the larger Hamiltonian cycle. A Hamiltonian cycle cannot contain a smaller cycle within it – if it did, at least one vertex from the smaller cycle would have to appear twice in the larger Hamiltonian cycle, which is not allowed.

Let's create a "truth-setting" component like the one in Figure 7.6 for each variable in the SAT instance, using the convention that taking the (L,R) edge in a truth-setting component corresponds to setting the associated variable to TRUE, while taking the (R,L) edge corresponds to setting the associated variable to FALSE. All of these truth-setting components would have to be connected in the larger graph or a Hamiltonian cycle could not exist, so let's create a vertex, B, from which to begin the cycle and a vertex, E, at which to end the cycle. Since we want to be able to traverse the component for x_1 in either direction, we will connect B to both sides of the component for x_1, as shown in Figure 7.7.

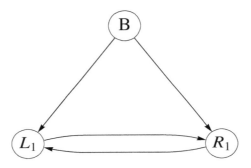

Figure 7.7: The beginning vertex, B, connected to both sides of the truth-setting component for x_1.

After connecting B to the x_1 component, we need to connect the x_1 component to the x_2 component. Since we want to have the ability to exit the x_1 component on either side and enter the x_2 component on either side, both sides of the x_1 component need to be connected to both sides of the x_2 component. Similarly, for x_2 to x_3, x_3 to x_4, and so on, until we connect both sides of x_n to E. Connecting E back to B then gives us a cycle. The entire truth-setting component for three variables would look like the graph in Figure 7.8.

As we discussed above, any Hamiltonian cycle in this graph can include at most one of the edges in each variable's truth-setting component. Furthermore, any Hamiltonian cycle must include *at least* one of these edges because there are no edges coming back into a variable's truth-setting component. For example, if we move from B to L_1 and then directly to L_2, there is no way to come back to include R_1 in the cycle. Therefore, we can associate a truth

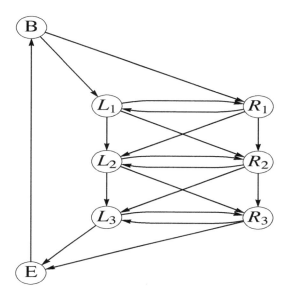

Figure 7.8: The truth-setting component of an instance of DIRECTED HAMILTO-NIAN CYCLE created from a SAT instance with three variables.

assignment with any Hamiltonian cycle in this graph as follows:

$$t(x_i) = \begin{cases} \text{TRUE} & \text{if the edge } (L_i, R_i) \text{ is in the cycle.} \\ \text{FALSE} & \text{otherwise} \end{cases}$$

We have successfully developed a correspondence between the choices made in the two problems. For every truth assignment, there is a cycle, and for every cycle, there is a truth assignment. However, the graph we have created so far has a Hamiltonian cycle whether or not the formula is satisfiable. Next, we must develop a correspondence between the constraints of the two problems so that a Hamiltonian cycle exists precisely when the formula is satisfiable. In particular, we need to establish a relationship between a clause being unsatisfied and something being missing from the cycle.

Let's create a vertex for each clause and connect it to the truth-setting component in such a way that the clause is satisfied by a truth assignment if and only if the cycle from B through the truth-setting components to E and back to B includes this vertex properly. Since each of the variables represented by a literal in a clause could be set in a way that satisfies the clause, the clause vertex

must be connected to each of its constituent variables' truth-setting components. For example, suppose we have the clause $c_1 = (x_1 \vee \overline{x_2})$. We'll create
a vertex C_1. If we set x_1 to TRUE or x_2 to FALSE, then we should be able to
include C_1 in our cycle, but if we set x_1 to FALSE and x_2 to TRUE, then we
should not be able to include C_1 in our cycle. For x_1, we can achieve this by
connecting L_1 to C_1 and C_1 to R_1. (See Figure 7.9.)

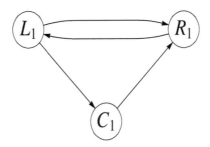

Figure 7.9: The truth-setting component for x_1 connected to clause vertex C_1. Rather
than taking the edge from L_1 to R_1, we can take L_1 to C_1 and then C_1 to R_1 to include
C_1 in the cycle through the larger graph.

If a cycle traverses x_1's component along the directed edge (L_1, R_1), which
corresponds to x_1 being set to TRUE, then we can take a detour from L_1 to C_1
and back to R_1 with no ill effects. However, if a cycle traverses x_1's component
along the directed edge (R_1, L_1), which corresponds to x_1 being set to FALSE,
the cycle cannot go back to pick up C_1 from x_1's component because C_1 will
be a dead end – the cycle cannot go to R_1 from C_1 because R_1 has already been
visited.

In the same way, we can connect the right side of x_2's component to C_1
and connect C_1 to the left side of x_2's component, giving us the graph in Figure 7.10. If a cycle did not pick up C_1 while traversing x_1's component and
traverses x_2's component along the directed edge (R_2, L_2), which corresponds
to x_2 being set to FALSE, then the cycle can take a detour through C_1 and continue on. However, if that cycle traverses x_2's component along the directed
edge (L_2, R_2), it cannot go to C_1 from x_2's component.

Of course, we need to be careful that we haven't destroyed the correspondence we had between cycles and truth assignments by adding this clause vertex. Unfortunately, as Figure 7.11 illustrates, we can create a Hamiltonian
cycle in the graph for $(x_1 \vee \overline{x_2})$ that is not consistent with our intent.

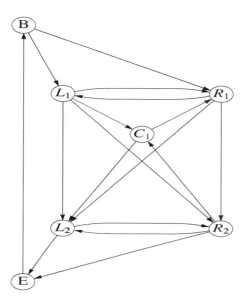

Figure 7.10: The graph created for the SAT instance consisting of the single clause $(x_1 \vee \overline{x_2})$.

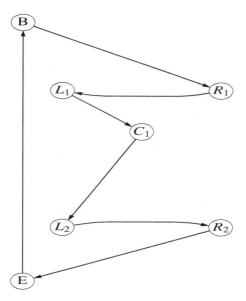

Figure 7.11: A Hamiltonian cycle, shown in darker edges, that we do not want to allow for the SAT instance consisting of the single clause $(x_1 \vee \overline{x_2})$.

Our interpretation of this bad Hamiltonian cycle is that the cycle corresponds to a truth assignment that assigns FALSE to x_1 and TRUE to x_2. This truth assignment does not satisfy the clause. What went wrong? Notice that the clause vertex, C_1, is entered from L_1 even though x_1's truth-setting component is traversed right to left. The clause vertex is being used as a bridge from x_1's truth-setting component to x_2's truth-setting component. This is not what we want.

Rather than complete the reduction here, let's see if you are ingenious enough to figure out for yourself what can be done to fix this. As usual, the solution is in the back of the book.

Exercise 7.5 *Complete the reduction from SAT to DIRECTED HAMILTO-NIAN CYCLE.*

Exercise 7.6 *Show that HAMILTONIAN CYCLE is NP-complete.*

Traveling Salesman Revisited.

We have just shown (sort of) that HAMILTONIAN CYCLE is NP-complete. In Section 6.3, we showed how HAMILTONIAN CYCLE can be reduced to the TRAVELING SALESMAN PROBLEM in polynomial time. If HAMILTONIAN CYCLE is NP-complete, then Thereom 6.5 implies that TSP is also NP-complete.

This is all very interesting, but what does it really mean to you that HAMILTONIAN CYCLE and TSP are NP-complete? Given that most computer scientists do not believe that P = NP and that each of these problems is as hard as any problem in NP, it means you shouldn't be sitting on your parents' couch trying to come up with polynomial time algorithms to solve these problems – unless you want to win a million dollars and your other alternative is to watch some silly reality TV show.

Chapter 8

Is it Better to Be a Pig?
Approximation Algorithms

Warning: There is quite a bit more algebra in this chapter than the others. Suck it up.

8.1 Introduction

Finally, you land a temporary job working for a small software company on a project for NASA. NASA is planning a robotic exploration of Neptune. They have a huge number of potential experiments they would like to perform. A panel of scientists has calculated the cost of each experiment and has assigned each a numeric value indicating the experiment's scientific merit. NASA has only budgeted a certain amount of money for the experiments and wants to choose a subset of experiments that maximizes the sum of the values without exceeding the budget.

Here is the problem, which is known as the **MAXIMUM KNAPSACK PROBLEM**:

GIVEN: 1. a set of objects A;
          2. for each object a in A, a value $v(a)$ and a cost $c(a)$;
          3. a total budget B.

OBJECTIVE: Find a subset of the objects, S, with maximum possible total value such that $\sum_{a \in S} c(a) \leq B$.

How should we go about solving this problem? We want to choose experiments that have high value but low cost, so why not take experiments based on the value to cost ratio? In other words, order the objects in decreasing order of their value per dollar and choose the experiments in order until we cannot take any more experiments without exceeding our budget. Does this work? Is it that simple? Will your friends and family finally realize that you are not wasting your time with idle thoughts and that all of this theoretical thinking has transformed you into a superior problem solver? Perhaps we should try this out on a few test cases before we get too carried away with the idea that instead of just proving a problem is hard, we have finally designed an algorithm to do something useful.

Suppose we have only three experiments to choose from: an Air experiment, a Water experiment, and a Temperature experiment. Let $B = 100$ be the budget. To see if we can break our algorithm, let's set up the costs of the experiments so that if we take one of the experiments, say Air, then we cannot take either of the other two. However, we should be able to take $Water$ and $Temp$ together if we don't take Air. If Air has the highest value to cost ratio, then our algorithm will choose Air as the only experiment since once Air is chosen, we cannot afford to take either of the other two experiments. If, in addition, the value of Air is not at least as large as the sum of the values of $Water$ and $Temp$, then our algorithm will not choose the experiments optimally. We can create these conditions by setting the cost of experiment Air to 51, $Water$ to 50, and $Temp$ to 50, and letting $v(Air) = 102$, $v(Water) = 75$ and $v(Temp) = 75$. (See Figure 8.1.) Then we have the following value to cost ratios:

$$\frac{v(Air)}{c(Air)} = 2; \qquad \frac{v(Water)}{c(Water)} = 1.5; \qquad \frac{v(Temp)}{c(Temp)} = 1.5.$$

Greedily choosing objects based on their value to cost ratio, results in Air being the only experiment taken – this provides a total value of 102. Taking the other two experiments instead of Air provides a total value of 150. Rats. This algorithm doesn't work. Optimism can turn to gloom very quickly in computer science.

We could just consider every possible combination of experiments to find the most valuable combination that we can afford. How long would that take? If we have n objects, there are $2^n - 1$ non-empty subsets of those n experiments to consider. As we saw earlier, n doesn't have to be too large for this brute-force algorithm to be completely useless, unless your boss is a very patient person.

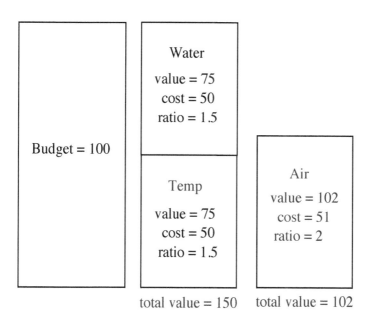

Figure 8.1: An example showing that the algorithm for MAXIMUM KNAPSACK that greedily chooses objects based on their value to cost ratio does not always find an optimal solution. The greedy algorithm will choose *Air* because it has the highest value to cost ratio. Once it has chosen *Air*, however, it cannot take either of the other two experiments. The value of *Air* is 102, while the value of taking both *Water* and *Temp*, which can be done without exceeding the budget, is 150. Therefore, the greedy algorithm does not return an optimal solution for this problem instance.

Given your recent experience with hard problems, you wonder whether or not you can prove that this problem is hard to solve. This problem is not a decision problem, though, and our theory so far has only dealt with decision problems. We can turn this optimization problem into a decision problem by adding a target value to shoot for. In other words, instead of trying to find an optimal solution, we are given a target value and are asked if there are any feasible solutions that achieve this target. This decision version of the problem is called **0-1 KNAPSACK** and is formulated as follows:

GIVEN: 1.   a set of objects A;
2.   for each object a in A, a value $v(a)$ and a cost $c(a)$;
3.   a total budget B;
4.   a target value T.

QUESTION: Is there a subset, S, of the objects such that:

$$\sum_{a \in S} c(a) \leq B \qquad \text{and} \qquad \sum_{a \in S} v(a) \geq T?$$

Exercise 8.1 *Design a polynomial time verifier for 0-1 KNAPSACK to show that 0-1 KNAPSACK is in* NP.

Of the problems that we have discussed so far, which problem does this look most like? We have objects that we are choosing and there are numbers associated with those objects, so this looks somewhat similar to SUBSET-SUM. Recall that SUBSET-SUM is defined as follows:

GIVEN: A finite set of nonnegative integers A and a target integer $T \geq 0$.

QUESTION: Is there a subset $S \subseteq A$ such that $\sum_{a \in S} a = T$?

SUBSET-SUM is actually a restricted version of 0-1 KNAPSACK in which $V = T$, $B = T$, $v(x) = x$, and $c(x) = x$, for all objects x. To see this, consider a solution, S, to an instance of this restricted 0-1 KNAPSACK problem. Because S is a 0-1 KNAPSACK solution, we have:

$$\sum_{a \in S} c(a) \leq B \qquad \text{and} \qquad \sum_{a \in S} v(a) \geq T.$$

But since $B = T$ and $v(a) = c(a)$ for each object a, it follows that:

$$\sum_{a \in S} c(a) \leq B \quad \text{implies} \quad \sum_{a \in S} v(a) \leq T.$$

Since $\sum_{a \in S} v(a) \leq T$ and $\sum_{a \in S} v(a) \geq T$, it must be the case that $\sum_{a \in S} v(a) = T$. In other words, in this restricted version of 0-1 KNAPSACK, we are looking for a subset of values that sum to a specific target value. That is exactly what is required for SUBSET-SUM.

The set of 0-1 KNAPSACK instances includes all of the problem instances from SUBSET-SUM plus a whole lot more, so 0-1 KNAPSACK cannot be easier to solve than SUBSET-SUM. Therefore, the 0-1 KNAPSACK problem must be NP-complete. Figure 8.2 illustrates this idea of proving a problem is NP-complete by showing that a restricted version of the problem is NP-complete.

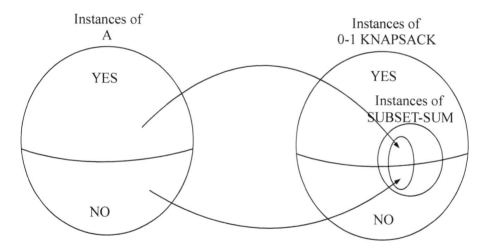

Figure 8.2: An illustration of proof by restriction. The instances of an arbitrary problem, A, in NP are mapped to a subset of the instances of the NP-complete problem SUBSET-SUM, which are themselves instances of 0-1 KNAPSACK. 0-1 KNAPSACK, therefore, must also be NP-complete.

Exercise 8.2 *Provide a formal instance mapping reduction of SUBSET-SUM to 0-1 KNAPSACK.*

What does knowing that 0-1 KNAPSACK is NP-complete tell us about the MAXIMUM KNAPSACK problem? Certainly, the MAXIMUM KNAPSACK problem is at least as hard as the 0-1 KNAPSACK problem since an algorithm to solve MAXIMUM KNAPSACK can be used to solve 0-1 KNAPSACK simply by checking the value of the solution returned against T. In other words, if we let FindMaxKnapsack(A, v, c, B) be a subroutine that finds an optimal solution to the MAXIMUM KNAPSACK problem, the following algorithm decides the 0-1 KNAPSACK problem:

Decide01Knapsack(A, v, c, B, T)

1   Set $x =$ FindMaxKnapsack(A, v, c, B)
2   **if** $x \geq T$
3   **then** return YES
4   **else** return NO

What we have here is a polynomial time Turing reduction – a hypothetical polynomial time subroutine for MAXIMUM KNAPSACK is used to solve 0-1 KNAPSACK in polynomial time. Since 0-1 KNAPSACK is NP-complete, the existence of a polynomial time algorithm for MAXIMUM KNAPSACK would imply that there are polynomial time algorithms for everything in NP. We cannot say MAXIMUM KNAPSACK is NP-complete, however, because it is not a decision problem and therefore cannot be in NP. Instead, we say that MAXIMUM KNAPSACK is NP-**hard**.

Definition 8.1 *A problem B is* NP-**hard** *if for every problem A in* NP*, there is a polynomial time Turing reduction from A to B, written* $A \leq^p_T B$.

With your newfound knowledge of NP-hardness and your proof in hand, you go to your boss with the news that there is no efficient algorithm to solve NASA's problem. You expect to be lavished in praise for your ingenious proof. Your boss's response, however, is a little different from what you expected:

> Boss: "So what should I do, tell NASA we quit because finding the best possible set of experiments is hard? If it was easy, NASA wouldn't pay us to do it. We just need a solution that is good enough for NASA to be satisfied. It doesn't have to be perfect."

Huh. You never thought of that. People might still need solutions to problems that are hard and they might be satisfied with solutions that aren't perfect.

8.2 Optimization problems

We have built our theory of the computational complexity of problems entirely based on decision problems. Some of the problems that we have encountered, such as the MAXIMUM KNAPSACK problem above, are more naturally viewed as **optimization problems**. These types of problems are called optimization problems because they require us to output a solution that is optimal according to some well-defined measure of optimality. The measure of optimality provides a way to compare different solutions. In the MAXIMUM KNAPSACK problem, the measure is the sum of the values of the objects chosen. MAXIMUM KNAPSACK is considered a **maximization problem** because it requires us to output a solution that has the maximum total value over all of the **feasible** solutions, where by feasible we mean a solution that satisfies the constraints of the problem.

We may also be faced with **minimization problems**. For example, our original optimization version of the TRAVELING SALESMAN PROBLEM required us to find a tour through the given cities that has the lowest cost. The **TRAVELING SALESMAN OPTIMIZATION PROBLEM** is a minimization problem defined as follows:

GIVEN: A set of cities and for each pair of cities, a and b, the cost of traveling between a and b.

OBJECTIVE: Find a tour through the cities such that the cost of the tour is minimized.

As with MAXIMUM KNAPSACK, the TRAVELING SALESMAN OPTIMIZATION PROBLEM can be proven to be NP-hard by a simple Turing reduction from the decision version of the problem.

Exercise 8.3 *Show that the TRAVELING SALESMAN OPTIMIZATION PROBLEM is NP-hard.*

Exercise 8.4 *It is generally straightforward to show that an optimization version of an NP-complete decision problem is NP-hard. However, an optimization problem may be "harder" than the corresponding decision problem. For example, consider an optimization version of 2SAT called* **MAX2SAT**:

GIVEN: 1. *a set of Boolean variables;*

2. *a collection of distinct clauses, each containing ex-
    actly two literals constructed from two different vari-
    ables.*

OBJECTIVE: *Find an assignment of values to the Boolean variables
such that the number of satisfied clauses is maximized.*

*To solve 2SAT, we must determine whether there exists a truth assignment
that satisfies every clause. In Exercise 6.3, we showed that this could be done
in polynomial time. To solve MAX2SAT, we need to return a truth assignment
that satisfies the maximum number of clauses possible. Show that MAX2SAT
is* NP-*hard.*

8.3   Approximately optimal solutions to hard problems

Here is a formal description of the algorithm we developed for the MAXIMUM
KNAPSACK problem:

GreedyKnapsack(A, v, c, B)

```
 1   Initialize G to be the empty set
 2   Sort A in decreasing order of v(a)/c(a)
 3   Initialize L to B          // L is the amount of money we have left
 4   for each a in A and while L > 0
 5       if c(a) ≤ L
 6       then begin
 7               Add a to G
 8               Decrease L by c(a)
 9           end
10   end for
11   return G.
```

We proved that this algorithm does not always return an optimal solution.
Might it return solutions that are "good enough"? Suppose our problem were
relaxed a bit so that we can take parts of objects rather than having to take objects in their entirety or not at all. This relaxed version of the problem is called
the **FRACTIONAL KNAPSACK** problem. Would the GreedyKnapsack algorithm appropriately modified to take fractions of objects find an optimal
solution to the FRACTIONAL KNAPSACK problem? Indeed it would. Let's

call this algorithm **SolveFractional**. SolveFractional differs from GreedyK-napsack only when it reaches an object that does not fit within the remaining budget. In that case, SolveFractional takes as much of the object as possible, while GreedyKnapsack moves on to the next object.

To understand why SolveFractional works, notice that when we can take fractional parts of objects, we will use every dollar of our budget (unless we can afford to take every object with money left over, in which case the problem instance is trivial). We want to get the most value for each of our dollars, so our first dollar should be spent on a portion of the object that provides the highest value per dollar. Furthermore, at any point in time, we should spend our next available dollar on getting one dollar's worth of the object that has the highest value per dollar among the remaining objects.

Notice that any feasible solution for a MAXIMUM KNAPSACK instance is also a feasible solution for the corresponding FRACTIONAL KNAPSACK instance. Expanding the set of feasible solutions for a problem instance cannot decrease the value of an optimal solution because the original optimal solutions are still feasible under the new constraints. Therefore, the value of an optimal solution to the FRACTIONAL KNAPSACK instance provides an upper bound on the value of an optimal solution to the MAXIMUM KNAPSACK instance. Let OPT be the value of an optimal solution for the MAXIMUM KNAPSACK instance and OPT_F be the value of an optimal solution to the corresponding FRACTIONAL KNAPSACK instance. We have:

$$OPT \leq OPT_F.$$

Let's look at the GreedyKnapsack algorithm again. Consider the objects in decreasing order of value to cost ratio as $a_1, a_2, \ldots, a_n$. Let a_j be the first object that is not taken by the greedy algorithm and let L_j be the amount of money left after taking objects 1 through $j - 1$. (Figure 8.3 illustrates the situation we are considering.) When object a_j is considered, it must be the case that the cost of a_j is greater than the amount of money left; otherwise a_j would have been taken. Since GreedyKnapsack took every object before a_j, we have:

$$L_j = B - \sum_{i=1}^{j-1} c(a_i).$$

Since $c(a_j) > L_j$, this implies that:

$$c(a_j) > B - \sum_{i=1}^{j-1} c(a_i).$$

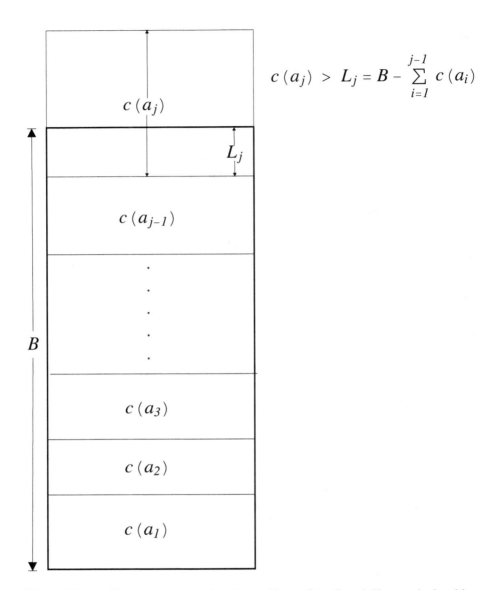

$$c\,(a_j) \;>\; L_j = B - \sum_{i=1}^{j-1} c\,(a_i)$$

Figure 8.3: An illustration comparing the workings of the GreedyKnapsack algorithm and the SolveFractional algorithm. After paying for the first $j-1$ objects, there will be L_j dollars left over. The j-th object does not fit at this point, so $c(a_j)$ must be more than L_j. GreedyKnapsack will skip object a_j and move on to consider object a_{j+1}. SolveFractional, on the other hand, will take as much of a_j as possible. In particular, SolveFractional will take L_j dollars worth of object a_j.

Let $Value(G)$ denote the total value of the objects in the solution, G, returned by the GreedyKnapsack algorithm. Since G includes the first $j-1$ objects, we have:

$$Value(G) \geq \sum_{i=1}^{j-1} v(a_i). \tag{8.1}$$

Furthermore, the behaviors of GreedyKnapsack and SolveFractional are identical up to the point at which a_j is considered. SolveFractional will take as much of a_j as possible, while GreedyKnapsack cannot take any of a_j at all. By taking as much of a_j as possible, SolveFractional exhausts the budget, so the value of an optimal solution to the FRACTIONAL KNAPSACK version of this problem is:

$$OPT_F = \sum_{i=1}^{j-1} v(a_i) + L_j \frac{v(a_j)}{c(a_j)} \tag{8.2}$$

Combining Equation (8.1) and Equation (8.2), we can conclude that:

$$OPT_F \leq Value(G) + L_j \frac{v(a_j)}{c(a_j)}$$

Since $OPT \leq OPT_F$, we then have:

$$OPT \leq Value(G) + L_j \frac{v(a_j)}{c(a_j)} \tag{8.3}$$

This gives us an upper bound on the value of an optimal solution in terms of the value of our greedy solution. To make this bound more informative, we need to evaluate the $L_j \frac{v(a_j)}{c(a_j)}$ term.

If $L_j \frac{v(a_j)}{c(a_j)} \leq Value(G)$, then $OPT \leq 2 \cdot Value(G)$, which we usually write as $Value(G) \geq \frac{OPT}{2}$. That's nice. With that bound, you could tell your boss that your algorithm finds a solution whose value is at least half of the value of an optimal solution. Telling her that the value of your solution will be at least $OPT - L_j \frac{v(a_j)}{c(a_j)}$ would probably not generate a polite response.

On the other hand, suppose $L_j \frac{v(a_j)}{c(a_j)} > Value(G)$. What does this inequality mean? It means we could get a better total value by taking a_j alone. To see this note that since a_j cannot fit within the remaining budget, we have $L_j < c(a_j)$. Because $Value(G) < L_j \frac{v(a_j)}{c(a_j)}$ and $L_j < c(a_j)$, we have:

$$Value(G) < c(a_j) \frac{v(a_j)}{c(a_j)} = v(a_j).$$

So when $L_j \frac{v(a_j)}{c(a_j)} > Value(G)$, GreedyKnapsack chooses a set of objects even though it would have been better off taking just one object, a_j. This is easy to correct by modifying the algorithm to take the object with the greatest value if this value is larger than the value of the greedy solution. The modified algorithm appears in Figure 8.4. Note that the algorithm assumes each object is affordable by itself given the budget constraints. If this is not the case, then the list of objects can be preprocessed to eliminate those that are too expensive to fit within the budget.

ModifiedGreedyKnapsack(A, v, c, B)

1   Initialize G to be the empty set
2   Sort A in decreasing order of $v(a)/c(a)$.
3   Initialize L to B // L is the amount of money we have left
4   **for** each a in A and **while** $L > 0$
5   **if** $c(a) \leq L$
6   **then begin**
7   Add a to G
8   Decrease L by $c(a)$.
9   **end**
10 **end for**
11 Let a_{max} be the object with maximum value.
12 **if** $v(a_{max}) > Value(G)$
13   **then return** $\{a_{max}\}$
14   **else return** G.

Figure 8.4: A greedy algorithm for MAXIMUM KNAPSACK modified to take the object with the highest value if that value is larger than the value of the greedy solution. The algorithm assumes each object is affordable by itself given the budget constraints. If this is not the case, then the list of objects can be preprocessed to eliminate those that are too expensive to fit within the budget.

Now let's see if we can come up with a nice clean formula to represent how close the value of the solution returned by ModifiedGreedyKnapsack is to an optimal solution. Let M be the solution returned by ModifiedGreedyKnapsack. Because the solution returned by ModifiedGreedyKnapsack is always as good if not better than the solution returned by GreedyKnapsack, $Value(G)$ is no more than $Value(M)$. We can use Equation (8.3) on page 133, then, to relate OPT and $Value(M)$ as follows:

$$OPT \leq Value(M) + L_j \frac{v(a_j)}{c(a_j)} \qquad (8.4)$$

Furthermore, our argument above showing $Value(G) \geq \frac{OPT}{2}$ when $L_j \frac{v(a_j)}{c(a_j)} \leq Value(G)$ also shows that $Value(M) \geq \frac{OPT}{2}$ when $L_j \frac{v(a_j)}{c(a_j)} \leq Value(G)$.

To show that $Value(M) \geq \frac{OPT}{2}$ when $L_j \frac{v(a_j)}{c(a_j)} > Value(G)$, we need to argue that $L_j \frac{v(a_j)}{c(a_j)} \leq Value(M)$. As we argued above, when $L_j \frac{v(a_j)}{c(a_j)} > Value(G)$, the algorithm is better off returning $\{a_{max}\}$, so ModifiedGreedyKnapsack does just that. Therefore, when $L_j \frac{v(a_j)}{c(a_j)} > Value(G)$, $Value(M) = v(a_{max})$. Furthermore, since a_j could not be taken without exceeding the budget, $L_j < c(a_j)$, which implies that $v(a_j) > L_j \frac{v(a_j)}{c(a_j)}$. This in turn implies that $Value(M) > L_j \frac{v(a_j)}{c(a_j)}$ because $Value(M) = v(a_{max})$ and $v(a_{max}) > v(a_j)$. Since $L_j \frac{v(a_j)}{c(a_j)} < Value(M)$, Equation (8.4) implies that $OPT \leq 2 \cdot Value(M)$.

In either case, we have $\frac{OPT}{Value(M)} \leq 2$. For this reason, ModifiedGreedyKnapsack is called a 2-approximation for the MAXIMUM KNAPSACK problem. The ratio, $\frac{OPT}{Value(M)}$, is called the algorithm's **approximation ratio**.

Exercise 8.5 *Show that the approximation ratio of GreedyKnapsack, the algorithm without the a_{max} modification, is arbitrarily bad.*

8.4 Fully polynomial time approximation schemes

With newfound confidence in your ability to design algorithms that come up with "good enough" solutions to hard problems, you present your approximation algorithm for MAXIMUM KNAPSACK to your boss.

Boss: Hmm....well, within half of optimal is better than noth-
            ing, I guess. I was hoping for something like no more
            than 5% away from optimal. Hey, how about this?
            What if I tell you how close to optimal I want the so-
            lution to be and you tell me approximately how much
            time your program is going to take. It seems like you
            should be able to write a program that gets closer to
            optimal the more time it is given, right? Let me know
            when you get that done. We need to finish this up
            before we meet with NASA next week.

Computer science is a frustrating discipline. No one is ever satisfied. You
meet one goal and they want something better, faster, simpler, ...

Your boss is going to give you a number, call it ε, that represents her tol-
erance for error. She wants the value of the solution returned to be within ε
of the value of an optimal solution. In other words, she wants the value of
the solution returned to be at least $(1 - \varepsilon) \cdot OPT$. The running time of your
algorithm can depend on ε, but suppose your algorithm runs in $O(n^{1/\varepsilon})$ time.
The running time would increase dramatically as ε decreases, as illustrated in
Figure 8.5.

ε	$(10^3)^{1/\varepsilon}$	Time
0.50	10^6	0.01 seconds
0.25	10^{12}	2.78 hours
0.10	10^{30}	3×10^{12} centuries
0.05	10^{60}	3×10^{42} centuries
0.01	10^{300}	3×10^{282} centuries

Figure 8.5: The growth of $n^{(1/\varepsilon)}$ for $n = 1000$ as ε decreases. The Time column
represents the time that would be taken by an algorithm executing the number of
instructions listed in the middle column on a machine capable of executing 100 million
of these instructions per second.

The data in the table makes clear that you really want your algorithm to be
polynomial in $1/\varepsilon$ as well as n. For example, Figure 8.6 shows the growth of
$\frac{1}{\varepsilon}n^3$ for $n = 1000$ as ε decreases. The growth of $\frac{1}{\varepsilon}n^3$ is, not surprisingly, much
more reasonable than the growth of $n^{(1/\varepsilon)}$.

ε	$\frac{1}{\varepsilon}(10^3)$	Time
0.50	2×10^9	20 seconds
0.25	4×10^9	40 seconds
0.10	1×10^{10}	1.67 minutes
0.05	2×10^{10}	3.33 minutes
0.01	1×10^{11}	16.67 minutes

Figure 8.6: The growth of $\frac{1}{\varepsilon}n^3$ for $n = 1000$ as ε decreases. The Time column represents the time that would be taken by an algorithm executing the number of instructions listed in the middle column on a machine capable of executing 100 million instructions per second.

A $(1 - \varepsilon)$-approximation algorithm that runs in time that is bounded by a polynomial in both n and $\frac{1}{\varepsilon}$ is called a **fully polynomial time approximation scheme (FPTAS)** – and you need one for MAXIMUM KNAPSACK before the next meeting with NASA.

Finding an optimal solution.

We are going to have to solve this problem nearly optimally in some cases, so let's design an algorithm to find an optimal solution and see if we can work from there. Sometimes it helps to look at things a little differently, so let's see if we can compute the cost of a minimum cost subset that achieves a given target value T. In essence, we have switched the roles of the budget constraint and the value – the value has now become a constraint and the budget, or total cost, is now the measure of optimality. Define $MinCost[i,t]$ to be the cost of a minimum cost subset of objects 1 through i whose total value is t or more. To find the value of an optimal solution to the MAXIMUM KNAPSACK PROBLEM, we need to find the maximum value of t such that $MinCost[n,t] \leq B$, where n is the number of objects.

For example, Figure 8.7 shows the table of $MinCost$ values for the example in Figure 8.1. The table shows only the points for t at which the minimum cost changes. We can see from the third row in the table that when the budget is 100, the maximum possible value is 150 since 100 is the minimum cost to achieve target value 150 and the cost of achieving target value 151 is 101, which is beyond the budget.

We can define $MinCost[i,t]$ recursively using the following idea. To choose

				76		103		150	151		178		253
	0	1	...	76	...	103	...	150	151	...	178	...	253
$i = 1$	0	51	...	51	...	∞	...	∞	∞	...	∞	...	∞
$i = 2$	0	50	...	51	...	101	...	101	101	...	∞	...	∞
$i = 3$	0	50	...	51	...	100	...	100	101	...	151	...	∞

target value

Figure 8.7: The *MinCost* table for the example in Figure 8.1. In the example, $v(a_1) = 102$, $c(a_1) = 51$, $v(a_2) = 75$, $c(a_2) = 50$, $v(a_3) = 75$, and $c(a_3) = 50$. The columns shown are the points at which the minimum cost changes. A target value of 253 is unachievable even with all three object available. The maximum achievable value with all three objects available and a budget of 100 is 150. This can be seen from the last row, which at column 151 shows a switch from a minimum cost of 100, which fits into the budget, to a minimum cost of 101, which does not.

a minimum cost subset of objects 1 through i that achieves a total value of at least t, we either include the i-th object or we do not include the i-th object. If we include the i-th object, then we have to pay $c(i)$ and choose a minimum cost subset of the first $i - 1$ objects that achieves a total value of at least $t - v(i)$. In this case, $MinCost[i,t] = c(i) + MinCost[i-1, t - v(i)]$. If we do not include the i-th object, then we must choose a minimum cost subset of the first $i - 1$ objects that achieves a total value of at least t, so $MinCost[i,t] = MinCost[i-1,t]$. We want to find the minimum cost, so we can define $MinCost[i,t]$ recursively as:

$$MinCost[i,t] = \min \left\{ \begin{array}{l} MinCost[i-1,t], \\ c(i) + MinCost[i-1, t - v(i)] \end{array} \right\}$$

As with any recursive definition, we need a base case. For this function, the base case occurs when t is 0 or i is 1. There is no cost to achieve a value of 0, so $MinCost[i,0]$ should be 0 for every i. If $i = 1$ and $v(1) < t$, then it is impossible to achieve a value of at least t using only the first object, so $MinCost[1,t]$ should be infinity. If $i = 1$ and $v(1) \geq t$, then we can achieve a value of at least t with the first object alone, so $MinCost[1,t]$ is the cost of the first object. This gives us the following complete recursive definition of $MinCost[i,t]$:

When $t = 0$, $MinCost[i, t] = 0$ for every object i;

$$\text{When } i = 1 \text{ and } t > 0, \;\; MinCost[1,t] = \begin{cases} \infty & \text{if } v(1) < t \\ c(i) & \text{if } v(1) \geq t \end{cases}$$

When $i > 1$ and $t > 0$:

$$MinCost[i,t] = \min \begin{cases} MinCost[i-1,t], \\ c(i) + MinCost[i-1, t-v(i)] \end{cases}$$

All we have left to do is to find an efficient way to compute $MinCost[n,t]$ for each possible value of t. We can compute the table of $MinCost$ values "bottom up", filling in $MinCost[1,t]$ for each possible t, then filling in $MinCost[2,t]$ for each t, and so on, until we have filled in $MinCost[n,t]$ for each t. To accomplish this, we need to know a maximum possible value for t. Since there are n objects and each has a value no more than $v(a_{max})$, the maximum possible target value is certainly no more than $n \cdot v(a_{max})$.

Figure 8.8 describes the complete algorithm, which is an example of a **dynamic programming** algorithm. The algorithm defines a *Take* table, where $Take[i,t]$ is YES if we take object i in our optimal solution to the subproblem consisting of the first i objects and target value t; otherwise, $Take[i,t]$ is NO. As the following exercise shows, this table can be used along with the $MinCost$ table to construct an optimal set of objects.

Exercise 8.6 *Design an algorithm that uses the MinCost and Take tables returned by SolveMaximumKnapsack from Figure 8.8 to construct the corresponding optimal set of objects for the given instance of MAXIMUM KNAPSACK.*

As we can see from pseudo-code in Figure 8.8, the first for-loop takes $\Theta(n)$ time, while the total running time for the second two for-loops is $\Theta(n \cdot v(a_{max}))$. The doubly nested for-loop beginning on Line 13 takes $\Theta(n^2 \cdot v(a_{max}))$ time. Therefore, the total running time of this algorithm is $\Theta(n^2 \cdot v(a_{max}))$. Hey, isn't this polynomial time? MAXIMUM KNAPSACK is NP-hard. If we just discovered a polynomial time algorithm to solve MAXIMUM KNAPSACK, then P $=$ NP. We're rich! We're rich! And everyone thought all of this time you spent laying around on the couch thinking about computational problems wouldn't get you anywhere.

Solving a long-standing open problem in an introductory course on the theory of computation seems like a little too much to ask, although one of my students did claim to do so the first time I taught this course. He spent

SolveMaximumKnapsack(A, v, c)

```
1    Set a_max to an object with maximum value.  // break ties however you like
2    for i = 1 to n                              // when target is 0, there is no cost
3        Set MinCost[i, 0] = 0
4    end for
     // when t ≤ v(1), target t can be achieved by taking object 1.
5    for t = 1 to v(1)
6        Set MinCost[1, t] = c(1)
7        Set Take[1, t] = YES
8    end for
     // when t > v(1), target cannot be reached with only object 1 available.
9    for t = v(1) + 1 to n · v(a_max)
10       Set MinCost[1, t] = Infinity
11       Set Take[1, t] = NO
12   end for
13   for i = 2 to n
14       for t = 1 to n · v(a_max)
15           Set NextT = max{0, t − v(i)}       // don't let index go below zero
16           if MinCost[i − 1, t] ≤ c(i) + MinCost[i − 1, NextT]
17               then begin      // don't include object i
18                   Set MinCost[i, t] = MinCost[i − 1, t]
19                   Set Take[i, t] = NO
20               end
21               else begin      // include object i
22                   Set MinCost[i, t] = c(i) + MinCost[i − 1, NextT]
23                   Set Take[i, t] = YES
24               end
25       end for
26   end for
27   return MinCost and Take
```

Figure 8.8: A dynamic programming algorithm to find an optimal solution to the MAXIMUM KNAPSACK problem. The first three for-loops fill in the first row and first column of the table in accordance with the base cases of the recursive definition. The for-loop beginning on Line 13 applies the recursive definition for the case $i > 1$. The body of the loop computes $MinCost[i, t]$ for each possible value of t based on the values in the previous row of the table. It records the choices made in the *Take* table. The algorithm returns the *MinCost* table and the *Take* table, from which a complete solution can be constructed, as demonstrated by Exercise 8.6.

most of his time trying to win a million dollars and not very much time on his homework, so he didn't do very well ... and he didn't win a million dollars either.

We should be careful before we pronounce SolveMaximumKnapsack to be a polynomial time algorithm. When we say an algorithm runs in polynomial time, we mean that the time required by the algorithm is bounded by a polynomial in the input size. What is the input size for MAXIMUM KNAPSACK? That depends on the encoding somewhat, but one thing we can be pretty sure of is that numbers in the problem instance are encoded in binary. In particular, $v(a_{max})$ is encoded in binary and contributes $\Theta(\log v(a_{max}))$ bits to the size of the input. Our algorithm takes $\Theta(n^2 \cdot v(a_{max}))$ time, which is *exponential* in the input size because $v(a_{max})$ is exponential in $\log v(a_{max})$. (Remember Figure 7.5.) We are not rich – at least not yet.

An algorithm such as the one above for MAXIMUM KNAPSACK whose running time would be polynomial if not for the fact that numbers are encoded in binary is said to be a **pseudo-polynomial time** algorithm.

Definition 8.2 *An algorithm is a* **pseudo-polynomial time algorithm** *if its running time is polynomial in the size of the problem instance and the magnitude of the numbers in the problem instance. In other words, if n is the size of the problem instance and M is the largest number in the problem instance, then there are constants c and d such that the running time of the algorithm is* $O(n^c M^d)$.

Pseudo-polynomial time algorithms are polynomial time algorithms when the numbers in the problem instances are known to be relatively small. For example, if we know that $v(a_{max}) = O(n^3)$ in all of the MAXIMUM KNAP-SACK problem instances that we are going to be given, then on this restricted version of the problem the running time of our dynamic programming algorithm above is $O(n^5)$, which is polynomial in the size of the restricted problem instance.

Isn't it reasonable to assume that the numbers in any practical problem instance will not be too big? Doesn't the fact that we have a pseudo-polynomial time algorithm for MAXIMUM KNAPSACK, which is NP-hard, imply that for all practical purposes P = NP? Not really. Recall we concluded that 0-1 KNAPSACK is NP-complete because it is a more general version of a known NP-complete problem, SUBSET-SUM. We proved that SUBSET-SUM is NP-complete using a reduction from 1in3SAT. How big were the numbers in the instances of SUBSET-SUM created in that reduction? Each number had one digit for each variable and one digit for each clause in the 1in3SAT instance. If the 1in3SAT instance contained n variables and m clauses, the magnitude of the numbers created for the SUBSET-SUM instance would be $\Theta(2^{n+m})$. Therefore, a pseudo-polynomial time algorithm for SUBSET-SUM would not provide a polynomial time algorithm for 1in3SAT. Pseudo-polynomial time algorithms are quite useful, however, in developing fully polynomial time approximation schemes.

From pseudo-polynomial time algorithms to fully polynomial time approximation schemes.

The difficulty with MAXIMUM KNAPSACK is that the range of numbers can be huge but the algorithm is required to be perfect. For example, suppose an optimal solution to a MAXIMUM KNAPSACK instance includes two objects with values 2 and 10^{10}, respectively. The value of the optimal solution is $10^{10} + 2$. Suppose that our algorithm outputs a solution consisting of two objects with values 1 and 10^{10}, respectively. The value of our solution is $10^{10} + 1$, which is not optimal but is extremely close.

Solving the problem optimally requires us to be able to deal with a completely fine grained space of values, but in the interest of time we could restrict the granularity with which we view values. If we were to shrink the range of values so that the values were bounded by a polynomial in n, then the pseudo-polynomial time dynamic programming algorithm above would run in polynomial time.

For example, suppose we were to divide the values by $v(a_{max})$. Consider what would happen to objects with values 1, 2, 1000, 1001, and 10000 when $v(a_{max}) = 10000$. Those values would become .00001, .00002, .1, .1001, and 1. This wouldn't be so good because our dynamic programming algorithm assumes we have values that are integers. It is also way too restrictive. We do not need the values to be between 0 and 1. We would be happy with values in the range 0 through $\left(\left(\frac{1}{\varepsilon}\right)^{c} n^{d}\right)$, for some constants c and d. If we multiplied the scaled values above by $\frac{1}{\varepsilon} n$, we would have numbers in the range 0 through $\frac{1}{\varepsilon} n$, which is polynomial in n and $\frac{1}{\varepsilon}$. The total running time of our dynamic programming algorithm operating on numbers in the range 0 through $\frac{1}{\varepsilon} n$ would be $\Theta(\frac{1}{\varepsilon} n^{3})$. The scaling algorithm is described formally in Figure 8.9, with the parameter F representing the scale factor that determines how much the values are scaled.

KnapsackApproxScheme$(objectList, v, c, F)$

    // compute the scaled values

1   **for** each a in $objectList$

2   set $scaled[a] = floor\left(\frac{v(a)}{F}\right)$

3   **end for**

    // solve using the *scaled* values.

4   $result = $ SolveMaximumKnapsack$(objectList, scaled, c)$

5   **return** $result$

Figure 8.9: A fully polynomial time approximation scheme for MAXIMUM KNAP-SACK. The parameter *scaleFactor* determines how much the values are scaled. As discussed in the main text, if the scale factor, F, is $\varepsilon \cdot \frac{v(a_{max})}{n}$, the running time will be $\Theta(\frac{1}{\varepsilon}n^3)$.

Suppose $\varepsilon = 1/2$ and the five objects above with values $1, 2, 1000, 1001$, and 10000 are just five of the 50 objects in the problem instance. Multiplying these values by $\frac{50}{1/2}\frac{1}{10000}$, which is 0.01, yields values 0.01, 0.02, 10, 10.01, and 100. Taking only the integer parts of these numbers gives us 0, 0, 10, 10, and 100. Objects 1 and 2 are now indistinguishable in terms of value, as are objects 3 and 4. We have lost some accuracy in the process of scaling, but we have sped up our algorithm by a factor of 100. The question we need to answer is: how much accuracy have we lost in general?

Let *Best* be an optimal solution and let *Good* be the solution output by the KnapsackApproxScheme algorithm from Figure 8.9. Since the algorithm would output an optimal solution if the scaled values were the true values, the sum of the scaled values of the objects in *Good* must be at least as large as the sum of the scaled values of the objects in *Best*. To evaluate the quality of our approximation scheme, however, we need to know how the sums of the original values of the objects in the two sets compare, not the sums of the scaled values.

If we had never applied the floor operator in Line 2 when we set $scaled[a] = floor\left(\frac{v(a)}{F}\right)$, then comparing the sums of the scaled values would be equivalent to comparing the sums of the actual values. (Without the floor, each object's scaled value would be the object's actual value multiplied by a constant.) Because we may have truncated the value when we applied the floor operator, however, we need to use a little more algebra. In particular, we need to use the fact that for any $t > 0$:

$$floor\left(\frac{v(a)}{t}\right) \geq \frac{v(a)}{t} - 1$$

With F representing the scale factor $\varepsilon \cdot \frac{v(a_{max})}{n}$, the algebra below shows that the value of the solution returned is at least $(1 - \varepsilon) \cdot OPT$:

$$\sum_{a \in Good} v(a) \geq F \cdot \sum_{a \in Good} scaled[a] \qquad \text{since } v(a) \geq F \cdot scaled[a]$$

$$\geq F \cdot \sum_{a \in Best} scaled[a] \qquad \text{since } Good \text{ was chosen over } Best$$

$$= F \cdot \sum_{a \in Best} floor\left(\frac{v(a)}{F}\right) \qquad \text{since } scaled[a] = floor\left(\frac{v(a)}{F}\right)$$

$$\geq F \cdot \sum_{a \in Best} \left(\frac{v(a)}{F} - 1\right) \qquad \text{since } floor\left(\frac{v(a)}{F}\right) \geq \frac{v(a)}{F} - 1$$

$$= \left(F \cdot \sum_{a \in Best} \frac{v(a)}{F}\right) - \left(F \cdot \sum_{a \in Best} 1\right) \qquad \text{since Algebra in 9th grade}$$

$$\geq \left(\sum_{a \in Best} v(a)\right) - F \cdot n \qquad \text{since } Best \text{ contains at most } n \text{ objects}$$

$$= \left(\sum_{a \in Best} v(a)\right) - \varepsilon \cdot v(a_{max}) \qquad \text{since } F = \frac{\varepsilon \cdot v(a_{max})}{n}$$

$$\geq \left(\sum_{a \in Best} v(a)\right) - \varepsilon \cdot \sum_{a \in Best} v(a) \qquad \text{since } Value(Best) \geq v(a_{max})$$

$$= (1 - \varepsilon) \cdot \sum_{a \in Best} v(a) \qquad \text{there's that 9th grade math again}$$

$$= (1 - \varepsilon) \cdot OPT \qquad \text{since } Best \text{ is an optimal solution.}$$

The dynamic programming algorithm using the scaled values gives us a fully polynomial time approximation scheme just in time for the meeting with NASA. For once you have satisfied your boss.

Boss: Nice.

8.5   Finding good enough solutions is not always easy.

Success has given you newfound confidence, so you decide to attack other optimization problems. You start with MAXIMUM SATISFIABILITY. Is it possible to come up with a pseudo-polynomial time algorithm for MAXSAT that could be turned into a fully polynomial time approximation scheme? Unfortunately, an instance of the MAXSAT optimization problem does not involve any numbers, only variables and clauses. A pseudo-polynomial time algorithm for MAXSAT would be a polynomial time algorithm, which does not exist unless $P = NP$.

That is disappointing, but what about TRAVELING SALESMAN? In a TRAVELING SALESMAN problem instance, there are costs given for each pair of cities, so a pseudo-polynomial time algorithm might be possible. Can we design a polynomial time algorithm for TSP when the costs are polynomial in the size of the problem instance?

Consider the reduction from HAMILTONIAN CYCLE to TSP that we used to prove that TSP is NP-complete. The distance between two cities was set to 1 if the corresponding edge was in the HAMILTONIAN CYCLE graph and set to 2 otherwise. The target cost was set equal to the number of cities. Clearly, all of the numbers in the problem instance created by this reduction are polynomial in the number of cities. A pseudo-polynomial time algorithm for TSP, therefore, would give us a polynomial time algorithm for HAMILTONIAN CYCLE, which does not exist unless $P = NP$.

Because there are no pseudo-polynomial time algorithms for TSP unless $P = NP$, TSP is said to be **strongly NP-hard**.

Definition 8.3 *If there is a constant k such that a problem B is NP-hard even when restricted to instances in which every number is $O(n^k)$, where n is the size of the problem instance, then B is said to be* **strongly NP-hard**.

Theorem 8.4 *If B is strongly NP-hard, then B cannot be solved by a pseudo-polynomial time algorithm unless $P = NP$.*

Exercise 8.7 *Prove Theorem 8.4.*

Not only is there no pseudo-polynomial time algorithm for TSP, but we can show that there is no c-approximation for TSP for any constant c. In the reduction of HAMILTONIAN CYCLE to TSP from Chapter 6, we assigned each edge in the TSP instance a cost of 1 if the edge appeared in the HAMIL-TONIAN CYCLE instance, while we assigned each edge in the TSP instance a cost of 2 if the edge did not appear in the HAMILTONIAN CYCLE instance. We set the budget for the TSP instance to n. This ensured that there was a TSP tour whose cost fit within the budget exactly when there was a HAMILTO-NIAN CYCLE in the original graph.

We are going to use the same trick here, assigning each edge a cost of 1 if the edge is in the HAMILTONIAN CYCLE instance, but instead of as-signing every other edge a cost of 2, we will assign every other edge a cost of $(c+1)n$. Any TSP tour that includes an edge that does not appear in the HAMILTONIAN CYCLE instance will have a cost of at least $(c+1)n$. On the other hand, any TSP tour consisting only of edges from the HAMILTO-NIAN CYCLE instance, will have a cost of n. This *gap* between the costs allows us to conclude that there is no c-approximation algorithm for TSP. For suppose there were such an algorithm. If there is a Hamiltonian cycle in the original HAMILTONIAN CYCLE instance, the value of an optimal solution to the TSP instance is n. A c-approximation algorithm would necessarily return a tour of cost no more than cn. However, there is no suboptimal tour whose cost is below $(c+1)n$ because the cost of any single suboptimal edge is $(c+1)n$. Therefore, any c-approximation algorithm must return an optimal tour, which corresponds to a Hamiltonian cycle in the HAMILTONIAN CYCLE instance. If there is no Hamiltonian cycle, a c-approximation algorithm will return a TSP tour with cost at least $(c+1)n$ because the tour must include an edge that is not in the HAMILTONIAN CYCLE instance. A c-approximation algorithm for TSP, then, can be used to solve HAMILTONIAN CYCLE by comparing the cost of the solution returned to n. If the cost is n, the HAMILTONIAN CYCLE instance is a YES instance. If the cost is not n, the HAMILTONIAN CYCLE instance is a NO instance. A c-approximation algorithm for TSP, therefore, cannot exist unless P = NP.

The graph we constructed to show there is no c-approximation algorithm for TSP is somewhat unlike many graphs we might expect to encounter in real life. Consider the TSP graph in Figure 8.11, which would be created from the HAMILTONIAN CYCLE instance shown in Figure 8.10 when $c = 2$.

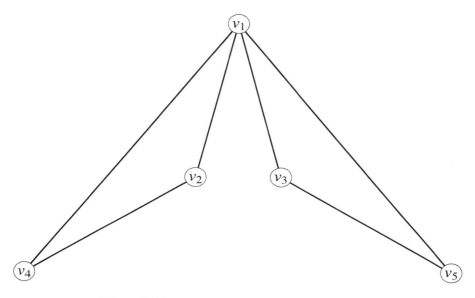

Figure 8.10: A graph without a Hamiltonian cycle.

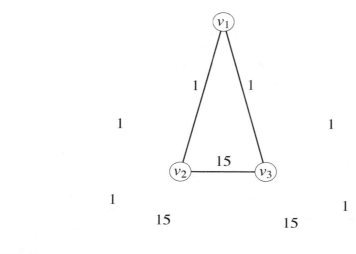

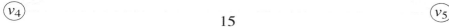

Figure 8.11: The TSP instance created from the graph in Figure 8.10 when $c = 2$. The darker edges in the center of the graph show a triangle that violates the triangle inequality because $c(v_2, v_3) > c(v_2, v_1) + c(v_1, v_3)$.

In the TSP graph created, shown in Figure 8.11, the cost of (v_2, v_3) is 3, while the costs of (v_2, v_1) and (v_1, v_3) are both 1. Such a graph could not, for example, represent cities on a map with the costs denoting the driving distances between cities. In real life, you can travel through v_1 to get from v_2 to v_3, so the distance from v_2 to v_3 cannot be more than the sum of the distances from v_2 to v_1 and v_1 to v_3. This property is known as the **triangle inequality**. A graph satisfies the triangle inequality if $c(x,z) \leq c(x,y) + c(y,z)$ for all vertices x, y, and z. Our proof above shows that there is no c-approximation algorithm for the TRAVELING SALESMAN PROBLEM when it is possible for the instances of the problem to violate the triangle inequality. When the instances of TSP are restricted to graphs in which the triangle inequality holds, the problem is called the **METRIC TRAVELING SALESMAN PROBLEM**. As the following exercise shows, there is a c-approximation algorithm for the METRIC TRAVELING SALESMAN PROBLEM. This illustrates an important point: when faced with a NP-hard optimization problem, it is crucial to consider whether the instances you will be given are restricted in some way that makes the problem easier.

Exercise 8.8 *Develop a polynomial time c-approximation algorithm for the METRIC TRAVELING SALESMAN PROBLEM. A $\frac{3}{2}$-approximation algorithm is known, but there are a couple of simpler 2-approximations. You may want to review what you know (or don't know) about* **minimum spanning trees**.

Chapter 9

Is It Better To Be an Ant? Heuristics For Hard Problems

9.1 Introduction

Always on the lookout for a permanent job, you decide to go to a job fair. You are ecstatic to discover that *The Tim and Francine Show* has a representative from their computing division at the fair. You immediately run up to the table and frantically explain what you know about computational complexity and approximation algorithms. You ask the rep how they go about solving their satisfiability problem and what kind of guarantee they have on the approximate optimality of the solution. The answer leaves you deeply disturbed.

Rep: "We don't get too complicated. We start with a random assignment of truth values. Then we repeatedly find the variable that appears in the most unsatisfied clauses and flip its value. After a large number of flips, we start over from a new random truth assignment. When we run out of time, we just take the best assignment we have seen so far. Our method usually finds a solution that satisfies a large majority of the clauses and it really isn't a big deal. *The Tim and Francine Show* is a pretty relaxed operation. We are looking to hire laid-back people. Next."

How can this be? 3SAT is NP-complete and these guys are treating it like they are playing a combination of Darts and King of the Hill.

What does it mean for 3SAT to be NP-complete? We measure complexity in terms of the *worst case* behavior of our algorithms. Assuming P $\neq$ NP, 3SAT being NP-complete means that for every algorithm that solves 3SAT, there are an infinite number of problem instances for which the algorithm takes more than polynomial time. There may, however, be infinitely many instances that can be solved quickly too. Perhaps this is what is happening with *The Tim and Francine Show*. Maybe something about the type of viewers watching the show leads them to collectively choose a set clauses that can be satisfied quickly by the show's algorithm.

9.2   Local Search

The algorithm described above is called **GSAT**. It has been shown to work fairly well in practice and it is worth investigating further. GSAT is an example of a general technique called **local search**. Local search algorithms start with some random or otherwise easy to compute candidate solution, which in all likelihood is suboptimal. At each iteration of the algorithm, a "local" change is made to the candidate solution in an attempt to move closer to an optimal solution. For instance, a local change in GSAT is a change to the value of a single variable – in particular, the variable that appears in the largest number of unsatisfied clauses.

In general, each local search algorithm must define the meaning of "local change" by specifying a **neighborhood relation** and a **selection mechanism**. The neighborhood relation defines for each candidate solution, a set of neighboring solutions. The selection mechanism is a procedure for selecting the neighboring solution to which the algorithm will move from the current candidate solution at each step. In GSAT, a candidate solution is any fully specified truth assignment, the neighbors of a truth assignment are those truth assignments that differ in the value of a single variable, and the selection mechanism is to choose the neighbor that satisfies the most clauses (where ties are broken randomly).

Local search algorithms can be effective, but unlike approximation algorithms, local search algorithms generally provide no guarantee on the quality of the solutions returned. Instead, local search algorithms are compared experimentally. Although, as the following exercise shows, there are times when local search does provide approximation guarantees.

Exercise 9.1 *Design a local search algorithm for the problem below, which is known as* **SCHEDULING ON IDENTICAL PARALLEL MACHINES**. *Show that your algorithm is a 2-approximation.*

GIVEN: 1. m identical machines that each can process one job at a time;

                2. n jobs, where each job j has a processing time p_j.

OBJECTIVE: Find an assignment of jobs to machines so that the time the last job completes is minimized. Note that each machine will be given a set of jobs. The total amount of processing time assigned to a machine is the time at which the last job on that machine is completed.

    For example, if we have 2 machines and 5 jobs with processing times 2, 4, 5, 8, and 10, the optimal schedule is to assign the jobs with processing times 4 and 10 to one machine and to assign the jobs with processing times 2, 5, and 8 to the other machine. The first machine finishes at time 14, while the second machine finishes at time 15. The last job, then, completes at time 15. A suboptimal solution would be to assign the jobs with times 10 and 8 to one machine and the jobs with times 2, 4, and 5 to the other. In this suboptimal schedule, the last job completes at time 18.

    As with any experimental technique, there are many difficulties in applying local search algorithms. For example, a local search algorithm may require a very large number of iterations to find an optimal solution. In fact, assuming that P $\neq$ NP and that each iteration of a local search algorithm takes a polynomial amount of time, the algorithm *must* require more than a polynomial number of iterations in the worst case to solve an NP-hard optimization problem. To avoid running for an exceedingly long time, local search algorithms limit the number of iterations before termination. This restricts the ability of the algorithm to find an optimal solution because the algorithm may bail out way too soon.

    The selection mechanism may provide an additional restriction on the algorithm's ability to find an optimal solution. For example, using GSAT's selection criteria there may be no way to get from a particular randomly chosen initial solution to an optimal solution. To see this, consider the 3SAT instance:

$$(\overline{x_1} \vee x_2 \vee x_4) \wedge (\overline{x_1} \vee x_2 \vee \overline{x_4}) \wedge (\overline{x_2} \vee x_3 \vee x_4) \wedge (\overline{x_2} \vee x_3 \vee \overline{x_4})$$
$$\wedge (\overline{x_1} \vee \overline{x_3} \vee x_4) \wedge (\overline{x_1} \vee \overline{x_3} \vee \overline{x_4}) \wedge (x_1 \vee x_2 \vee x_5) \wedge (x_1 \vee x_4 \vee x_5)$$

The truth assignment ($x_1 = $ FALSE, $x_2 = $ TRUE, $x_3 = $ TRUE, $x_4 = $ TRUE, $x_5 = $ FALSE) satisfies every clause. However, if GSAT starts with the truth assignment ($x_1 = $ TRUE, $x_2 = $ TRUE, $x_3 = $ TRUE, $x_4 = $ FALSE, $x_5 = $ FALSE), which satisfies 7 of the 8 clauses, changing the value of a single variable cannot increase the number of clauses satisfied. This solution is referred to as a **local optimum**. It is not an optimal solution, but the algorithm cannot find a neighboring solution that is closer to optimal. Therefore, it has no neighbor to which it can move according to the selection mechanism.

Various techniques are used to alleviate the problem of local optima. For example, some algorithms restart from another randomly generated initial candidate solution after no improvement can be made; others make random moves instead of solution-improving moves some percentage of the time.[1] The latter approach leads to another problem, however. When a local search algorithm does not strictly move to more optimal neighbors, it may cycle over a large number of candidate solutions. One approach used to avoid this cycling behavior is called **Tabu Search**. In this variant of the local search paradigm, each candidate solution is marked with the last time step it was encountered and is restricted from being reached again for a certain period of time. This period is called the **tabu tenure**.

As local search algorithms become more and more sophisticated, there is an increasing number of parameters to specify. (In our short discussion of local search, we have already encountered at least three potential parameters: tabu tenure length, probability of exploring moves, and the maximum number of moves before restarting.) The effectiveness of the algorithm may depend heavily on the settings of these parameters. This makes applying local search techniques more of an art than a science. Local search has, however, proved effective in solving some NP-hard problems in practice, which may be something you wish to remember the next time you start blabbering on about how hard SAT is to solve.

9.3 SAT Solvers

Your temporary consulting job for NASA is about to expire. However, NASA has awarded your firm another project – developing an autonomous deep-space probe. You are hopeful that your contract will be renewed. The software on

---

[1]The real GSAT algorithm, in fact, allows moves that do not improve the candidate solution. See the chapter notes for details.

the probe must plan out each sequence of actions required for the probe to rendezvous with objects in the Kuiper belt, one of which was formerly known as a planet. Because of the long time required to transmit instructions from Earth to the outer reaches of the solar system, the probe's software must develop its plan without help from flight control operators on Earth. The NASA design team has figured out a way to convert the entire planning problem into a satisfiability problem. Your boss, who has had to endure many of your animated, lunchtime mini-lectures about SAT, approaches you about the possibility of staying on to help design an algorithm to solve SAT. "That's easy," you blurt, trying somewhat unsuccessfully to keep your pizza in your mouth. "We just start with a random initial assignment and repeatedly flip the value of the variable that most reduces the number of unsatisfied clauses."

Your boss looks as though she began to regret approaching you about the problem as soon as you opened your mouth to respond. As she grabs a napkin from the napkin dispenser thingy, she says, "Local search will not do here. We need to know for sure when the instance is unsatisfiable."

A week later you are back on your parents' couch explaining that your contract simply expired and that you were *not* really fired again. A year later you still have trouble concentrating on the TV. Disappointing your boss a week before your contract was due to end was unfortunate. What has you truly disturbed, however, is that she expected you to be able to solve SAT quickly enough to control a billion-dollar spacecraft and she wouldn't even consider using a local search algorithm. Local search is good enough for Tim and Francine, isn't it? That show probably does more to make people comfortable and happy in their lives than some stupid, ridiculously expensive, deep-space probe. You would rather sit around watching Tim and Francine than help develop some doomed space probe anyway.

Exasperated, you drop onto your couch, lay your head back on your temper-foam pillow, and click on the TV.

TV: "And here's a breaking news update. NASA's new space probe, which at least one vocal internet critic had argued was doomed due to the complexity of its software, has successfully rendezvoused with an object that was formerly considered a planet but is now simply named ⚥, a symbol with no known pronunciation."

How could we design an algorithm to solve SAT – not approximately solve

SAT, not solve SAT most of the time, but actually *solve* SAT? We know such an algorithm will take more than a polynomial amount of time in the worst case, but maybe we can design an algorithm that will run reasonably quickly on the specific problem instances generated by converting NASA's planning problem into SAT. Unfortunately, we do not know much about those instances. We need to develop a general algorithm that has some hope of doing well on a large number of potential SAT instances.

We could "blindly" search for a solution by evaluating every one of the 2^n possible truth assignments. But maybe there is a more intelligent way to go about searching for a solution that will reduce the number of truth assignments we need to evaluate. Consider the following instance of SAT:

$$(x_1) \wedge (\overline{x_1} \vee x_2) \wedge (\overline{x_1} \vee \overline{x_3} \vee x_4) \wedge (\overline{x_2} \vee x_3) \wedge (x_1 \vee x_4)$$

To satisfy the formula, we must set x_1 to TRUE because x_1 appears in a clause by itself. Such a clause is called a **unit clause**. Setting x_1 to TRUE immediately satisfies both the first clause and the last clause, leaving us with just the middle three clauses left to satisfy. However, once we set x_1 to TRUE, the only way to satisfy $(\overline{x_1} \vee x_2)$ is to set x_2 to TRUE because $\overline{x_1}$ is FALSE. In other words, setting x_1 to TRUE transforms the clause $(\overline{x_1} \vee x_2)$ into (x_2). For the same reason, setting x_1 to TRUE transforms the clause $(\overline{x_1} \vee \overline{x_3} \vee x_4)$ into $(\overline{x_3} \vee x_4)$. In general, once we decide that x_1 will be TRUE, we can remove $\overline{x_1}$ from every clause in which it appears because $\overline{x_1}$ will be FALSE and cannot be used to satisfy any clause. Setting x_1 to TRUE, then, transforms the formula above into:

$$(x_2) \wedge (\overline{x_3} \vee x_4) \wedge (\overline{x_2} \vee x_3)$$

Notice that our new formula also contains a unit clause, (x_2), so we are forced to set x_2 to TRUE. Using the ideas above, this transforms the formula into:

$$(\overline{x_3} \vee x_4) \wedge (x_3)$$

Once again, we have a unit clause, (x_3). This forces us to set x_3 to TRUE, which in turn forces us to set x_4 to TRUE, at which point we have found a satisfying truth assignment for the original formula. We found this truth assignment not by considering every possible truth assignment but by following the dictates of the formula itself. The unit clause in the original formula forced us to set x_1 to TRUE. The logical implications in the formula then told us that

x_2 must also be TRUE, which in turn told us that x_3, and then x_4, must be TRUE as well.

This process of satisfying a unit clause and then transforming the formula by following simple logical consequences of that action is called **unit propagation**. Perhaps we can use it to develop an algorithm to solve SAT efficiently enough to be useful for a wide range of problem instances even though we have no hope of developing an algorithm that will be efficient on all problem instances.

Before we get too carried away by our initial success, let's consider how unit propagation would work on an unsatisfiable formula. Figure 9.1 summarizes the progression of clauses generated by unit propagation starting with the formula: $(x_1) \wedge (\overline{x_1} \vee x_2) \wedge (\overline{x_1} \vee x_3 \vee \overline{x_4}) \wedge (\overline{x_2} \vee \overline{x_3}) \wedge (x_3 \vee x_4)$.

	(x_1)	$(\overline{x_1} \vee x_2)$	$(\overline{x_1} \vee x_3 \vee \overline{x_4})$	$(\overline{x_2} \vee \overline{x_3})$	$(x_3 \vee x_4)$
1. $x_1 = $ TRUE	TRUE	(x_2)	$(x_3 \vee \overline{x_4})$	$(\overline{x_2} \vee \overline{x_3})$	$(x_3 \vee x_4)$
2. $x_2 = $ TRUE	TRUE	TRUE	$(x_3 \vee \overline{x_4})$	$(\overline{x_3})$	$(x_3 \vee x_4)$
3. $x_3 = $ FALSE	TRUE	TRUE	$(\overline{x_4})$	TRUE	(x_4)
4. $x_4 = $ FALSE	TRUE	TRUE	TRUE	TRUE	EMPTY

Figure 9.1: A trace of the execution of the Unit Propagation algorithm on the formula $(x_1) \wedge (\overline{x_1} \vee x_2) \wedge (\overline{x_1} \vee x_3 \vee \overline{x_4}) \wedge (\overline{x_2} \vee \overline{x_3}) \wedge (x_3 \vee x_4)$.

Following the progression in the table, we recognize the first clause as a unit clause, so we start by setting x_1 to TRUE. This implies that $\overline{x_1}$ is FALSE, so as before, we can remove $\overline{x_1}$ from the clauses in which it appears. This gives us the formula:

$$(x_2) \wedge (x_3 \vee \overline{x_4}) \wedge (\overline{x_2} \vee \overline{x_3}) \wedge (x_3 \vee x_4)$$

Notice that this formula also has a unit clause, (x_2), so we must set x_2 to TRUE to satisfy the formula. When we do this, we remove $\overline{x_2}$ from the clauses in which it appears, just as we removed $\overline{x_1}$. We can also now remove the clause

(x_2) from the formula because it has been satisfied. This gives us the following formula, which includes the unit clause $(\overline{x_3})$:

$$(x_3 \vee \overline{x_4}) \wedge (\overline{x_3}) \wedge (x_3 \vee x_4)$$

We propagate the newly created unit clause through the formula by setting x_3 to FALSE, giving us the formula:

$$(\overline{x_4}) \wedge (x_4)$$

Now, we have two unit clauses, $(\overline{x_4})$ and (x_4). We can tell at this point that the formula cannot be satisfied because if we set x_4 to TRUE, we do not satisfy $(\overline{x_4})$, and if we set x_4 to FALSE, we do not satisfy (x_4). Alternatively, we can propagate one of these unit clauses, say $(\overline{x_4})$, through the formula by setting x_4 to FALSE, removing the satisfied clause $(\overline{x_4})$, and removing x_4 from every clause in which it appears. This leaves us with a formula containing a single clause with nothing in it. What does this empty clause represent? To produce an empty clause, we must have removed every literal that appeared in the original clause. Since we remove literals from a clause only when we have chosen their values to be FALSE in a unit propagation step, this empty clause represents a clause that cannot be satisfied by the truth assignment we have constructed so far. This means that when unit propagation generates an empty clause in the formula, the formula is unsatisfiable. The complete pseudocode for the unit propagation algorithm is given in Figure 9.2.

While the unit propagation algorithm gives us hope that we may be able to develop a decent algorithm for SAT, unit propagation by itself is not enough. There is no guarantee we will be given a formula that contains a unit clause. There is also no guarantee that unit propagation will generate a formula that contains a unit clause at each step along the way. Our examples above were way too easy. We need to build a more general algorithm around the unit propagation subroutine.

Let's consider the formula from the previous example but without the unit clause (x_1):

$$(\overline{x_1} \vee x_2) \wedge (\overline{x_1} \vee x_3 \vee \overline{x_4}) \wedge (\overline{x_2} \vee \overline{x_3}) \wedge (x_3 \vee x_4)$$

We cannot apply unit propagation directly to this formula because the formula does not contain a unit clause. However, we have to assign some value

UnitPropagation(*formula, truthAssignmentSoFar*)

1   **while** *formula* contains a unit clause but not an empty clause
2   Let x_j be the variable in some unit clause
3   **if** x_j appears positively in the unit clause
4   **then begin**
5   Add $x_j =$ TRUE to *truthAssignmentSoFar*
6   Remove every clause that contains x_j from *formula*
7   Remove $\overline{x_j}$ from every clause in *formula* containing $\overline{x_j}$
8   **end**
9   **else begin**
10   Add $x_j =$ FALSE to *truthAssignmentSoFar*
11   Remove every clause that contains $\overline{x_j}$ from *formula*
12   Remove x_j from every clause in *formula* containing x_j
13   **end**
14 **end while**
15 **return** *truthAssignmentSoFar* and *formula*

Figure 9.2: Pseudocode for the Unit Propagation algorithm.

to x_1, so why not just try $x_1 =$ TRUE? This is equivalent to trying to satisfy our original formula, the one containing the unit clause (x_1):

$$(x_1) \wedge (\overline{x_1} \vee x_2) \wedge (\overline{x_1} \vee x_3 \vee \overline{x_4}) \wedge (\overline{x_2} \vee \overline{x_3}) \wedge (x_3 \vee x_4)$$

This next statement is important (you can tell by the exclamation mark). Trying a particular value for a variable is equivalent to adding a unit clause to the formula! We can now apply unit propagation, which as demonstrated in Figure 9.1, will tell us that the formula is unsatisfiable. This implies that it is impossible to satisfy the formula with $x_1 =$ TRUE. Our only other choice is for x_1 to be FALSE.

Setting x_1 to FALSE is equivalent to adding the unit clause $(\overline{x_1})$ to the formula, giving us:

$$(\overline{x_1}) \wedge (\overline{x_1} \vee x_2) \wedge (\overline{x_1} \vee x_3 \vee \overline{x_4}) \wedge (\overline{x_2} \vee \overline{x_3}) \wedge (x_3 \vee x_4)$$

Applying unit propagation, we set x_1 to FALSE and remove the first three clauses because they are satisfied, leaving us with:

$$(\overline{x_2} \vee \overline{x_3}) \wedge (x_3 \vee x_4)$$

Unfortunately, this formula does not have a unit clause, so again we have to create one, this time by choosing a value for x_2. Choosing x_2 to be TRUE is equivalent to adding (x_2) to the formula, which yields:

$$(x_2) \wedge (\overline{x_2} \vee \overline{x_3}) \wedge (x_3 \vee x_4)$$

Applying another unit propagation step generates the formula:

$$(\overline{x_3}) \wedge (x_3 \vee x_4)$$

Applying unit propagation one more time yields:

$$(x_4)$$

This formula can be satisfied with $x_4 =$ TRUE, thus proving that the original formula was satisfiable with $x_1 =$ FALSE and in particular by the truth assignment $(x_1 =$ FALSE$, x_2 =$ TRUE$, x_3 =$ FALSE$, x_4 =$ TRUE$)$.

The algorithm described above is known as the **Davis Putnam Logemann Loveland (DPLL)** algorithm. The complete pseudocode appears in Figure 9.3.

We can view DPLL as performing depth-first search on a binary tree in which each node represents a variable. Taking the left branch off of a node represents setting the variable to TRUE, while taking the right branch represents setting the variable to FALSE. Figure 9.4 shows the tree representing the execution of DPLL on the formula in the previous example.

After each new assignment to a variable, we perform unit propagation to determine the implications of the assignment. If unit propagation establishes that the formula is satisfiable, we return the assignment we have built so far as the satisfying truth assignment for the formula. The values of any variables we have not assigned are chosen arbitrarily. If unit propagation establishes that the formula is unsatisfiable given the values we have chosen so far, we backtrack to the previous node at which a branch has not yet been considered and restart the process from that point with a new assignment for the corresponding variable. The last possibility is that unit propagation transforms the formula into a new formula that does not include a unit clause. At that point, we have another decision to make about the value of a variable. This is the situation in which we find ourselves after setting x_1 to FALSE in the example illustrated in Figure 9.4.

Algorithms based on DPPL have been successful in solving SAT instances with millions of variables and clauses. Despite being the prototypical NP-complete problem, large SAT instances that arise in practice are often solvable

DPLL($formulaSoFar, truthAssignmentSoFar$)

1   Call UnitPropagation($formulaSoFar$, $truthAssignmentSoFar$)
2   Set *newFormula* to the formula returned by UnitPropagation
3   Set *newAssignment* to the truth assignment returned by UnitPropagation
4   **if** *newFormula* is empty
5   **then return** SATISFIABLE with *newAssignment* as the solution
6   **if** *newFormula* contains an empty clause
7   **then return** UNSATISFIABLE
8   Let x_i be the first variable that is not assigned in *newAssignment*
9   Add clause (x_i) to *newFormula*
10   Add $x_i =$ TRUE to *newAssignment*
11   Set *result* = DPLL(*newFormula*, *newAssignment*)
12   **if** *result* is SATISFIABLE
13   **then return** SATISFIABLE with *newAssignment* as the solution
14   **else begin**
15   Replace (x_i) with $(\overline{x}_i)$ in *newFormula*
16   Replace $x_i =$ TRUE with $x_i =$ FALSE in *newAssignment*
17   **return** DPLL(*newFormula*, *newAssignment*)
18   **end**

Figure 9.3: Pseudocode for the Davis-Putnam-Logemann-Loveland algorithm.

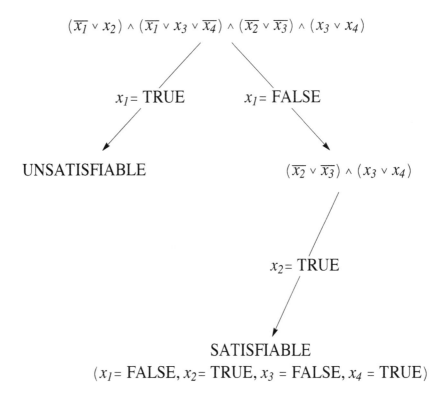

Figure 9.4: A tree representation of the execution of DPLL on the formula $(\overline{x_1} \vee x_2) \wedge$ $(\overline{x_1} \vee x_3 \vee \overline{x_4}) \wedge (\overline{x_2} \vee \overline{x_3}) \wedge (x_3 \vee x_4)$. After DPLL sets x_1 to TRUE by adding (x_1) to the formula, UnitPropagation will determine that the formula is unsatisfiable. DPLL will then backtrack and set x_1 to FALSE by adding $(\overline{x_1})$ to the formula. UnitPropagation will not be able to determine whether the formula is satisfiable. Instead, it will return the formula $(\overline{x_2} \vee \overline{x_3}) \wedge (x_3 \vee x_4)$. DPPL will then try setting x_2 to TRUE. With this setting, UnitPropagation will determine that the formula is satisfied by the assignment $(x_1 = \text{FALSE}, x_2 = \text{TRUE}, x_3 = \text{FALSE}, x_4 = \text{TRUE})$.

in a matter of minutes. So why don't we consider NP rather than P to be the set of problems that can be solved in practice? The success of modern SAT solvers notwithstanding, SAT is still a very hard problem. No SAT solver will be fast on all instances of SAT. DPLL works well on some types of instances but works very poorly on others.

For example, suppose we randomly generate a large number of clauses using a small number of variables. Odds are that the formula will not be satisfiable. To see this, consider the extreme case of generating eight distinct 3SAT clauses over three variables. Every possible combination of three literals will be used, giving us the formula:

$$(x_1 \lor x_2 \lor x_3) \land (x_1 \lor x_2 \lor \overline{x_3}) \land (x_1 \lor \overline{x_2} \lor x_3) \land (x_1 \lor \overline{x_2} \lor \overline{x_3})$$
$$\land (\overline{x_1} \lor x_2 \lor x_3) \land (\overline{x_1} \lor x_2 \lor \overline{x_3}) \land (\overline{x_1} \lor \overline{x_2} \lor x_3) \land (\overline{x_1} \lor \overline{x_2} \lor \overline{x_3})$$

You should be able to verify that there is no way to satisfy this formula or any formula that contains all possible 3-literal clauses made from the given variables. While this is an extreme example, the principle applies generally – if the formula contains a large percentage of the possible clauses, the formula is likely to be unsatisfiable. On the other hand, if we randomly generate a small number of clauses over a large number of variables, odds are that the formula will be satisfiable. DPLL works well in either of these cases. It has the most difficulty on randomly generated formulas that about as equally likely to be satisfiable as to be unsatisfiable. This occurs in the neighborhood of what is called the **critical point**. For 3SAT, experiments indicate that the critical point is the point at which the ratio of clauses to variables is about 4.26. Understanding the behavior of SAT solvers on instances in the region around the critical point is a major area of research.

So is SAT easy or hard? Theory tells us that SAT is hard, but just because a problem is hard doesn't mean we should stop trying to come up with good algorithms to solve it. DPLL is an exponential-time algorithm and local search algorithms do not always guarantee they will find a satisfying truth assignment when one exists, but these algorithms often work well in practice. If you are going to solve SAT instances in practice, however, you need to understand something about the type of instances with which your algorithm will be presented. Some algorithms may be more appropriate than others in your particular situation. Algorithm designers cannot ignore theory but theorists cannot forget that algorithms operate in the real world, a world that is often very different from the abstract world we create to make theoretical work possible.

Exercise 9.2 *Implement the DPPL algorithm in your favorite programming language and run experiments on randomly generated 3SAT instances with varying ratios of clauses to variables. Keep track of the running time of your program and plot the running time against the clause to variable ratio. Pay particular attention to the behavior of the algorithm near the critical point.*

Chapter 10

Space

10.1 Introduction

Epiphanies don't happen very often – for you, maybe never – but you suddenly realize you are better off working for yourself. Rejection after rejection could have had something to do with your newfound wisdom. You decide to learn how to develop apps for mobile phones. There must be money in that. Mobile apps were new fairly recently and almost everyone carries a mobile phone with them. Surely you can design apps that people will buy and still have enough free time to think about P and NP – and watch TV. At the very least, you are certain your plan will mollify your parents. Your initial forays into app development are not terribly successful, however. Phones have a limited amount of space with which to work. Throughout your short and relatively unsuccessful career, you have been entirely focused on the *time* taken by your algorithms, not the space. Frustrated, you sit down to watch the final episode of *The Tim and Francine Show*.

Host: "Welcome to the final episode of *The Tim and Francine Show*, recorded tonight in front of a live studio audience. By now you have probably heard that Tim and Francine are in the process of breaking up. So, we have changed the format of the show to reflect the more competitive nature of their relationship.

As usual, each viewer will express his or her preference using a clause containing any number of literals. Tim's goal is to satisfy all of the viewers, while Francine's goal is to ensure that at least one viewer remains unsatisfied. Tim moves first, choosing the value of the first variable. Francine responds by choosing the value of the second variable. Tim then chooses the value of the third variable and Francine responds by choosing the value of the fourth variable. The game proceeds like this, with Tim choosing the values of the odd numbered variables and Francine choosing the values of the even numbered variables, until every variable has been given a value. At that point, the formula is evaluated. Tim wins if the formula evaluates to TRUE; Francine wins if the formula evaluates to FALSE. Whoever wins gets to keep the cat.

Enough with the formalities. Let's bring out America's favorite couple and get this show started.

Audience: (Applause, Applause, Applause)

Host: Tim, I have to ask the question that all of our viewers are no doubt asking – why are you wearing a football helmet?

Tim: Well, given the circumstances, I wasn't sure how this show would go tonight.

Host: Francine, what exactly are the circumstances that Tim is referring to?

Francine: I found out that Tim has been having an affair with that woman from the farm who delivered the pigs for our first episode – OUR FIRST EPISODE!

Audience: Booooooooo.

Francine: The PIG has been sneaking out to the farm all season!

Host: The pig has been sneaking out to the farm all season? How is that possible?

Francine: No, *Tim* is the pig, you moron.

Host: Oh ... right ... Tim is the pig and I am a moron. Well folks, this should be an interesting show tonight.

You are dumbfounded (or something) – not by Tim and Francine breaking up, but by this new competitive scenario. How can this be formulated as a computational problem? Let's start by looking at the case in which there are only three variables: x_1, x_2, and x_3. Tim needs to find a value for x_1 so that *for any* value Francine chooses for x_2, *there is* some value for x_3 that causes the formula to evaluate to TRUE. Is it possible for Tim to come up with a strategy that guarantees he will win no matter how Francine responds to each of his choices.

To formulate the problem using a logical formula, we'll need a way to express the phrases "for any" and "there is" using logical operators. We'll use the symbol $\forall$ to represent "for any" and the symbol $\exists$ to represent "there is." These symbols, which almost certainly have Satanic origins, are usually read as "for all" and "there exists." The formula $\exists x_1 \forall x_2 \exists x_3 [x_1 \lor x_2 \lor \overline{x_3}]$, would be read as, "There exists a value for x_1 such that for all values of x_2, there exists a value of x_3 such that $(x_1 \lor x_2 \lor \overline{x_3})$ evaluates to TRUE."

Here's how these operators work. If $f(x)$ is a Boolean formula using the variable x, then $\forall x[f(x)]$ is TRUE if and only if $f(x)$ is TRUE regardless of whether x is assigned TRUE or x is assigned FALSE. For example, $\forall x[x \lor \overline{x}]$ is TRUE because $(x \lor \overline{x})$ is TRUE when x is assigned TRUE *and* when x is assigned FALSE. On the other hand, $\forall x[\overline{x}]$ is FALSE because $(\overline{x})$ is FALSE when x is assigned TRUE.

The formula $\exists x[f(x)]$ is TRUE if and only if $f(x)$ is TRUE for at least one of the two values of x. For example, $\exists x[\overline{x}]$ is TRUE because there is a value for x, namely FALSE, that causes $(\overline{x})$ to evaluate to TRUE. For $\exists x[f(x)]$ to be FALSE, $f(x)$ must be FALSE regardless of the value assigned to x. The formula $\exists x[x \land \overline{x}]$ is FALSE because $(x \land \overline{x})$ is FALSE no matter what value we plug in for x.

Formulas built using $\forall$ and $\exists$ are called **quantified Boolean formulas**, with $\forall$ referred to as the **universal quantifier** and $\exists$ referred to as the **existential quantifier**. Quantified Boolean formulas can be combined to create ever longer quantified Boolean formulas. For example, the following formula is a quantified Boolean formula with three quantified variables:

$$\exists x \forall y \exists z [(x \lor y) \land (\overline{y} \lor z)]$$

With quantifiers, we can formulate the computational problem of determining whether Tim has a strategy that guarantees a win as a quantified satisfiability problem known as **QSAT** and defined as follows:

GIVEN: 1.   a sequence of n Boolean variables: $x_1, \ldots, x_n$;
              2.   a set of clauses over $\{x_1, \ldots, x_n\}$.

QUESTION: If $f(x_1, \ldots, x_n)$ is the Boolean formula consisting of an AND of the given clauses and we take Q_i to be either $\forall$ or $\exists$ depending on whether the index is even or odd, is the following quantified Boolean formula true?

$$\exists x_1 \forall x_2 \exists x_3 \forall x_4 \ldots Q_{n-1} x_{n-1} Q_n x_n [f(x_1, \ldots, x_n)]$$

Is QSAT in P? It seems unlikely given what we know about 3SAT.

Exercise 10.1 *Reduce 3SAT to QSAT to show that QSAT is* NP-*hard.*

Is QSAT even in NP? Let's try to come up with a simple verifier. All of the verifiers we have developed so far have used a solution to the problem instance as a certificate – SAT's verifier used a truth assignment, SUBSET-SUM's verifier used a subset of the numbers, HAMILTONIAN CYCLE's verifier used a cycle, etc. Consider the following QSAT instance:

$$\exists x_1 \forall x_2 \exists x_3 [(x_1) \wedge (x_2 \vee x_3) \wedge (\overline{x_2} \vee \overline{x_3})].$$

The solution for this formula is to set x_1 to TRUE and to set x_3 to FALSE if x_2 is TRUE, but to set x_3 to TRUE if x_2 is FALSE. This example suggests that a solution may be an entire plan in which the values of the existentially quantified variables are contingent on the values of the universally quantified variables. Since there are $n/2$ universally quantified variables, there are $2^{(n/2)}$ different combinations of values for the universally quantified variables. Depending on the formula, for each of these combinations we may have to specify a different set of values for the existentially quantified variables. In that case, using a solution as a certificate creates a certificate with size that is exponential in the size of the problem instance. A polynomial time verifier wouldn't even have enough time to read the entire certificate!

Finding a polynomial time verifier for QSAT seems a lot harder than finding a polynomial time verifier for SAT or HAMILTONIAN CYCLE. Indeed, no one knows whether QSAT is in NP, or for that matter, whether QSAT is in

P. It would be nice to say something about the complexity of QSAT, though, so let's design an algorithm to solve QSAT and see what resources are required by our algorithm.

To solve QSAT, we can use a simple backtracking search like that used in the DPPL algorithm from Chapter 9 but without the unit propagation step. Start by setting x_1 to TRUE and then consider each possible value for x_2. For each of these two values, we need to be able to choose a value for x_3 to make the remaining formula evaluate to TRUE. If for some value of x_2, it is impossible to choose a value for x_3 that causes the remaining formula to evaluate to TRUE, then we have to backtrack and try again with x_1 assigned FALSE. Figure 10.1 illustrates this idea for the quantified formula:

$$\exists x_1 \forall x_2 \exists x_3 [(\overline{x_1} \vee x_3) \wedge (\overline{x_2} \vee \overline{x_3})].$$

The algorithm can be implemented recursively using one subroutine for the existentially quantified variables and one for the universally quantified variables. (Figure 10.2 describes the algorithm in detail.) In the example shown in Figure 10.1, the entire search tree does not have to be explored. For example, once it has been determined that the formula cannot be satisfied when both x_1 and x_2 are TRUE, there is no point in checking the formula with x_1 set to TRUE and x_2 set to FALSE because x_2 is a universally quantified variable. In the worst case, however, the algorithm would have to explore the entire search tree. The algorithm, then, takes $\Omega(2^n)$ time in the worst case.

Have you ever had a stack overflow exception when testing a recursive program? Stack overflow exceptions are common when recursive programs are run on large inputs because data needs to be stored on the call stack to keep track of the recursion. Whenever we deal with recursive algorithms, we need to to be conscious of the amount of space the recursion will use on the call stack. If we use too much stack space, then we get a stack overflow exception.

The amount of stack space required by SolveQSAT from Figure 10.2 will depend on the depth of the recursion and the size of each stack entry. We have one local variable, i, which is incremented by 1 in each recursive call. Since i starts at 1 and the recursion ends when i is $n+1$, the depth of the recursion is n. Each stack entry must include a value for i. (Note that we are treating n, *clauses*, and t as global variables.) It takes $\Theta(\log n)$ space to store i in binary, so the total space required is $\Theta(n \log n)$.

Exercise 10.2 *Design an algorithm to solve QSAT using $O(n)$ space.*

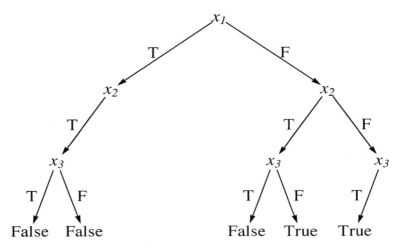

Figure 10.1: A tree representation of the execution of our SolveQSAT algorithm on the formula $\exists x_1 \forall x_2 \exists x_3 [(\overline{x_1} \vee x_3) \wedge (\overline{x_2} \vee \overline{x_3})]$. After the algorithm sets x_1 to TRUE, it checks to see if there is a way to satisfy all of the clauses no matter what value is chosen for x_2. When that check fails, the algorithm tries again with x_1 set to FALSE. Notice that because x_2 is a universally quantified variable, the algorithm does not need to try setting x_2 to FALSE if it has determined that there is no way for the clauses to be satisfied when x_2 is TRUE. This happens at the leftmost x_2 node. On the other hand, because x_3 is an existentially quantified variable, the algorithm does not need to try setting x_3 to FALSE once it has determined that the clauses *can* be satisfied with x_3 set to TRUE. This happens at the rightmost x_3 node.

Exists(i)   // i is the index of the next existential variable to consider
1 **if** i is $n+1$ // we have assigned a value to every variable
2   **then if** all clauses are satisfied by the truth assignment t
3   **then return** TRUE
4   **else return** FALSE
5   **else begin**
6   Set $t[x_i]$ to TRUE
7   **if ForAll**($i+1$) returns TRUE
8   **then return** TRUE
9   **else begin**
10   Set $t[x_i]$ to FALSE
11   **return ForAll**($i+1$)
12   **end**
13   **end**

ForAll(i)   // i is the index of the next universal variable to consider
1 **if** i is $n+1$ // we have assigned a value to every variable
2   **then if** all clauses are satisfied by the truth assignment t
3   **then return** TRUE
4   **else return** FALSE
5   **else begin**
6   Set $t[x_i]$ to TRUE
7   **if Exists**($i+1$) returns FALSE
8   **then return** FALSE
9   **else begin**
10   Set $t[x_i]$ to FALSE
11   **return Exists**($i+1$)
12   **end**
13   **end**

SolveQSAT($n, clauses$)
1 **for** $i = 1$ to n
2   Initialize $t[x_i]$ to *undefined*   // truth assignment t is a global variable
3 **end for**
4 **return Exists**(1)

Figure 10.2: A recursive algorithm to solve QSAT, where n is the number of variables and *clauses* is the set of clauses.

Although SolveQSAT uses an exponential amount of time, it certainly uses a reasonable amount of memory, which we will refer to as **space**. The amount of space used by an algorithm could be as important to us as the amount of time used. Before we start classifying problems based on the amount of space needed to solve them, however, we need to define exactly how we measure space.

We measure space slightly differently than we measure time. When a machine is given an input string, we don't think of that process as taking up any time. We do not want to think of a that process as taking up any space either. However, the input string does take up space on the tape. To rectify this situation, we define space in terms of a Turing machine with a read-only input tape and a read-write work tape. We say the machine uses $S(n)$ space if $S(n)$ is the maximum number of distinct tape squares accessed on the work tape for any input of size n.

Definition 10.1 *A problem can be* **solved using** $S(n)$ **space** *if there is a Turing machine with a read-only input tape and a read-write work tape that decides the problem using* $S(n)$ *space.*

As the following exercise demonstrates, we could have equivalently defined space in terms of a Turing machine with a read-only input tape and multiple read-write work tapes. In that case, the space could be measured as the maximum number of tape squares used on any single work tape. We are free, then, to use Turing machines with multiple work tapes when analyzing the space needed to solve a problem.

Exercise 10.3 *Consider any problem that can be solved by a Turing machine with k work tapes such that the maximum number of tape squares accessed on any single work tape is* $S(n)$*. Show that that problem can solved using* $S(n)$ *space by a Turing machine with a read-only input tape and a single work tape.*

Because we are ignoring the space taken up by the input string, we can discuss space requirements that are smaller than n. For example, our Turing machine to decide the language $\{0^n 1^n : n \geq 0\}$, which appears in the solution to Exercise 3.7, uses a work tape to count the number of 0's at the beginning of the input string. It then decrements the counter as it read the 1's, ensuring at the end that the number of 0's and 1's are equal. The machine does not write to the input tape. Since the number of bits in the counter is $\Theta(\log n)$, the amount of space used by this machine is $\Theta(\log n)$.

We use L to denote the set of decision problems that can be solved in $O(\log n)$ space.

Definition 10.2 **L** *is the set of decision problems that can be solved using* $O(\log n)$ *space.*

Exercise 10.4 *Show that the problem of determining whether a string is palindrome is in* L.

QSAT is said to be in PSPACE because it can be solved using a polynomial amount of space.

Definition 10.3 **PSPACE** *is the set of decision problems that can be solved in* $O(n^k)$ *space for some constant* $k > 0$.

10.2 Hierarchy Theorems

It is certainly true that L $\subseteq$ PSPACE, but is it possible that everything that can be decided using polynomial space can actually be decided using logarithmic space? In other words, is it possible that these two classes of problems are equal? That seems unlikely. It would make sense that with more space available, we could solve more problems. For example, it seems like there must be problems that can be solved using n^2 space that cannot be solved using $\log n$ space. After all, a machine with n^2 space has exponentially more space with which to work than a machine with $\log n$ space.

To prove that machines with more space can solve more problems, we will use a universal Turing machine that limits the amount of space available to the simulated machine. Let ExecuteBounded(Source, Input, Space) be a subroutine that executes the Turing machine program represented by Source on the input string Input when the simulation limits the work tape for the simulated machine to be at most Space tape squares long. We will assume that Source describes a Turing machine with a read-only input tape and a single read-write work tape.

ExecuteBounded can be implemented using a slightly modified version of the universal Turing machine code described in the solution to Exercise 3.10. The universal machine would have to be expanded to handle instructions that specify whether they are operating on the input tape or the work tape. This can be done by simply adding a parameter to each encoded instruction. For

example, WI1 would represent the instruction Write 1 to the input tape
and MWR would represent the instruction Move Right on the work tape.
Prior to simulating the machine, ExecuteBounded will mark off Space tape
squares on the work tape. If the simulation ever tries to access a tape square
outside of the marked off region on the work tape, ExecuteBounded will halt
and return No.

Consider the following program, which uses ExecuteBounded in much
the same way that Weird uses Accepts in the proof from Chapter 4 that the
ACCEPTANCE PROBLEM is undecidable:

```
Strange(Source):
    run ExecuteBounded(Source, Source, length(Source)²)
    if ExecuteBounded returned YES
      then return NO
      else return YES
```

Strange is given the source code for a machine as input and determines
whether that machine not only returns YES when given its own source code
as input but does so using no more than n^2 space, where n is the length of the
source code. How much space does Strange use? Strange doesn't do much
other than compute $(\text{length}(\text{Source}))^2$ and run ExecuteBounded. As the
following exercise shows, it takes n^2 space to compute length(Source)²:

Exercise 10.5 *Design a Turing machine that writes exactly n^2 symbols to the
work tape when given any string of length n on the input tape.*

ExecuteBounded needs to keep track of the source code of the simulated machine, the contents of the simulated machine's work tape, the position of the head on the simulated machine's input tape, and the label for
which it is searching when simulating an if-goto instruction. The length
of the source code is n, the length of any label is less than the length of the
source code itself, the simulated machine's input tape has n possible position for the head, and the simulated machine's work tape has n^2 tape squares.
Therefore, ExecuteBounded uses $\Theta(n^2)$ space. Since ExecuteBounded uses
$\Theta(n^2)$ space and it takes n^2 space to compute length(Source)², the overall
space required by Strange is $\Theta(n^2)$.

Could there be a different program that uses $O(\log n)$ space and whose output matches the output of Strange for every input? Because of Exercise 10.3,
we know that if there is such a program, there is such a program that uses a

single work tape. Let's see if we can prove, by contradiction of course, that there is no such program.

Let Match be a program for a Turing machine with a read-only input tape and a single read-write work tape. Assume that the output of Match matches that of Strange on every input and that Match uses $O(\log n)$ space. What would happen if we ran Strange with the source code for Match as input? Because Match uses $O(\log n)$ space, ExecuteBounded has more than enough space to run Match to completion on every input, doesn't it? Actually, not. We need to be careful here. Because Match and Strange decide the same language, we can assume that the input alphabets for the two programs are the same. In particular, we can assume that Match's input alphabet consists of the symbols used to encode Turing machine programs for our universal Turing machine, namely $\{0, 1, \beta, *, \#, :, W, M, R, L, I, T, E\}$. Since Match has a read-only input tape, these are the only symbols that will appear on the input tape. We can make no such assumption about Match's work tape, however. Match could have a completely different set of symbols that it writes to the work tape. For ExecuteBounded to be able to simulate Match, these symbols must be encoded using some binary code. The encoded version of Match, then, could use more space than the non-encoded version. For example, if Match has 32 symbols in its tape alphabet, the encoded version of Match will use a 5-bit code to represent each of these symbols. That means for each square Match uses on the work tape, the encoded version of Match uses 5 squares. Consequently, the encoded version of Match uses 5 times as much space as the non-encoded version. Luckily, the tape alphabet is fixed, so if Match uses $O(\log n)$ space, the encoded version of Match also uses $O(\log n)$ space.

Still, when we say that Match uses $O(\log n)$ space, we mean that there are constants c and B such that Match uses at most $c \log n$ space when $n \geq B$. When n is smaller than B, it could be that Match uses more than n^2 space. Here n is the length of the source code for Match, so when the length of the source code for Match is too small, ExecuteBounded may not have allocated enough space for Match to run to completion. What's to say there isn't a really short program that uses $O(\log n)$ space and that matches the output of Strange on every input?

So, what do we do? I once asked a student who had come to me for help why he had repeatedly included a strange piece of perfectly legal but completely useless code in his program. He explained that he couldn't get his program to compile, so he typed in some random code in an attempt to stop the compiler from complaining. We are going to do the same sort of thing.

Suppose we add two lines to the beginning of the source code for Match:

```
Move Right
Move Left
```

Those lines don't change the output of Match and change the space used by at most one square, so this expanded program still uses $O(\log n)$ space and still matches the output of Strange. We can keep adding these two lines to the beginning of the source code until the length of the expanded source code is so large that we have:

$$\text{length}(\text{expandedSource})^2 \geq c \cdot \log(\text{length}(\text{expandedSource})).$$

ExecuteBounded allocates enough space to run the program with the expanded source code to completion. We can assume, then, that the length of the source code passed in for Match is large enough for Match to be run to completion when n^2 space is allocated for the work tape.

When Match is run to completion, ExecuteBounded returns exactly what Match returns. Strange is designed to return the opposite of what is returned by ExecuteBounded, so Strange returns the opposite of what Match returns. But we assumed that Match matches the output of Strange on every input. Here we have an input for which the outputs do not match. We must have made another assumption that was invalid, but the only other assumption we made was that Match uses $O(\log n)$ space. We can conclude, then, that the problem decided by Strange cannot be solved using $O(\log n)$ space. Consequently, $\mathsf{L} \neq \mathsf{PSPACE}$.

Exercise 10.6 *Wait a minute!! In Chapter 6 we said that encoding schemes for inputs to our programs must "not create inputs that are unnecessarily large." Haven't we violated that principle by padding the source code for Match with useless instructions?*

Nothing in our argument above relied on the exponential difference between $\log n$ and n^2. The same argument holds for any function that is asymptotically smaller than n^2. Our argument also did not rely heavily on the properties of n^2. Our argument, however, did rely on the fact that n^2 can be computed in n^2 space. A function $S(n)$ that shares this property with n^2 is said to be **fully space-constructible**.

Definition 10.4 *A function $S(n)$ is* **fully space-constructible** *if there is a Turing machine that writes exactly $S(n)$ symbols to the work tape when given any string of length n on the input tape.*

The argument above, then, can be generalized to prove the following result, known as the **Space Hierarchy Theorem**.

Theorem 10.5 (Space Hierarchy Theorem) *Let $g(n)$ be any function that is fully space-constructible. Let $f(n)$ be a function that is asymptotically smaller than $g(n)$. Then there is a problem that can be solved using $\Theta(g(n))$ space that cannot be solved using $O(f(n))$ space.*

There is an analogous **Time Hierarchy Theorem**, which we will state but not prove.

Theorem 10.6 (Time Hierarchy Theorem) *Let $g(n)$ be any function such that for all $n \geq 0$, $g(n) \geq n$ and there is a Turing machine that uses exactly $g(n)$ time when given an input of size n. (Such a function is said to be* **fully time-constructible**.*) Let $f(n)$ be a function such that $f(n) \log f(n)$ is asymptotically smaller than $g(n)$. Then there is a problem that can be solved in $\Theta(g(n))$ time that cannot be solved in $O(f(n))$ time.*

The hierarchy theorems tell us that there is an infinite hierarchy of complexity classes – any time we are given a little more time or space, we can solve more problems. This is good for theoretical computer scientists. No matter what technological progress we make, there will always be problems that can be solved in theory but not in practice and someone is going to need to study the problems at the boundary.

10.3 Relating Space, Time, and Everything Else

We now have the space complexity classes L and PSPACE and the time complexity classes P and NP. We also have the decidable problems, the recognizable problems, and the problems that can be represented by regular languages – that is, those that can be decided by a finite automaton. How are these classes related to each other?

Certainly, anything that can be solved in polynomial time can be solved in polynomial space because a Turing machine can access only a constant number of tape squares in a single time step. Therefore, $P \subseteq PSPACE$. But what about NP? Does PSPACE contain every problem in NP? To answer that question, we'll need to measure the space used by a nondeterministic Turing machine.

We say a nondeterministic Turing machine with a read-only input tape and a read-write work tape uses $S(n)$ space if $S(n)$ is the maximum number of distinct tape squares accessed on the work tape in any single nondeterministic computation path on any input of size n.

Definition 10.7 NPSPACE *is the set of decision problems that can be solved by a nondeterministic Turing machine with a read-only input tape and a read-write work tape that uses $O(n^k)$ space for some constant $k > 0$.*

Is it possible that $PSPACE = NPSPACE$, or is this another annoying question for which we do not have an answer? Fortunately, unlike P and NP, we can prove that $PSPACE = NPSPACE$ using a proof similar to the one we used in Chapter 5 to prove that any problem that can be solved using a nondeterministic Turing machine can be solved using a deterministic Turing machine In that proof, we created a deterministic machine for each nondeterministic machine. The deterministic machine searched for an accepting configuration in the configuration graph of the nondeterministic machine. We would like to do the same thing here. Unfortunately, in the process of searching the configuration graph, the deterministic machine could use exponentially more space than the nondeterministic machine. Perhaps we can use the same idea but perform the search through the configuration graph more efficiently.

To simplify things a little, let's assume there is a unique accepting configuration for the nondeterministic machine no matter what the input. To ensure this, we can modify the nondeterministic machine to clear its tape and move the head all the way to the leftmost tape square before accepting. Our problem is then one of determining whether it is possible to reach the unique accepting configuration from the starting configuration.

Let $S(n)$ be the amount of space used by the the nondeterministic machine. Then there are $S(n)$ different possible head positions on the work tape and n different possible head positions on the read-only input tape. Furthermore, each of the tape squares contains one of the symbols from the tape alphabet, so if a is the size of the tape alphabet, there are $a^{S(n)}$ different sequences of tape symbols that the machine can see on the tape. (Note that the symbols on the read-only input tape are fixed and so don't need to be part of the configuration.) If l is the number of lines in the program, then the total number of distinct configurations the machine can visit along a computation path is at most $l \cdot n \cdot S(n) \cdot a^{S(n)}$. This is exponential in $S(n)$. If we want our deterministic machine to use no more than a polynomial amount of space, the deterministic machine cannot keep track of the entire path. Instead, let's use a divide and conquer strategy.

If we follow a path in the configuration graph from a configuration u to a configuration v, then we must reach some configuration halfway between u and v before we get to v. This insight leads to the recursive algorithm described in Figure 10.3 to find a path from a configuration u to a configuration v of length at most some given number *maxLength*. The algorithm checks every possible configuration, *mid*, to see if *mid* is reachable from u using at most *maxLength*/2 steps and v is reachable from *mid* in *maxLength*/2 steps. If such a configuration exists, then v is reachable from u in *maxLength* steps.

Zeno($u, v, maxLength$):

1   **if** *maxLength* is 1 and ($u = v$ or v follows from u in one step)
2   **then return** YES
3   **else for** each possible configuration *mid*
4   **if** Zeno($u, mid, maxLength/2$) returns YES
                AND
           Zeno($mid, v, maxLength/2$) returns YES
5   **then return** YES
6   **return** NO

Figure 10.3: A recursive algorithm to find a path from the configuration u to the configuration v of length at most *maxLength*. (Minutes after typing Zeno in for the name of this algorithm, I opened Papadimitriou(1994) to the page containing the proof of Savitch's Theorem. In that proof, z was used to indicate the intermediate configuration "in honor of Zeno of Elea." So much for being clever and original.)

To determine whether the unique accepting configuration is reachable from the starting configuration, we can call Zeno with u set to the starting configuration and v set to the accepting configuration. To avoid truncations in the divisions by 2 in Line 4, we will initialize *maxLength* to next largest power of 2 at or above $l \cdot n \cdot S(n) \cdot a^{S(n)}$, which is the maximum length of any computation path in the configuration graph.

To determine how much space Zeno uses, we need to consider the size of each entry on the call stack and the depth of the recursion. Each stack entry includes the parameters u, v, and $maxLength$, as well as the local variable mid. Since u, v, and mid are configurations of the nondeterministic machine, we can write them down by writing down the line number that is about to be executed, the position of the head on the input tape (which we can write in binary), the position of the head on the work tape, and the contents of the $S(n)$ squares on the work tape. The number of lines in the program is constant; the number of head positions on the input tape is n, so writing this in binary takes $\Theta(\log n)$ space; the number of head positions on the work tape is $S(n)$; and the number of symbols on the work tape is $S(n)$. If we assume that $\log n$ is $O(S(n))$, then the total space needed to write down a single configuration is $O(S(n))$. The maximum value for $maxLength$ is its initial value, $l \cdot n \cdot S(n) \cdot a^{S(n)}$, so encoding $maxLength$ in binary requires $O(\log_2(l \cdot n \cdot S(n) \cdot a^{S(n)}))$ bits. Again, if we assume $\log n$ is $O(S(n))$, then this is also $O(S(n))$. The size of each stack entry is therefore $O(S(n))$ when $\log n$ is $O(S(n))$.

Since each recursive call cuts $maxLength$ in half, the depth of the recursion will be $O\left(\log_2\left(l \cdot n \cdot S(n) \cdot a^{S(n)}\right)\right)$, which again is $O(S(n))$ if $\log n$ is $O(S(n))$. Because the depth of the recursion and the size of each stack entry are both $O(S(n))$, the total amount of space required by our deterministic algorithm to determine whether the nondeterministic algorithm accepts a particular input string is $O(S(n)^2)$.

We have just proven the following result, which is known as **Savitch's Theorem**.

Theorem 10.8 (Savitch's Theorem) *Any decision problem that can be solved nondeterministically using $O(S(n))$ space can be solved deterministically using $O(S(n)^2)$ space as long as $S(n)$ is fully space-constructible and $\log n$ is $O(S(n))$.*

Because the square of a polynomial is itself a polynomial, Savitch's Theorem implies that PSPACE = NPSPACE. Furthermore, NP is a subset of NPSPACE because a nondeterministic Turing machine can access at most one new tape square in any single time step. We can conclude then that NP is a subset of PSPACE. That is the final piece we need to relate all of the classes of problems we have considered in this book. We have the following:

$$\text{Regular} \subsetneq \text{L} \subseteq \text{P} \subseteq \text{NP} \subseteq \text{PSPACE} \subsetneq \text{Decidable} \subsetneq \text{Recognizable}$$

Exercise 10.7 *All of the relationships in the list above were either established earlier in the book or are straightforward to prove. Make sure you understand why each of the classes is a subset of the subsequent class, paying particular attention to the subsets that are proper subsets. You'll need to prove that* Regular $\subsetneq$ L *and that* L $\subseteq$ P.

We know that L $\neq$ PSPACE, so it must be the case that L $\neq$ P, P $\neq$ NP, or NP $\neq$ PSPACE. However, we currently don't know which of those three statements is true or if more than one of them is true. So now you have three open problems to think about in your abundant free time. That should keep you busy for a while, so let's wrap things up.

Chapter 11

Conclusion

We started with a simple question, what is a computer and what can it do? By using a simple model of a computer to solve decision problems, we have developed a powerful and rich theory of computation. We have investigated problems that cannot be solved, even when we ignore practical resource bounds, and problems that can be solved in theory but cannot be solved in practice. We expanded our discussion to include optimization problems and considered algorithms that provide good enough solution in a reasonable amount of time. We also discussed heuristic algorithms, which have exponential running times in the worst case but often have acceptable performance for the problem instances we face in the real world. Finally, we proved the hierarchy theorems and were able to relate all of the disparate classes of problems we defined. Not bad for a theory built on a primitive machine with four instructions.

The story of the theory of computation is never ending and there is much more we could discuss. It is time, however, for you to get your head out of the clouds and get a job.

Finally, you have the job you have dreamed of for years – designing algorithms for a company in California. Driving home late one night, you are listening to the news on your phone.

> Phone: A rather bizarre news story just came in. A series of accidents has occurred throughout the country. In each case, a spider web is present that appears to spell out the word "Wilbur". The FBI's data mining team has found an unusual association among the victims.

181

> Each of the victims voted for pig's tongue on the pilot
> episode of *The Tim and Francine Show*.

You: I don't remember how I voted.

Phone: You voted for pig's tongue.

You: Wow, this new interactive news app is pretty impres-
            sive. I wish I had written it.

Phone: Thank you.

It is night. It is dark. You have been working too hard. You look into your rearview mirror. Is that a spider web? It is a strange looking web. That first part looks like a "W". You pull over. Your seat belt is jammed. No, it isn't jammed; there is a spider web holding it latched. You reach for your phone.

You: Where is my phone?

Phone: I'm over here!

It is dangling by a thread just out of your reach.

Phone: Help me!

You: Call the police!

Phone: What? I can't hear you. My ears are covered in silk.

You: You don't have ears, you stupid phone.

Phone: I heard that!

You speed off, trying to get to a police station (or an exterminator) as fast as you can. The windshield is getting foggier and foggier. The defroster does no good. You reach up to wipe the windshield. Yuk, it is covered with silk. Your steering wheel locks. You crash through a guard rail and over a cliff. You are falling, falling,....

Phone: Good Morning, San Francisco!

Your alarm wakes you. At breakfast, you pass on the bacon and tell your parents you are quitting your job at the local library. Story time is too stressful.

Solutions to Exercises

Cheater.

Solutions for Chapter 1: Introduction

If you are looking for solutions to the exercises from Chapter 1, you must not have read the chapter very carefully.

Solutions for Chapter 2: Finite Automata

Solution to Exercise 2.1 *Design finite automata for each of the following languages.*

a) $L = \{x \in \{0, 1\}^* : \text{the length of } x \text{ is a multiple of } 4\}$.

What information does the machine need to keep track of as it reads the input? It seems like it needs to keep track of the length of the input, but we know it cannot do that using a finite memory because the input could be larger than the machine's memory. In other words, the machine cannot keep track of the length of the input using a finite number of states. So what should we do? What did we do to solve the problem of determining whether the number of 1's in the data stream was even? Isn't this problem very similar to that one?

Consider the algorithm we designed in Chapter 1 (Figure 1.6) to decide the even number of 1's problem using a finite number of states. If we think of the Boolean variable *isEven* as a 1-bit counter, the algorithm can be viewed as counting the number of 1's in the input string but re-setting the counter to 0 whenever it gets to 2. To determine if a length of the string is a multiple of 4, we repeatedly count to 4 as we read the input symbols, resetting to 0 each time the counter gets to 4. Here is a complete description of the algorithm:

```
1    set NumberSinceLastMultiple to 0
2    while input remains to be read
3        read the next input symbol
4        if NumberSinceLastMultiple is 3
5            then set NumberSinceLastMultiple to 0
6            else increment NumberSinceLastMultiple
7    end while
8    if NumberSinceLastMultiple is 0
9        then return YES
10       else return NO
```

Once you convince yourself that this algorithm works, it is not hard to see that a machine can execute this algorithm using a finite number of states. There is one variable, *NumberSinceLastMultiple*, which can take on one of only four values. Therefore, the algorithm uses a fixed amount of memory. In fact, we should be able to construct a finite state automaton with four states to decide this language, one for each possible value of *NumberSinceLastMultiple*. See Figure S.1.

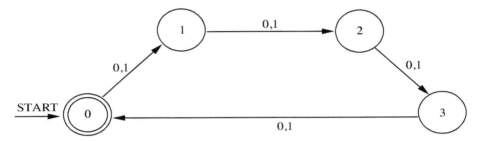

Figure S.1: A finite automaton that decides the language $\{x \in \{0,1\}^* :$ the length of x is a multiple of 4}. The numbers inside the states indicate the number of symbols read since the last time the length of the input to that point was a multiple of 4.

b) $L = \{x \in \{0,1\}^* : x \text{ ends with a 1 followed by at least two 0's}\}$.

Let's think about designing an algorithm to decide this language. We don't know when we are close to the end of the input stream, so any-time we see a 1, we need to be on the look-out for at least two 0's to end the input. Until we see a 1, there is nothing to do, so we need to consume all of the 0's we see before the first 1 is encountered. Once we read a 1, we can create a variable called *NumZerosNeeded* that keeps track of the number of 0's that we need to read. We need to see at least two 0's, so we will set our variable to 2. When we read a 0, we decrement the variable. Anytime we read another 1, we reset the variable to 2. Can this algorithm be executed using only a finite number of states? Because we decrement *NumZerosNeeded* every time we read a 0, *NumZerosNeeded* could go arbitrarily far below zero. We need to fix that. Knowing how far *NumZerosNeeded* is below zero is not useful to us, so instead of decrementing every time we see a 0, let's decrement only when *NumZerosNeeded* is not already zero. Figure S.2 describes the final algorithm. This algorithm has one variable and that variable can take on only three values. We can implement this algorithm with the finite state machine shown in Figure S.3.

```
1   read the next input symbol
2   while symbol is a 0 and input remains to be read
3       read the next input symbol
4   end while
5   initialize NumZerosNeeded to 2
6   while input remains to be read
7       read the next input symbol
8       if the symbol is a 0 and NumZerosNeeded > 0
9           then decrement NumZerosNeeded
10          else if the symbol is a 1
11                  then reset NumZerosNeeded to 2
12  end while
13  if NumZerosNeeded is 0
14      then return YES
15      else return NO
```

Figure S.2: An algorithm to decide the language $L = \{x \in \{0,1\}^* :$ x ends with a 1 followed by at least two 0's$\}$ using a finite number of states.

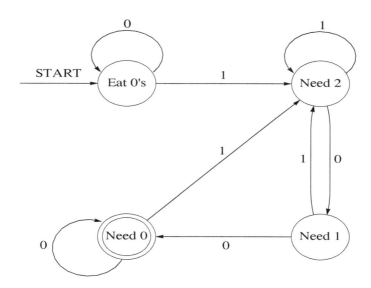

Figure S.3: A finite automaton that decides the language $L = \{x \in \{0,1\}^* :$ x ends with a 1 followed by at least two 0's$\}$.

c) $L = \{x \in \{0,1\}^* : x \text{ does not contain two consecutive 0's}\}$.

The automaton needs to remember the last symbol read to make sure it does not see two consecutive 0's, so it will require two states: one to indicate that the last symbol read was a 0 and one to indicate that the last symbol read was a 1. An additional state will be required to indicate that two consecutive 0's have already been read, in which case the input should be rejected no matter what symbols remain to be read. Figure S.4 defines the automaton.

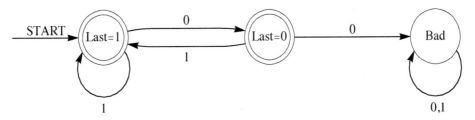

Figure S.4: A finite automaton that decides the language $L = \{x \in \{0,1\}^* : x \text{ does not contain two consecutive 0's}\}$.

Solutions for Chapter 3: Turing Machines

Solution to Exercise 3.1 *How would the code in Figure 3.2 handle an empty input string?*

This first line of the program would see the head pointing to a β symbol. This is not a 1, so the program would move to the line labeled READ-0. At that line, the program would move right on the tape where another β awaits. The next two if-statements would cause the program to move to the line labeled END-0. The machine would move left on the tape, encountering a β again. Since this is not 0, the next if-statement would cause the program to move to the line labeled REJECT, at which point the program would return No. In short, the program would reject the empty string.

It is debatable whether this is the desired behavior. The definition of the language isn't entirely clear on whether the empty string is or is not in the language. You could argue that the empty string begins and ends with a blank, or you could argue that the empty string doesn't begin with anything and so cannot begin and end with the same symbol. We assume that the empty string is not in the language.

Solution to Exercise 3.2 *By expanding the code in Figure 3.2, describe a Turing machine that determines whether the input string is a palindrome, that is, the string reads the same forward as it does backward.*

The code appears in Figure S.5. It begins by reading the first symbol from the left, remembering it by using the labels just like in the code in Figure 3.2, and then writing a new tape symbol, $\times$, over the first symbol to mark the first symbol as having been read. It then moves to the last symbol and compares it to the first symbol. If the symbols do not match, the string is rejected. If the symbols do match, a blank is written over the last symbol so that the next time through we will compare the next symbol in from the right. The program then moves left to the $\times$. This marks the last symbol on the left side of the string that was matched. The program moves one square to the right and repeats the process with the next symbol found. If the next symbol found is β, the program has matched all of the pairs and can accept the string.

The one tricky thing here is dealing with strings of an odd length. For example, 01010 is a palindrome. Figure S.6 shows the execution of the code with

input string 01010. The first pair of 0's and the first pair of 1's will be matched.
The third symbol to match will be 0. There is, however, no corresponding symbol with which to match it. When we move left from the first blank at the line
labeled END-0, we will read the × symbol that we just wrote. This indicates
that the string has odd length and that we are at the middle symbol. In this
case, the string should be accepted. In the code, this check is handled by the
if-statements at the lines labeled ELSE-1× and ELSE-0×.

```
LOOP:     if head is 1 then goto READ-1 else goto READ-0
READ-1:   Write ×
LOOP-1    Move Right
          if head is 0 then goto LOOP-1 else goto ELSE-1
ELSE-1:   if head is 1 then goto LOOP-1 else goto END-1
END-1:    Move Left
          if head is 1 then goto NEXT else goto ELSE-1×
ELSE-1×:  if head is × then goto ACCEPT else goto REJECT
READ-0:   Write ×
LOOP-0:   Move Right
          if head is 0 then goto LOOP-0 else goto ELSE-0
ELSE-0:   if head is 1 then goto LOOP-0 else goto END-0
END-0:    Move Left
          if head is 0 then goto NEXT else goto ELSE-0×
ELSE-0×:  if head is × then goto ACCEPT else goto REJECT
NEXT:     Write β
FIND×:    Move Left
          if head is 0 then goto FIND× else goto ELSE-N
ELSE-N:   if head is 1 then goto FIND× else goto END-N
END-N:    Move Right
          if head is β then goto ACCEPT else goto LOOP
ACCEPT:   Return YES
REJECT:   Return NO
```

Figure S.5: A Turing machine program to decide whether an input string is a palindrome.

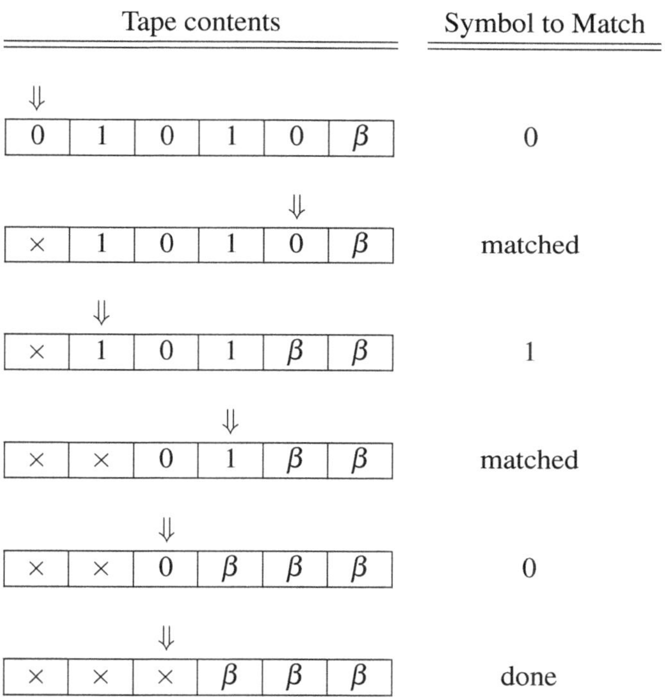

Tape contents	Symbol to Match

Figure S.6: The execution of the Turing machine program from Figure S.5 to determine if a string is a palindrome. The tape contents is shown on the left, with the arrow indicating the head position. The symbol read that must be matched is shown on the right. When the program reads the × while trying to match a 0, the program can terminate with success because this indicates the input string is an odd length string and all pairs have been matched.

Solution to Exercise 3.3 *As demonstrated by the code in Figure 3.2, we can find the last input symbol by moving right until we reach the first blank and then moving left one square. But what if we then needed to move back to the first input symbol? There is nothing to the left of the first input symbol, so we can't move beyond it to the left and then move back one tape square to the right analogous to what we do with the last input symbol. The way our Turing machine is defined, when the head is at the position of the first input symbol, a* Move Left *does nothing at all and provides no indication that we are already at the left end of the tape. How can we design a Turing machine program capable of determining that it has reached the leftmost input symbol?*

We can create a left end of tape indicator by expanding the tape alphabet. For each symbol in the original tape alphabet, we create a new symbol to indicate that the original symbol is at the left end of the tape. For example, if our tape alphabet is $\{0, 1, \beta\}$, we expand the tape alphabet to be $\{0, 1, \beta, \lceil 0, \lceil 1, \lceil \beta\}$. The symbol $\lceil 0$ indicates that there is a 0 in the tape square and that the tape square is the leftmost tape square on the tape. At the start of our program, we can replace the first input symbol with one of these new symbols. In that way, we create an left end of tape indicator without losing the original symbol stored at that position. At every line in our code where we would normally check for a symbol, we would now have to check for that symbol or its companion left end of tape symbol. For example, any if-goto that compares the head to 0 would have to be rewritten to test for either 0 or $\lceil 0$. If we want to test to see if we are at the left end of the tape, we need only test to see if the head is pointing to one of our left end of tape symbols. Including compound symbols in the tape alphabet is a very useful technique that we will see again. Because our tape alphabet is still fixed and finite, this is perfectly legal.

Solution to Exercise 3.4 *For each of the structured programming constructs, write the equivalent Turing machine code using the four basic instructions.*

Below are the three structured programming constructs along with the equivalent Turing machine code. Each lines that says:

```
if head is any symbol then goto ...
```

would need to be replaced by multiple if-goto statements, one for each symbol in the tape alphabet.

if-then-else:

> **if** head is x
> **then begin**
>   ⟨execute some block of code⟩
>   **end**
> **else begin**
>   ⟨execute a different block of code⟩
>   **end**

Equivalent Turing machine code:

```
        if head is x then goto THEN else goto ELSE
THEN:   ⟨execute some block of code⟩
        if head is any symbol then goto END
ELSE:   ⟨execute a different block of code⟩
END:    ⟨do whatever comes after the if-then-else⟩
```

while loop:

> **while** head is x
>   ⟨execute some block of code⟩
> **end while**

Equivalent Turing machine code:

```
LOOP: if head is x then goto BODY else goto END
BODY: ⟨execute some block of code⟩
      if head is any symbol then goto LOOP
END:  ⟨do whatever comes after the the while⟩
```

repeat-until loop:

repeat
   ⟨execute some block of code⟩
until head is x

Equivalent Turing machine code:

```
LOOP: ⟨execute some block of code⟩
        if head is x then goto END else goto LOOP
END:    ⟨do whatever comes after the repeat-until⟩
```

Solution to Exercise 3.5 *Design a Turing machine to increment a counter using only the four basic instructions.*

We assume the head starts at the tape square just before the counter. The machine will move right to enter the counter. Then the machine will write a 0 over every 1 that occurs before the first 0 in the counter. This has the effect of "carrying" a 1 until there is no longer a need to carry. Remember that we are keeping the counter in reverse order so the counter can grow without having to shift all of the symbols down. In the code, which is shown in Figure S.7, the loop labeled GO-BACK moves the head back to the tape square preceding the counter. Figure S.8 shows the execution of two successive increments starting from a zero counter.

```
LOOP:      Move Right
           if head is 1 then goto CARRY else goto ENDLOOP
CARRY:     Write 0
           if head is any symbol then goto LOOP
ENDLOOP:   Write 1
GO-BACK:   Move Left
           if head is 0 then goto GO-BACK else goto CHECK-1
CHECK-1:   if head is 1 then goto GO-BACK else goto END
END:
```

Figure S.7: The Turing machine code to increment a binary counter. The counter is kept in reverse order so as to avoid having to shift the counter down when we need to expand the number of bits in the counter.

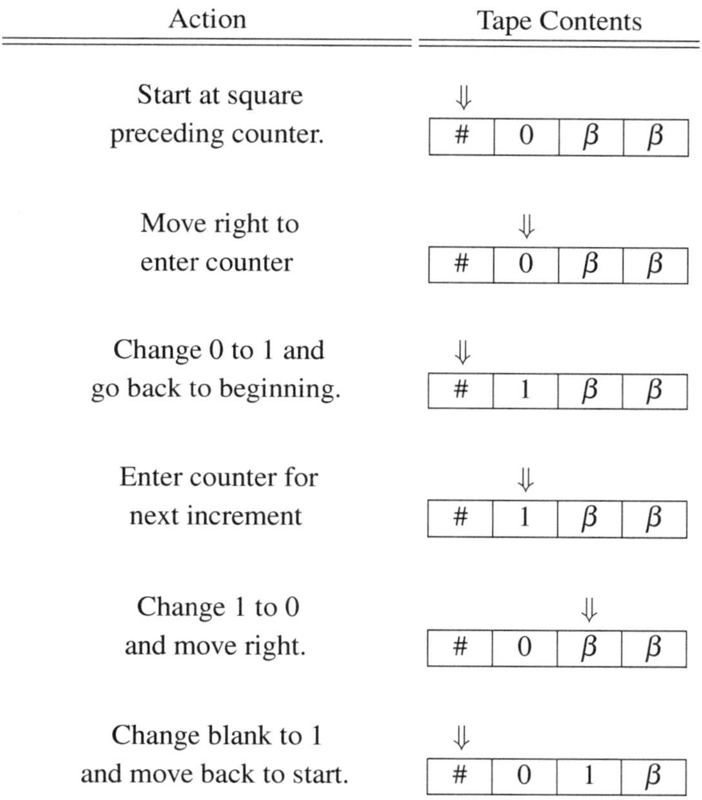

Action	Tape Contents
Start at square preceding counter.	⇓ `#	0	β	β`
Move right to enter counter	⇓ `#	0	β	β`
Change 0 to 1 and go back to beginning.	⇓ `#	1	β	β`
Enter counter for next increment	⇓ `#	1	β	β`
Change 1 to 0 and move right.	⇓ `#	0	β	β`
Change blank to 1 and move back to start.	⇓ `#	0	1	β`

Figure S.8: The execution of the Turing machine program for Exercise 3.5 to increment a binary counter. The arrow indicates the position of the tape head. The execution is shown for two successive increments, leaving the counter at 01. This represents 2 because we keep our counter in reverse order to avoid having to shift the counter down when we need to expand the number of bits in the counter.

Solution to Exercise 3.6 *Design a Turing machine to decrement the counter. (You can choose whether to use only the four basic instructions or the structured programming constructs.)*

This solution will use the structured programming constructs. The idea is simple. If the first bit is a 1, we change it to a 0. If the first bit is a 0, then we change it to a 1 and move on to decrement the counter at the second bit. For simplicity, we will assume that no one will decrement the counter when the counter is already 0. We also assume that the head starts at the tape square immediately preceding the first bit in the counter, but we do not do any error checking to make sure these assumptions are true. Figure S.9 shows the code.

```
1  repeat
2      Move Right
3      if the head is 0
4          then Write 1
5  until head is 1
6  Write 0
```

Figure S.9: The Turing machine code to decrement a binary counter kept in reverse order.

Solution to Exercise 3.7 *Write the complete description of a Turing machine that decides the language $L = \{0^n 1^n : n \geq 0\}$ using a second tape as a work tape to keep track of the counter.*

A Turing machine program to decide $\{0^n 1^n : n \geq 0\}$ is described in Figure S.10 using the structured programming constructs as well as the increment and decrement code from the previous two exercises. Where we say "increment the counter," the increment code should be inserted, while the decrement code should be inserted in place of "decrement the counter." In the last if-statement, we compare the counter to 0. This can be done by simply checking that the first symbol of the counter is 0 and that the second symbol is blank. Again, for the purposes of writing code that is readable, we simply say, "if the counter is 0," and assume the code that actually performs this check would be inserted. This is similar to what we do daily when writing in high-level programming languages. Once we know that machine code can be generated for a high-level operation, we do not often worry about the actual machine code generated by the compiler.

```
     // initialize the counter
 1   Write # on the work tape
 2   Move Right on the work tape
 3   Write 0 on the work tape
 4   Move Left on the work tape

     // increment for each 0 read
 5   while head on the input tape is 0
 6       increment the counter
 7       Move Right on the input tape
 8   end while

     // decrement for each 1 read
 9   while head on the input tape is 1
10       if the counter is 0   then return NO        // too many 1's
11       decrement the counter
12       Move Right on the input tape
13   end while

     // verify that no 0's appear after the 1's and that
     // the number of 0's and 1's are the same.
14   if the head on the input tape is 0
15     then return NO              // we just saw a 0 after a 1
16     else if the counter is 0
17             then return YES      // equal number of 0's and 1's
18             else return NO       // too many 0's
```

Figure S.10: A Turing machine program to decide the language $\{0^n 1^n : n \geq 0\}$.

Solution to Exercise 3.8 *Show how a Turing machine with one tape can sim-ulate a Turing machine with k tapes, for any fixed number k. Remember the set of symbols that can be written to the tape is not restricted to the input alpha-bet. As long as we have a finite number of tape symbols, we can write whatever symbols we like to the tape. We could even have symbols in our tape alphabet* *to represent k other symbols. For example, in a single tape square we could write a compound symbol, $(0,1,1,1,0,\beta,1)$, to represent the contents of the tape squares of seven different tapes. Though I typed 15 symbols to write this compound symbol, to a Turing machine this will be a single symbol. (Imagine a civilization of aliens who use only one symbol, a straight line. Residents of that civilization would think that H requires three symbols, yet we think of H as a single symbol.) As long as there are a finite number of tapes on the machine with multiple tapes, there are a finite number of different symbols in the tape alphabet of the one-tape machine.*

For simplicity we will show that a two-tape machine can be simulated by a one-tape machine. The idea is easily generalized to any fixed number of tapes. As indicated in the description of the exercise, we can add symbols to our tape alphabet as long as the alphabet is finite and remains fixed once the machine is defined. In this case, we are going to define symbols that represent the contents of both tapes. We also have to keep track of the location of the head on each tape.

Assuming our original tape alphabet consists of the symbols 0, 1, and β, we will define our new tape alphabet to consist of the original three symbols plus the following symbols:

- All pairs of symbols from the original tape alphabet:

  $(\beta,\beta), (\beta,0), (\beta,1), (0,\beta), (0,0), (0,1), (1,\beta), (1,0), (1,1)$

- All pairs of symbols but with the head at the first symbol in the pair. The head position is indicated by a bar over the top of the symbol:

  $(\bar{\beta},\beta), (\bar{\beta},0), (\bar{\beta},1), (\bar{0},\beta), (\bar{0},0), (\bar{0},1), (\bar{1},\beta), (\bar{1},0), (\bar{1},1)$

- All pairs of symbols but with the head at the second symbol in the pair:

  $(\beta,\bar{\beta}), (\beta,\bar{0}), (\beta,\bar{1}), (0,\bar{\beta}), (0,\bar{0}), (0,\bar{1}), (1,\bar{\beta}), (1,\bar{0}), (1,\bar{1})$

- All pairs of symbols but with the head at both symbols in the pair:

  $(\bar{\beta},\bar{\beta}), (\bar{\beta},\bar{0}), (\bar{\beta},\bar{1}), (\bar{0},\bar{\beta}), (\bar{0},\bar{0}), (\bar{0},\bar{1}), (\bar{1},\bar{\beta}), (\bar{1},\bar{0}), (\bar{1},\bar{1})$

Remember, these are individual symbols in our tape alphabet. Each tape square will include exactly one of these symbols. For example, our tape may look like this:

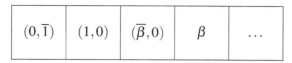

This single tape represents the content of two tapes. The first tape contains 01 followed by blanks. The second tape consists of 100 followed by blanks. The head of the first tape is on the third tape square, while the head of the second tape is on the first tape square.

Now that we have the ability to represent the contents of any two-tapes using a single tape, we must show it is possible to simulate the execution of a two-tape machine using a one-tape machine. The two-tape machine is presented with the input string on the input tape. The second tape is initially blank. The one-tape machine is also presented with the input string on its single tape. However, the one-tape machine must do some work to initialize its "virtual" second tape. In particular, it must replace each input symbol with the corresponding compound symbol from the expanded tape alphabet. For example, if given 101 as the input, the single-tape machine must replace the contents of the first three squares on its tape with $(\overline{1},\overline{\beta})(0,\beta)(1,\beta)$. This indicates that the two-tape machine begins with the head of each tape at the tape's first square, the first tape contains 101, and the second tape is blank. The code in Figure S.11 describes how to implement this initialization procedure.

Notice that the initialization procedure stops replacing symbols when it reaches the first blank on the input tape. This blank indicates the end of the input. What should we do about all of the blanks that appear after the last symbol of the input string? At each of these positions, both of the tapes in the two-tape machine are blank. It seems, then, that we should replace each β with (β,β). Doing so, however, might take a while because there are an unlimited number of blanks to replace. Instead, we will simply leave a single β in each of these tape squares, replacing them only when the simulated operations requires us to access these squares.

The entire process of simulating a single instruction of the two-tape machine entails first having the one-tape machine search for the head position of the tape on which the instruction operates. Then the instruction itself would be simulated. For example, to simulate a Write 1 on first tape instruction, the one-tape machine must first search for the compound symbol that has the bar over the first symbol in the pair. It would then execute the Write instruction.

The search code, shown in Figure S.12, begins by moving to the first actual β on the tape. We know the head position of each tape will be to the left of

```
1    if head is β
2       then Write (β̄, β̄)
3       else begin
4              if head is 1
5                 then Write (1̄, β̄)
6                 else Write (0̄, β̄)
7              Move Right
8              while head is not β
9                 if head is 1
10                   then Write (1, β)
11                   else Write (0, β)
12                Move Right
13             end while
14       end
```

Figure S.11: The code to initialize a one-tape machine's representation of the two tapes of a two-tape machine.

this square.

Simulating the individual instructions themselves is fairly straightforward. For example, for an if-goto to compare the tape square at the head on the second tape to a 1, it must compare the compound symbol on the one-tape machine's tape to the six compound symbols corresponding to having a 1 on the second tape, namely $(\beta, \bar{1})$, $(0, \bar{1})$, $(1, \bar{1})$ $(\bar{\beta}, \bar{1})$, $(\bar{0}, \bar{1})$, and $(\bar{1}, \bar{1})$. A single if-goto instruction would be replaced by six if-goto instructions as shown in Figure S.13.

To simulate a Write instruction, the one-tape machine needs to look at the current compound symbol under the tape head to determine the correct compound symbol to write to the tape. Figure S.14 shows the code to replace Write 1 on the second tape.

A similar conditional structure is required to simulate a Move. To indicate the new head position, the simulated Move would change the compound symbol of both the current tape square and one of the adjacent squares, either to the left or to the right of the current tape square depending on the direction of the Move.

SearchForFirstTapeHead:

1 **while** head is not β
2   Move Right
3 **end while**
4 Move Left
5 **while** head is not $(\overline{s_1}, s_2)$ for some symbols, s_1 and s_2, from the
            original tape alphabet.
6   Move Left
7 **end while**

Figure S.12: Turing machine code to search for the head position on the first tape in the simulation of a two-tape machine by a one-tape machine.

Two-tape machine

```
if head on second tape is 1 then goto THEN else goto ELSE
```

One-tape machine

```
        if head is (β,1̄) then goto THEN else goto NEXT-1
NEXT-1: if head is (0,1̄) then goto THEN else goto NEXT-2
NEXT-2: if head is (1,1̄) then goto THEN else goto NEXT-3
NEXT-3: if head is (β̄,1̄) then goto THEN else goto NEXT-4
NEXT-4: if head is (0̄,1̄) then goto THEN else goto NEXT-5
NEXT-5: if head is (1̄,1̄) then goto THEN else goto ELSE
```

Figure S.13: A single if-goto instruction in the two-tape machine would be replaced by these six if-goto instructions in the one-tape machine.

Two-tape machine

```
Write 1 on the second tape
```

One-tape machine

if head is $(\beta, \overline{\beta})$ or $(\beta, \overline{0})$ or $(\beta, \overline{1})$
  then Write $(\beta, \overline{1})$
else if head is $(\overline{\beta}, \overline{\beta})$ or $(\overline{\beta}, \overline{0})$ or $(\overline{\beta}, \overline{1})$
  then Write $(\overline{\beta}, \overline{1})$
else if head is $(0, \overline{\beta})$ or $(0, \overline{0})$ or $(0, \overline{1})$
  then Write $(0, \overline{1})$
else if head is $(\overline{0}, \overline{\beta})$ or $(\overline{0}, \overline{0})$ or $(\overline{0}, \overline{1})$
  then Write $(\overline{0}, \overline{1})$
else if head is $(1, \overline{\beta})$ or $(1, \overline{0})$ or $(1, \overline{1})$
  then Write $(1, \overline{1})$
else if head is $(\overline{1}, \overline{\beta})$ or $(\overline{1}, \overline{0})$ or $(\overline{1}, \overline{1})$
  then Write $(\overline{1}, \overline{1})$

Figure S.14: The code required by a one-tape machine to simulate a Write 1 instruction. We use the structured programming constructs to shorten the description.

Solution to Exercise 3.9 *Suppose we allow a Turing machine with k tapes to work with all k tapes simultaneously. This modified Turing machine is called a* **multi-tape Turing machine.** *Show how a Turing machine with k tapes that is restricted to working with one tape at a time can simulate a multi-tape Turing machine that has k tapes. From this exercise and the last exercise, we can conclude that any multi-tape Turing machine can be simulated by a one-tape Turing machine. Therefore, the multi-tape Turing machine does not solve any decision problems beyond those that can be solved by a one-tape Turing machine.*

Each instruction of the multi-tape Turing machine with k tapes can be viewed as k identical instructions of a k-tape machine. Write $(s_1, s_2, \ldots, s_k)$, for example, is equivalent to Write s_1 on tape 1, followed by Write s_2 on tape 2, etc, up to Write s_k on tape k. The Move instruction for a multi-tape Turing machine specifies the direction to move on each tape. It can also specify to stay put on individual tapes. A Move(Right, Left, ..., Right) is equivalent to Move Right on tape 1, followed by Move Left on tape 2, etc, up to Move Right on tape k. If the instruction specifies that the tape head stay where it is on a particular tape, the instruction for that tape can simply be omitted. Finally, if $(s_1, s_2, \ldots, s_k)$ goto THEN else goto ELSE, is equivalent to the following code:

```
        if head on tape 1 is s₁ goto COND-2 else goto ELSE
COND-2: if head on tape 2 is s₂ goto COND-3 else goto ELSE
⋮
COND-k: if head on tape k is sₖ goto THEN else goto ELSE
THEN:   <do whatever the THEN part is supposed to do>
ELSE:   <do whatever the ELSE part is supposed to do>
```

Solution to Exercise 3.10 *Write a complete description of a universal Turing machine.*

As the solution to Exercise 3.8 shows, anything that can be done with k tapes can be done with one tape, so we will assume the source code we are given is the source code for a single-tape machine. The first thing we need to do is to specify how the source code will be encoded when it is given to our universal machine. The tape alphabet for our universal machine will include symbols to represent each of the four instructions: *I* for if, *M* for Move, *W* for Write, and *R* for Return. It will also include symbols for the direction of the move and the value to be returned: *L* for Left, *R* for Right, *Y* for Yes, and *N* for No. (Although we are using *R* for both Return and Right, the symbol will appear in different contexts, so there will be no confusion.) We will also need symbols in the tape alphabet to represent labels. Let's assume the symbols in the labels are restricted to be either 0 or 1. A colon will separate the label from the instruction. Each encoded instruction will have the form:

$$\langle label \rangle : \langle instruction \rangle \langle arguments \rangle$$

Instructions will be separated from each other by #'s. We will use * to mark the beginning and the end of the program. The if-goto will use T to mark the beginning of the then label and E to mark the beginning of the else label.

There is one more important issue regarding the tape alphabet. Each Turing machine that our universal Turing machine may be asked to simulate could have a different tape alphabet. In fact, there are infinitely many tape alphabets that our universal Turing machine will have to handle. The universal Turing machine clearly cannot directly represent the symbols of infinitely many tape alphabets using a finite tape alphabet of its own. Instead, the tape alphabet of the given machine will be encoded using a fixed length binary code. For example, if the machine's tape alphabet has eight symbols other than β, these symbols will be encoded with 000 representing the first symbol, 001 representing the second symbol, etc. The eighth and last symbol will be represented by 111. Blanks must be handled explicitly because the tape itself contains an unlimited number of blanks after the input string.

For example, to encode the program from the solution to Exercise 3.2 in Figure S.5, we would first encode the labels in binary as shown in Figure S.15. Then we would encode the instructions and tape symbols as shown in Figure S.16. There are three non-blank tapes symbols in the tape alphabet used by the original machine: 0, 1, and ×. These will be encoded as 00, 01, and 10 for the universal machine.

The universal machine will use three tapes – one tape to store the given source code, one tape to simulate the program's input tape, and one tape to process if-goto instructions. In particular, this third tape will be used to hold the label of the instruction to which the if-goto is moving in order to facilitate comparisons with the labels in the source code.

```
00000:   if head is 1 then goto 00001 else goto 00110
00001:   Write ×
00010    Move Right
         if head is 0 then goto 00010 else goto 00011
00011:   if head is 1 then goto 00010 else goto 00100
00100:   Move Left
         if head is 1 then goto 01011 else goto 00101
00101:   if head is × then goto 01111 else goto 11111
00110:   Write ×
00111:   Move Right
         if head is 0 then goto 00111 else goto 01000
01000:   if head is 1 then goto 00111 else goto 01001
01001:   Move Left
         if head is 0 then goto 01011 else goto 01010
01010:   if head is × then goto 01111 else goto 11111
01011:   Write β
01100:   Move Left
         if head is 0 then goto 01100 else goto 01101
01101:   if head is 1 then goto 01100 else goto 01110
01110:   Move Right
         if head is β then goto 01111 else goto 00000
01111:   Return YES
10000:   Return NO
```

Figure S.15: The code from Figure S.5 with the labels replaced using a 5-bit code.

```
*
#00000:I01T00001E00110
#00001:W10
#00010:MR
#:I00T00010E00011
#00011:I01T00010E00100
#00100:ML
#:I01T01011E00101
#00101:I10T01111E11111
#00110:W10
#00111:MR
#:I00T00111E01000
#01000:I01T00111E01001
#01001:ML
#:I00T01011E01010
#01010:I10T01111E11111
#01011:Wβ
#01100:ML
#:I00T01100E01101
#01101:I01T01100E01110
#01110:MR
#:IβT01111E00000
#01111:RY
#11111:RN
#
*
```

Figure S.16: An encoding of the Turing machine from Figure S.15 to be presented to our universal Turing machine. The encoding uses a 2-bit code for the tape symbols other than β, with 0 encoded as 00, 1 encoded as 01, and $\times$ encoded as 10. (There would be no line breaks in the actual encoding.)

The universal Turing machine will start with its input tape containing $P*w$, where P is the encoding of the program to be executed and w is the input string to be given to P. The universal machine will first copy P to the second tape, which we call the source tape. The head of the input tape will be moved to the first symbol in w. At this point, the input tape will be ready to be used as the input tape for P. The universal machine will then move to the beginning of the source tape to read the first instruction.

Figure S.17 shows the main program that performs the initialization steps and then repeatedly runs the code in Figure S.18 to execute instructions until a Return instruction is executed, causing the entire program to return. You should not think of the code in Figure S.18 as a subroutine that is being run. Our Turing machine does not have the built-in ability to run subroutines. Instead, you should view this code as being inserted into the main program.

As can be seen from the code in Figure S.18, simulating the Move, Write, and Return instructions is fairly easy. Simulating the if-goto is a little more complicated. We need to do two things. First, based on the symbol at the head, we must decide whether we should move to the label in the then part of the instruction or to the label in the else part of the instruction. Once this is determined, we need to search the source tape for the corresponding instruction. To facilitate the label search, we will copy the label to the third tape, then walk through the source code from the beginning to find a matching label. Once we have found the matching instruction, we will be in position to execute that instruction.

The code in Figure S.19 uses the code in Figure S.20 to move to the correct label and then copies the label to the label tape. The initial while-loop in Figure S.20 compares the encoded symbol on the input tape with the encoded symbol on the source tape that appears directly after the I for the if-goto instruction. This is the symbol on which the if-goto instruction is basing its decision. If the symbols do not match, the code moves the head on the source tape to the symbol directly following the E marking the else label. If all of the symbols match, the head on the source tape will be at the symbol directly following the T marking the then label. Once it has found the appropriate label, the code in Figure S.19 copies the label to the label tape. The final piece of code for the if-goto appears in Figure S.21. This code reads the label tape and moves to the corresponding labeled instruction on the source tape.

Taken together, the code is these five figures represents a complete universal Turing machine.

UniversalTuringMachine:

    // Mark the beginning of label tape so we can find it later

1   Write * on label tape

    // Copy the source code to the source tape.

2   **while** head on input tape is not *

3   **if** head on input tape is #

4   **then** Write # on source tape

5   **else if** head on input tape is T

6   **then** Write T on source tape

7   **else if** head on input tape is E

8   **then** Write E on source tape

9   **else if** head on input tape is :

10   **then** Write : on source tape

11   **else if** head on input tape is M

12   **then** Write M on source tape

13   **else if** head on input tape is W

14   **then** Write W on source tape

15   **else if** head on input tape is R

16   **then** Write R on source tape

17   **else if** head on input tape is I

18   **then** Write I on source tape

19   **else if** head on input tape is L

20   **then** Write L on source tape

21   **else if** head on input tape is 0

22   **then** Write 0 on source tape

23   **else if** head on input tape is 1

24   **then** Write 1 on source tape

25   **else return** No // bad source code

26 **end while**

    // Put head on input tape at beginning of input string.

27 Move Right on input tape

28 **repeat** // repeatedly simulate instructions until hitting a Return

29   insert **ExecuteNextInstruction** code from Figure S.18.

30 **until** the cows come home

Figure S.17: The main program for our universal Turing machine. After initializing the source tape, the program repeatedly runs the ExecuteNextInstruction code until a Return is executed, at which point the entire universal Turing machine returns.

ExecuteNextInstruction:

```
 1    if head on source tape is M
 2      then begin
 3              Move Right on source tape
 4              if head on source tape is R
 5                then Move Right on input tape
 6                else begin
 7                        Move Left on input tape
 8                        if head on input tape is *    // we moved past input string
 9                          then Move Right on input tape
10                      end
11          end
12      else if head on source tape is W
13        then begin
14                Move Right on source tape
15                while head on source tape is not #
16                    if head on source tape is 0
17                      then Write 0 on input tape
18                      else if head on source tape is 1
19                          then Write 1 on input tape
20                          else Write β on input tape
21                end while
22            end
23      else if head on source tape is R
24        then begin
25                Move Right on source tape
26                if head on source tape is Y then return YES else return NO
27            end
28      else insert Handle-If-Goto code from Figure S.19.
        // Move to the next instruction
29    while head on source tape is not a colon
30      Move Right
31    end while
32    Move Right
```

Figure S.18: Turing machine code to simulate the three simple instructions: Move, Write, and Return. The if-goto instruction is handled by the code shown Figure S.19.

Handle-If-Goto:

1   Move Right on source tape
2   insert **MoveToThenOrElsePosition** code from Figure S.20.
    // move back to the beginning of the label tape and clear the label tape
3   **while** the head on label tape is not *
4   Move Left on label tape
5   **end while**
6   Move Right on label tape
7   **while** the head on label tape is not β
8   Write β on label tape
9   Move Right on label tape
10 **end while**
    // move back to the beginning of label tape
11 **while** the head on label tape is not *
12   Move Left on label tape
13 **end while**
14 Move Right on label tape
    // copy label to label tape
15 **while** the head on source tape is not E or #
16   **if** head on source tape is 0
17   **then** Write 0 on label tape
18   **else** Write 1 on label tape
19   Move Right on label tape
20   Move Right on source tape
21 **end while**
    // move back to the beginning of the label tape
22 **while** the head on label tape is not *
23   Move Left on label tape
24 **end while**
25 Move Right on label tape
    // move to the correct instruction
26 insert **GoTo-Instruction-With-Label** code from Figure S.21.

Figure S.19: Turing machine code to process an if-goto instruction. First, it finds the correct label of the if-goto instruction using the MoveToThenOrElsePosition code from Figure S.20. After moving to the correct label, the label is copied from the source tape to the label tape. Then the tape head on the source tape is moved to the correct instruction using the GoTo-Instruction-With-Label code from Figure S.21.

MoveToThenOrElsePosition:

// skip over then-label if symbols do not match

```
1    while head on source tape is not T or E
2      if head on source tape is 0
3        then if head on input tape is 1 or β
4            then begin // skip to Else label
5                    while head on source tape is not E
6                        Move Right on source tape
7                    end while
8                end
9          else if head on source tape is 1
10             then if head on input tape is 0 or β
11                 then begin // skip to Else label
12                         while head on source tape is not E
13                             Move Right on source tape
14                         end while
15                     end
16             else if head on source tape is β
17                 then if head on input tape is 0 or 1
18                     then begin // skip to Else label
19                             while head on source tape is not E
20                                 Move Right on source tape
21                             end while
22                         end
23                 else return No // source code has bad format
24    end while
     // move to the label
25   Move Right on source tape
```

Figure S.20: Turing machine code to move the head of the source tape into position to read the correct label on an if-goto instruction.

GoTo-Instruction-With-Label:

    // move to the beginning of the source tape
1 **while** head on source tape is not *
2   Move Left on source tape
3 **end while**
4 Move Right   // to get to first instruction
    // match each symbol in the label on the source tape with the
    // label on the label tape
5 **while** head on source tape is not a colon
    // if we reach the end of source before we find the label
    //   then this is bad source code, so Return No
6   **if** head on source tape is * **then return** No
    // if at some point the labels do not match,
    //   then start over with the next instruction
7   **if** head on source tape does not match the head on label tape
8   **then begin**
9   // find next instruction on the source tape
10   **while** head on source tape is not #
11   Move Right on source tape
12   **end while**
13   Move Right on source tape
14   // go back to beginning of label tape
15   **while** head on label tape is not *
16   Move Left on label tape
17   **end while**
18   Move Right on label tape
19   **end**
20   **else begin**
21   Move Right on label tape
22   Move Right on source tape
23   **end**
24 **end while**

Figure S.21: Turing machine code to read the label off of the label tape and move the source tape head to the corresponding instruction.

Solutions for Chapter 4: Unsolvable Problems

Solution to Exercise 4.1 *In the proof of Rice's Theorem, we assumed that the empty language does not have the property. How can we make such an assumption? Prove that Rice's Theorem holds when the empty language has the property in question.*

In the proof of Rice's Theorem, we created the source code for the following program:

```
Source = "DoNotRunThis(x):
            if Execute(P,w) returns YES
              then return Execute(M,x)
              else return NO"
```

The idea was to make sure that if P accepts w, then the language recognized by DoNotRunThis has the property, but if P does not accept w, then the language recognized by DoNotRunThis is the empty language, which we assumed did not have the property. In this exercise, we need to prove Rice's Theorem when the empty language *has* the property in question.

Because the property is non-trivial, we know there is some recognizable language that does not have the property. So let's assume there is some Turing machine program, DoesNotHaveProperty, such that the language recognized by DoesNotHaveProperty does not have the property and create the source code as follows:

```
Source-Bad = "DoNotRunThis(x):
               if Execute(P,w) returns YES
                 then return NO
                 else return Execute(DoesNotHaveProperty,x)"
```

This source code appears to do what we want. When P accepts w, the language recognized by DoNotRunThis is empty and so has the property. When Execute(P,w) returns NO, the language recognized by DoNotRunThis is the language recognized by the program DoesNotHaveProperty, which does not have the property. Unfortunately, Execute(P,w) returning NO is not the only way in which P can reject w. P may run forever when given w as input, in which case the else part of the code will never be executed and the language recognized by DoNotRunThis is the empty language, which HAS THE PROPERTY!

It seems we can't get away from using the empty language. What to do? Instead of showing that the property testing problem is undecidable, we will use the same proof to show that the problem of testing whether a recognizable language does *not* have the property is undecidable. This is the complement of our original problem. Exercise 4.3 shows that if the complement of a problem is undecidable, then so is the problem.

Our original source code works to show that the problem of testing whether the recognizable language does not have the property is undecidable. This time we assume that the empty set has the property and that M is a Turing machine program such that $L(M)$ does not have the property. We know such an M exists because the property is not trivial. We define Source as in our original proof:

```
Source = "DoNotRunThis(x):
              if Execute(P,w) returns YES
                  then return Execute(M,x)
                  else return NO"
```

If P accepts w, then the language recognized by DoNotRunThis is $L(M)$ which we assume does not have the property. If P rejects w, by either returning NO or running forever, then the language recognized by DoNotRunThis is the empty language, which has the property. Thus, by testing whether the language recognized by DoNotRunThis does not have the property, we can determine whether P accepts w.

Solution to Exercise 4.2   *We have seen problems that are undecidable. Is it possible there are problems that are* **unrecognizable,** *by which we mean there is no algorithm that returns* YES *for each* YES *instance and returns* NO *or runs forever for each* NO *instance? Let's consider a problem called the* **REJECTION PROBLEM:**

GIVEN: *Two strings, P and w.*

QUESTION: *Is P either not the source code for any program or the source code for a program that rejects input string w?*

Prove that the REJECTION PROBLEM is unrecognizable.

We have a program Execute that recognizes YES instances of the ACCEPTANCE PROBLEM. Let's suppose we also have a program that *recognizes* YES instances of the REJECTION PROBLEM called RecognizeRejection. Consider the following program:

Accepts(P, w):

1 Set $i = 1$
2 **while true**   // Continue the loop until a **return** is executed.
3   Run Execute(P,w) for i steps.
4   **if** Execute(P,w) returned YES **then return** YES
5   Run RecognizeRejection(P,w) for i steps.
6   **if** RecognizeRejection(P,w) returned YES **then return** NO
7   Increment i
8 **end while**

First, we need to convince ourselves that we can run a program or sub-routine for i steps. Our universal Turing machine construction can easily be modified to accomplish this by keeping a counter indicating the number of instructions that have been executed so far and comparing the counter to i before executing the next instruction. Therefore, the program above is valid.

Suppose P accepts w. Then Execute(P,w) will return YES after some number of steps. Consequently Accepts(P,w) will return YES. Suppose P rejects w. Then RecognizeRejection(P,w) will return YES after some number of steps and Accepts(P,w) will subsequently return NO. This is true even if P runs forever when given w. Consequently, if RecognizeRejection(P,w) recognizes YES instances of the REJECTION PROBLEM, then it must be the case that Accepts(P,w) decides the ACCEPTANCE PROBLEM. Since the ACCEPTANCE PROBLEM is undecidable, the REJECTION PROBLEM cannot be recognizable.

Solution to Exercise 4.3   *The result of the previous exercise shouldn't be all that surprising. The set of YES instances of the REJECTION PROBLEM is the set of NO instances of the ACCEPTANCE PROBLEM. Being able to recognize both YES and NO instances of a problem implies that we are able to decide the problem. We already have* Execute(P,w) *to recognize the YES instances of the ACCEPTANCE PROBLEM. If in addition we had a program to recognize NO instances of the ACCEPTANCE PROBLEM, we could decide the ACCEPTANCE PROBLEM.*

This specific argument can be generalized to any problem.

Theorem S.1 *Let L be the set of YES instances for a given problem. Let $\overline{L}$ be the set of NO instances for the problem. (Note: $\overline{L}$ is simply the complement of L.) Then L is decidable if and only if $\overline{L}$ is decidable.*

Prove this theorem formally.

Let M be a Turing machine program that recognizes L and let $\overline{M}$ be a Turing machine program that recognizes $\overline{L}$. We will write another program `Alternate` that alternates between executing one line of M and one line of $\overline{M}$. For every input string, x, one of these machines will eventually return YES, because either x is in L or x is in $\overline{L}$. If M returns YES, then `Alternate` will return YES. If $\overline{M}$ returns YES, then `Alternate` will return NO. `Alternate`, then, always halts. Moreover, `Alternate` will return YES if and only if x is in L. Therefore, `Alternate` decides L.

We can write `Alternate` by making use of our universal Turing machine capabilities. `Alternate` begins by writing the source code for M and $\overline{M}$ on two different tapes. M and $\overline{M}$ are constant strings as far as `Alternate` is concerned, so this code is just a large sequence of Write instructions. `Alternate` then copies the input string to two other tapes, one to simulate M's input tape and the other to simulate $\overline{M}$'s input tape. At this point, `Alternate` can use the universal Turing machine code to execute the first instruction in M, leaving the head on the source tape for M at the next instruction to execute. After executing the first instruction from M, `Alternate` executes the first instruction of $\overline{M}$, similarly leaving the head on the source tape for $\overline{M}$ at the next instruction to execute. `Alternate` continues to alternate between executing one instruction of M and one instruction of $\overline{M}$ until one of the two programs YES.

Solution to Exercise 4.4 *We have developed a theory of computation based on decision problems – our machines are given inputs and must respond by saying* YES *or* NO. *More formally, we have defined computation as determining whether a given string is in a particular language. Maybe this way of viewing computation is all wrong. Great time to think of that, isn't it? Suppose we have a machine that simply generates information without any input whatsoever. For example, what if a machine generates all the digits of π or all prime numbers – just for fun or perhaps to transmit into space to attract aliens who like donuts. Such a machine would never even halt. Is that machine computing? It seems like it is. Does our theory give us any information about this type of computation? Modify the Turing machine model so that a Turing machine generates a language rather than decides a language. Relate the set languages generated by your model to the decidable and recognizable languages.*

Let's replace the input tape in the Turing machine model with an output tape and have the machine write strings to the output tape separated by some symbol, say #. Such a machine is called an **enumerator**.

Definition S.2 *An **enumerator** is a Turing machine with two tapes: a work tape and an output tape. The output is a write-once tape whose tape head never moves left. Initially both tapes are blank. As the enumerator proceeds, it writes strings to the output tape separated by #'s.*

*We say a string w is **generated** by enumerator E if and only if E eventually writes w on the output tape between two #'s. The set of strings generated by an enumerator E is denoted $G(E)$. Unless E runs forever, $G(E)$ is finite.*

*A language that can be generated by an enumerator is called **recursively enumerable (r.e.)**.*

Let's see how we could generate $\{0^n1^n : n \geq 0\}$ with a Turing machine? On the work tape, we will have a main counter that indicates which string we are generating. At the beginning of each new string generation, we make two copies of this counter for the 0's and 1's respectively. We then use these two counters to generate the correct number of 0's followed by the correct number of 1's. Once the string is written to the output tape, we append a # to separate it from the next string, increment the main counter, and repeat. Figure S.22 describes the algorithm in detail.

Notice that this enumerator enumerates the strings in $\{0^n1^n : n \geq 0\}$ in order of length. That $\{0^n1^n : n \geq 0\}$ can be enumerated in order is an important property of the language. The "order" of strings in $\{0^n1^n : n \geq 0\}$ is naturally defined as smaller strings come before larger strings. However, many languages have multiple strings with the same length. Therefore, in general, we define a **lexicographic ordering** on a language as an ordering such that smaller strings precede larger strings and strings of the same length are ordered "alphabetically" (in our case 0 comes before 1). A language that can be enumerated by a Turing machine in lexicographic order is said to be **recursive**.

Are recursive languages decidable? Suppose we have an enumerator E that enumerates a language L in lexicographic order. Let's assume L is infinite. If L is not infinite, then it can be decided by a finite automaton and so is decidable. Given an input string x, a Turing machine could decide L by using the universal Turing machine to simulate E and comparing the strings generated by E to x. If x is ever generated by E, then the Turing machine should answer YES. If x is not generated by E and some string that appears after x in the lexicographic

Generate():

```
1   Initialize the main counter to 0
2   repeat the following Forever
3       Copy the main counter to Counter0 and Counter1
4       while counter0 > 0
5           Write 0 to the output tape
6           Decrement counter0
7       end while
8       while counter1 > 0
9           Write 1 to the output tape
10          Decrement counter1
11      end while
12      Write # to the output tape to separate this string from the next string
13      Increment the main counter
14  until whenever forever ends
```

Figure S.22: An enumerator to generate the language $\{0^n 1^n : n \geq 0\}$.

ordering is generated by E, then the Turing machine should answer No. In this way, the Turing machine decides L. Recursive languages are, therefore, decidable.

Are decidable languages recursive? Let M be a Turing machine that decides a language L. We can create an enumerator E to enumerate L in lexicographic order as follows. E simply generates every possible string in lexicographic order. Each time it creates a new string x, and before writing x to the output tape, it uses a portion of the work tape to simulate M with input x. If M accepts x, then E writes x to the output tape. Otherwise, E moves on to the next string.

We have proven the following result:

Theorem S.3 *A language L is recursive if and only L is decidable.*

What about the recursively enumerable languages? For any enumerator E that generates a language L, we can use the same idea as above to create a Turing machine to recognize L. The Turing machine simulates E and examines the strings generated. If the input string is ever generated by E, the Turing machine returns YES. Because the strings may not be generated in lexicographic order, however, the Turing machine does not when to stop simulating E. In other words, the Turing machine will not halt if the input string is not in L. Of course, for a Turing machine to recognize L, it need not halt for strings that are not in the language.

We have proven that recursively enumerable languages are recognizable, but are recognizable language necessarily recursively enumerable. In our proof that decidable languages are recursive, our enumerator generated strings in order and ran the Turing machine on each string. If the Turing machine accepted the string, the enumerator wrote the string to the output tape. This relied on the fact that the Turing machine was guaranteed to halt. We have no such guarantee here, so we have to be more careful. In particular, for each string, we need to stop the Turing machine after some number of steps before moving on to the next string. But we don't know how many steps to run before stopping. Furthermore, the number of steps needed will be different for different strings. We'll need to run every string for every number of possible steps. Here's the idea. We will generate the first string. Run the Turing machine on that string for one step. Then generate the second string. Run the Turing machine on both of the strings we have generated so far for two steps. Then generate the third string and run the Turing machine on all three strings for three steps. We continue like this forever. Here is the code for this enumerator:

Generate():

```
1   Initialize stepCounter to 1
2   repeat the following Forever
3        Generate the next string in lexicographic order on the work tape.
4        for each string x generated so far
5             Run the Turing machine for stepCounter steps with x as input
6             if the Turing machine accepts x
7               then begin
8                       Write x to the output tape.
9                       Write # to the output tape.
10              end
11       end for
12       Increment stepCounter by 1.
13  until we are done, which is never
```

If x is a string in the language recognized by the Turing machine, then the enumerator will eventually generate x and run the Turing machine for long enough on x for the Turing machine to return YES. At that point, the enumerator will write x to the output tape. Since only strings that the Turing machine accepts are written to the output tape, the language generated by the enumerator is the language recognized by the Turing machine.

We have proven the following result:

Theorem S.4 *A language L is recursive enumerable if and only L is recognizable.*

Solutions for Chapter 5: Nondeterminism

Solution to Exercise 5.1 *You may be wondering why we allow some possible sequences of nondeterministic choices to return* NO *when given* YES *instances yet still consider the algorithm to solve the decision problem. Suppose we required all possible sequences of choices to return the correct answer for every instance of the problem. Show that with these requirements nondeterminism would not provide any additional power by providing a simple way to convert any such nondeterministic algorithm to a deterministic one.*

If we required a nondeterministic algorithm to return the correct answer no matter what sequence of choices the algorithm followed, it is trivial to prove that nondeterministic algorithms are equivalent to deterministic algorithms with respect to the problems that can be solved. For any nondeterministic algorithm, the equivalent deterministic algorithm could simply use one fixed sequence of choices as the deterministic computation path. For example, we can create a deterministic Turing machine program from a nondeterministic Turing machine program by replacing each nondeterministic if-goto with an equivalent deterministic if-goto as follows:

Replace:	with:

if *symbol*
     then goto $\{then_1, \ldots, then_k\}$
     else goto $\{else_1, \ldots, else_l\}$
	if *symbol*
	     then goto *$then_1$*
	     else goto *$else_1$*

The sequence of labels seen by this deterministic Turing machine corresponds to a possible sequence of nondeterministic choices for the nondeterministic Turing machine. If each such sequence returns the correct answer, the deterministic machine solves the problem. This type of nondeterminism, therefore, provides no additional power.

Solution to Exercise 5.2 *Modify the argument preceeding Theorem 5.4 to prove Theorem 5.5.*

We must show that any language that can be recognized by a nondeterministic machine can be recognized by a deterministic machine. We can use the same simulation that we used to show that any language that can be *decided* by a nondeterministic machine can be decided by a deterministic machine. In particular, run breadth-first search on the configuration graph. Breadth-first search is guaranteed to find the shortest path from the starting configuration to a goal configuration. If the goal is in the graph, then breadth-first search will return YES as required. If the goal is not in the graph, breadth-first search may run forever if there is a cycle or if the configuration graph is infinite. Running forever is fine, however, since the definition of recognize does not require the algorithm to halt on NO instances.

Solutions for Chapter 6: Computational Complexity

Solution to Exercise 6.1 *What type of reduction did we just use to argue that MAX2SAT is at least as hard as 2SAT?*

The reduction from 2SAT to MAX2SAT is a Turing reduction. If we had a hypothetical, polynomial-time algorithm to find a truth assignment that satisfied the maximum possible number of clauses, we could use that algorithm to decide 2SAT in polynomial time.

Solution to Exercise 6.2 *Show that if the RAM described above includes multiplication in its instruction set and we measure the memory consumed by the machine as the number of bits needed to write down the largest number created at any point in the computation, the RAM would not obey our restriction on the relationship between time and memory.*

Consider the following algorithm:

RepeatedSquaring(n)

```
1   result = 2
2   for i = 1 to n
3       result = result * result
4   end for
5   return result
```

The algorithm squares the number 2, then squares the result, then squares that result, and so on, performing a total of n squares. The resulting number is $2^{(2^n)}$, which requires 2^n bits to store in binary. In contrast, the number of instructions performed is $O(n)$. Writing 2^n bits using $O(n)$ instructions violates our restriction that *reasonable* machine models use only a constant amount of memory in any single instruction.

Solution to Exercise 6.3 *Show that 2SAT is in* P.

The proof below is based on the proof of Theorem 9.1 from Papadimitriou (1994).

The idea of the algorithm follows from the equivalence of $(x \lor y)$ and $\bar{x} \Rightarrow y$. Create a directed graph as follows. For each variable x, create two vertices, x and $\bar{x}$. For every clause $(x \lor y)$ in the formula, create edges $(\bar{x}, y)$ and $(\bar{y}, x)$. These edges correspond to two implications, $\bar{x} \Rightarrow y$ and $\bar{y} \Rightarrow x$, that can be derived from the clause $(x \lor y)$. If there is a path in the graph from a vertex x to vertex $\bar{x}$, then there is a series of implications that would force $\bar{x}$ to be TRUE whenever x were TRUE. This is a logical contradiction because x and $\bar{x}$ must have opposite values. If there is also a path from $\bar{x}$ to x, then we can assign neither TRUE nor FALSE to x without creating a contradiction. Therefore, if the graph contains a cycle that includes both x and $\bar{x}$ for some variable x, then the formula is unsatisfiable.

Furthermore, if the graph does not contain such a cycle, the formula is satisfiable. To see this, first notice that the graph has a symmetry to it. If there is a path from u to v in the graph, there must also be a path from $\bar{v}$ to $\bar{u}$. (Here we assume that if u is a vertex corresponding to a literal l, then $\bar{u}$ is the vertex corresponding to the literal $\bar{l}$. For example, if u represents the literal $\bar{x}$, then $\bar{u}$ represents the literal x.) We can prove that the graph has this symmetry using mathematical induction on the length of the path as follows.

Suppose there is a path from u to v that contains a single edge (u, v). Recall that edges are added to the graph in pairs. If $(x \lor y)$ were a clause in the 2SAT instance, the graph would include edges $(\bar{x}, y)$ and $(\bar{y}, x)$. Therefore, if (u, v) is an edge in the graph, then $(\bar{v}, \bar{u})$ is an edge in the graph, and so there is a path from $\bar{v}$ to $\bar{u}$.

Next, for some $k \geq 1$, assume that whenever there is a path of length k from a vertex u to a vertex v, there is also a path from $\bar{v}$ to $\bar{u}$. This is our induction hypothesis.

Consider a path of length $k+1$ from u to v. Let (w, v) be the last edge on this path. Then there is a path of length k from u to w. Our induction hypothesis then implies that there is a path from $\bar{w}$ to $\bar{u}$. But if the graph contains the edge (w, v), it must also contain the edge $(\bar{v}, \bar{w})$. Prepending this edge to the path from $\bar{w}$ to $\bar{u}$ gives us a path from $\bar{v}$ to $\bar{u}$.

Since we have proven that the statement is true for paths of length 1 and we have proven that if the statement is true for paths of length k, it must be also true for paths of length $k+1$, the statement must be true for any path. (This is the principle of mathematical induction.) Thus, we have proven that if there is a path from u to v in the graph, there must also be a path from $\bar{v}$ to $\bar{u}$.

So what? How do we use this symmetry to prove that the formula is satisfiable if it does not contain one of the contradictory cycles. Well, suppose we have a graph that does not contain a cycle including both x and $\bar{x}$ for any variable x. Consider the truth assignment created as follows. For each literal l such that l cannot reach $\bar{l}$ and l has not been previously assigned a value, assign TRUE to l and assign TRUE to every literal reachable from l in the graph.

Since there is no variable x such that $\bar{x}$ is reachable from x and x is reachable from $\bar{x}$, every variable must eventually be assigned a value. To ensure that our truth assignment is well-defined, we also need to show that we never try to assign two different values to a variable. For example, suppose that we assign TRUE to x because x has not yet been given a value and $\bar{x}$ is not reachable from x. Suppose in addition that y is reachable from x. Is it possible for y to have previously been given the value FALSE? There are two ways y could have previously been assigned FALSE: either $\bar{y}$ was one of the literals previously chosen for assignment or $\bar{y}$ is reachable from another of the literals previously chosen for assignment. In either case, we would also have assigned TRUE to anything reachable from $\bar{y}$. The symmetry of the graph, however, tells us that because y is reachable from x, $\bar{x}$ is reachable from $\bar{y}$. But then x was assigned to FALSE when y was. This contradicts our assumption that x was not yet assigned a value at the time we chose it for assignment. Therefore, we will never try to assign a different value to a variable that has previously been assigned.

Finally, we need to show that this truth assignment satisfies every clause. Consider a clause $(x \lor y)$. Suppose x is assigned a value before y. If x is assigned FALSE, then because $(\bar{x}, y)$ is an edge in the graph, y is reachable from $\bar{x}$ and will be assigned TRUE. The clause will therefore be satisfied.

We can conclude that the 2SAT formula is satisfiable if and only if there is a cycle containing both x and $\bar{x}$ in the graph. Any polynomial-time cycle detection algorithm, such as breadth-first search, can be used to solve 2SAT in polynomial time. Therefore, 2SAT is in P.

Solution to Exercise 6.4   *Compute the times for an algorithm with running time $2^{n^{1/(100)}}$ as we did in Figure 6.1. You should see fairly reasonable running times unless n is impracticably large. Algorithms with exponential running times but where the exponent is much smaller than n would certainly be practical. On the other hand, try to design an algorithm that does something useful and has running time $2^{n^{1/(100)}}$.*

The time required by a machine with running time $2^{n^{1/(100)}}$ on various input sizes is shown below. Note: s represents seconds in the table. The machine is assumed to be capable of executing 250 trillion instructions per second. I finally got it over a second when I used $n = 10^{168}$.

Input Size	Running Time
10	8e-15 s
100	8e-15 s
1000	8e-15 s
10000	9e-15 s
100000	9e-15 s
1000000	9e-15 s

Solution to Exercise 6.5 *Argue that the nondeterministic algorithm described on Page 85 correctly solves the* Hamiltonian Cycle *problem.*

Consider any graph that contains a Hamiltonian cycle. Let $v_1, v_2, \ldots, v_k$ be a Hamiltonian cycle in the graph. Assume the algorithm begins by setting *start* to v_1. (If not, the same argument works starting somewhere else in the cycle.) Since v_2 follows v_1 in the cycle, v_2 is adjacent to v_1. Therefore, there is a nondeterministic choice that sets u to v_2 during the first iteration of the loop. Similarly, v_3 is adjacent to v_2, so there is a nondeterministic choice that sets u to v_3 in the next iteration of the loop. The algorithm can continue in this fashion until it reaches v_n and then *start*, at which point the loop terminates and returns YES. Therefore, for any YES instance, there is a sequence of nondeterministic choices that leads the algorithm to return YES.

If the graph does not contain a Hamiltonian cycle, then no matter what sequence of choices are made, the algorithm must hit a vertex a second time within $|V|$ iterations of the loop, at which point the algorithm returns NO in line 6.

Solution to Exercise 6.6 *Show that a decision problem is in* NP *if and only if the problem has a polynomial time verifier.*

We need to show that we can convert a polynomial time verifier for a decision problem into polynomial time nondeterministic algorithm to decide the problem and vice versa.

Suppose we are given a polynomial time verifier V for the decision problem. V takes at most $an^k + b$ steps on inputs of length n, for some constants a, b and k. Therefore, V can access at most the first $an^k + b$ symbols of the given certificate. Construct a nondeterministic machine such that each sequence of nondeterministic choices creates a different certificate of length $an^k + b$ and such that every certificate of length $an^k + b$, is created by some sequence of nondeterministic choices. After creating the certificate, run V with the input string and the certificate created, returning whatever V returns, like so:

NondeterminsticAlgorithmForVerifier(w)

    // Given input w of length n
1   Nondeterministically create a certificate of length at most $an^k + b$.
2   Run V with input w and the nondeterministically created certificate.
3   **if** V returns YES
4   **then return** YES
5   **else return** NO

This nondeterministic algorithm runs in polynomial time since V runs in $O(n^k)$ time and it should only take $O(n^k)$ steps to nondeterministically create a certificate of length at most $an^k + b$. Therefore, the decision problem is in NP.

Now suppose we have a polynomial-time nondeterministic algorithm to decide the problem. If the algorithm accepts an input, there is some sequence of nondeterministic choices that leads the algorithm to return YES. We will create a verifier that takes the sequence of choices made by the nondeterministic algorithm as the certificate. The verifier will then simulate the nondeterministic algorithm. Every time the nondeterministic algorithm has a choice to make, the verifier will look to the certificate to determine the choice to simulate. Because the nondeterministic algorithm runs in polynomial time, the verifier will run in polynomial time.

Solution to Exercise 6.7 *Prove Theorem 6.5.*

We can simply insert A for HAMILTONIAN CYCLE and B for TSP in the argument that a polynomial time algorithm for TSP can be used in conjunction with a polynomial time reduction from HAMILTONIAN CYCLE to TSP to create a polynomial time algorithm for HAMILTONIAN CYCLE.

Solution to Exercise 6.8   *Why did we need to use $cn^k + 2$ instead of cn^k?*

Because the Turing machine is the underlying machine model for our entire theory, we must consider the case when the input is the empty string. In this case, n is 0. To figure out that the input is empty, the machine must at least take time to execute an `if-goto` instruction and a `Return` instruction. The proof tacitly assumes that all of the nondeterministic machines have such a special case. This is legitimate since for any machine that does not have the special case code, there is an equivalent machine that does. Thus, we have a lower limit of 2 instructions whenever n is 0. Had we used cn^k instead of $cn^k + 2$, we would not have created any clauses or variables at all in our reduction when n is 0.

Solution to Exercise 6.9   *Verify that the number of clauses created in the proof of the Cook-Levin Theorem is polynomial in n.*

Let l be the number of lines in the program for the nondeterministic machine. Let a be the number of symbols in our tape alphabet. The formula created by the reduction in the proof of the Cook-Levin Theorem consists of:

1. clauses forcing any satisfying truth assignment to assign values to variables that are consistent with our interpretation of the variables;

2. clauses ensuring that any satisfying truth assignment corresponds to a valid sequence of line numbers executed in the program;

3. clauses ensuring the contents of the tape are updated properly;

4. a clause ensuring that the machine starts in the starting configuration;

5. a clause ensuring that the machine ends in an accepting configuration.

In the set of clauses that ensure the consistent interpretation of variables, there are $l^2(cn^k + 2)$ clauses involving LINE variables, $(cn^k + 2)^3$ clauses involving HEAD variables and $a^2(cn^k + 2)^2$ clauses involving SYMBOL variables. In the set of clauses that ensure the consistent progression through program, there are at most $2l(cn^k + 2)^2$ clauses. (If all instructions in the program were if-goto instructions, there would be exactly that many clauses in the set.) In the set of clauses to ensure the consistency of the tape contents, there are at most $l(cn^k + 2)^2$ clauses ensuring that the head is moved properly and $la(cn^k + 2)^2$ clauses ensuring that the symbols on the tape are updated properly. Finally, there is one clause ensuring that we begin in the start configuration and one clause to ensure that we end in an accepting configuration. The total number of clauses is therefore $O(l^2a^2(cn^k + 2)^3)$. Because l, a, c, and k are constants, this is polynomial in n.

Solutions for Chapter 7: Reduce, Reuse, Recycle

Solution to Exercise 7.1 *Prove Theorem 7.1.*

The theorem states that if B is NP-complete, C is in NP, and $B \leq^p_m C$, then C is also NP-complete. Consider any problem A that is in NP. We can reduce A to C as follows:

1. Given an instance x of A.

2. Transform x into an instance y of B. Because B is NP-complete, this can be done in polynomial time.

3. Transform y into an instance z of C. We know this can be done in polynomial time because $B \leq^p_m C$.

The transformation of x to y runs in time that is polynomial in the size of x, that is, it takes $O(|x|^k)$ time, where k is a constant and $|x|$ is the size of x. The transformation of y to z runs in time that is polynomial in the size of y, that is, it takes $O(|y|^d)$ time, for some constant d. We need to show that the entire transformation from x to z takes time that is polynomial in the size of x. Because y was created using $O(|x|^k)$ instructions and each instruction can access only a constant amount of memory, we know that $|y| = O(|x|^k)$. Therefore, the running time of the entire reduction is $O((|x|^k)^d) = O(|x|^{kd})$, which is a polynomial in $|x|$, the size of the instance of A.

Solution to Exercise 7.2 *In the reduction from SAT to 3SAT, we created many new variables. Show that other variables from the SAT instance could be used instead of new variables when the number of literals in the SAT clause is 1 or 2. Also show that new variables are necessary (at least for this particular reduction) for a SAT clause in which the number of literals is 4.*

Let's consider a clause with one literal, l. The reduction to 3SAT creates two new variables, y and z, in expanding this clause to four three-literal clauses: $(l \vee y \vee z)$, $(l \vee \bar{y} \vee z)$, $(l \vee y \vee \bar{z})$, and $(l \vee \bar{y} \vee \bar{z})$. Satisfying all four of these clauses requires l to be assigned TRUE, but the values assigned to y and z are completely irrelevant. There are no constraints placed on y and z by these four clauses, so we could use any variables, even variables that occur elsewhere in the formula, in place of y and z. The same argument applies to the case of a two-literal clause.

When the number of literals is more than three, however, the new variables are required because their values are essential. For example, consider a four-literal clause $(l^1 \lor l^2 \lor l^3 \lor l^4)$. The reduction creates one new variable, u^1, and two clauses, $(l^1 \lor l^2 \lor u^1)$ and $(\overline{u^1} \lor l^3 \lor l^4)$. We need to satisfy both of these clauses whenever we would satisfy the original four-literal clause. If we satisfied the original clause with l^1 set to TRUE and the others set to FALSE, then the value of u^1 must be FALSE to satisfy the second of the clauses created by the reduction. Using an existing variable in place of u^1 would place an additional constraint on the value of this variable, a constraint that did not exist in the original formula.

Solution to Exercise 7.3   *Prove that 1in3SAT is NP-complete.*

The solution below is adapted from Moret (1998).

We must first show that 1in3SAT is in NP. Similar to the verifier for SAT, we can guess a truth assignment and verify that it satisfies every clause by setting exactly one literal in each clause to true.

Next, we will reduce 3SAT to 1in3SAT. Consider a clause $(l_1 \lor l_2 \lor l_3)$ in the original 3SAT instance. We need to do something to create a clause or group of clauses so that there is a truth assignment that satisfies the original clause if and only if there is a truth assignment that satisfies exactly one literal in each clause of the group.

Since l_1, l_2 and l_3 appear together in a clause of the 1in3SAT instance, no more than one of them can be set to TRUE. However, the 3SAT instance could be satisfied by setting all three of these literals to TRUE, so we need to separate l_1, l_2 and l_3 in the 1in3SAT instance. Let's create a separate clause for each literal. As we did in the SAT to 3SAT reduction, we need to create new variables to expand these clauses into clauses that contain three literals each. We also need to do something to tie the clauses together to ensure that we maintain the relationships among the original three literals. In particular, we must ensure that at least one of the original literals is set to TRUE.

Let's create four new variables, a, b, c, and d, and three clauses: $(l_1 \lor a \lor b)$, $(b \lor l_2 \lor c)$, and $(c \lor d \lor l_3)$. Now suppose t is a satisfying truth assignment for the original 3SAT instance. Let's see if we can expand this truth assignment to include values for a, b, c, and d in such a way that exactly one literal in each of the new clauses is TRUE. Suppose, for example, that $t(l_1) = $ TRUE, $t(l_2) = $ FALSE, and $t(l_3) = $ TRUE. Because $t(l_1)$ is TRUE, we must set the values of a and b to FALSE; otherwise, we would have more than one literal in the first clause set to TRUE. Similarly, because $t(l_3)$ is TRUE, we must set the values of c and d to FALSE so that no more than one literal in the third clause is set to TRUE. But then each of the three literals in the second clause is FALSE, which is bad.

We need to try something else. Let's think about the middle clause more carefully since that links the other two clauses together. If l_2 is FALSE, then either b or c has to be TRUE. Suppose b is TRUE. Since b appears with l_1 in the first clause, l_1 has to be set to FALSE. On the other hand, if c is TRUE, then l_3 must be set to FALSE because c appears with l_3 in the third clause. In the 3SAT instance, setting l_2 to FALSE forces at least one of l_1 and l_3 to be TRUE. In the 1in3SAT clauses we created, setting l_2 to FALSE forces at least one of l_1 and l_3 to be FALSE, which is exactly the opposite of what we want. So why not just negate l_1 and l_3? Our three clauses would then be $(\overline{l_1} \vee a \vee b)$, $(b \vee l_2 \vee c)$, and $(c \vee d \vee \overline{l_3})$. Now, setting l_2 to FALSE forces at least one of l_1 and l_3 to be TRUE, which is what we want.

Let's see if this works. Suppose we have a truth assignment, t, that satisfies the original 3SAT instance. The table below lists the possible values for $t(l_1)$, $t(l_2)$, and $t(l_3)$, along with values for a, b, c, and d that satisfy the three corresponding clauses in the 1in3SAT instance. This shows that a truth assignment that satisfies the 3SAT instance can be expanded to satisfy the 1in3SAT instance.

$t(l_1)$	$t(l_2)$	$t(l_3)$	a	b	c	d
TRUE	TRUE	TRUE	TRUE	FALSE	FALSE	TRUE
TRUE	TRUE	FALSE	TRUE	FALSE	FALSE	FALSE
FALSE	TRUE	TRUE	FALSE	FALSE	FALSE	TRUE
FALSE	TRUE	FALSE	FALSE	FALSE	FALSE	FALSE
TRUE	FALSE	FALSE	FALSE	TRUE	FALSE	FALSE
FALSE	FALSE	TRUE	FALSE	FALSE	TRUE	FALSE
TRUE	FALSE	TRUE	FALSE	TRUE	FALSE	TRUE

Now suppose t is a truth assignment for the 1in3SAT instance that satisfies exactly one literal in each of the three clauses but does not satisfy the original 3SAT formula. Let $(l_1 \vee l_2 \vee l_3)$ be a clause in the original 3SAT instance that

t does not satisfy. The 1in3SAT formula must include the clauses $(\overline{l_1} \vee a \vee b)$, $(b \vee l_2 \vee c)$, and $(c \vee d \vee \overline{l_3})$. Because t does not satisfy $(l_1 \vee l_2 \vee l_3)$, $t(l_1)$ must be FALSE, which of course implies that $t(\overline{l_1})$ must be TRUE. But, since t satisfies the 1in3SAT instance by setting exactly one literal in each clause to TRUE, $t(a)$ and $t(b)$ must both be FALSE. Similarly, $t(\overline{l_3})$ must be TRUE, which implies that $t(c)$ and $t(d)$ are both FALSE. The middle clause, then, cannot be satisfied by t because $t(l_2)$ is also FALSE. This contradicts the assumption that t satisfied the 1in3SAT instance. We can conclude, then, that the 3SAT instance is satisfiable if and only if the 1in3SAT instance can be satisfied by setting exactly one literal in each clause to TRUE.

To complete the proof, we must argue the reduction can be computed in polynomial time. The reduction does nothing terribly complicated. For each clause in the 3SAT instance, we create 4 new variables and 3 clauses. Therefore, the reduction takes a constant amount of time per clause in the original 3SAT instance. This is certainly polynomial in the size of the 3SAT instance.

Solution to Exercise 7.4   *Like 1in3SAT, other variants of 3SAT can also be useful in reductions. For example, in* **Not-All-Equal-3SAT** *(***NAE3SAT***), satisfying truth assignments are restricted from setting all three literals in any clause to* TRUE. *Prove that NAE3SAT, defined formally below, is* NP-*complete.*

GIVEN: 1.   *a set of Boolean variables,*
                    2.   *a collection of clauses formed from these variables and containing three distinct literals each.*

QUESTION: *Is there an assignment of values to the variables that satisfies every clause but does not set all of the literals in any clause to* TRUE?

To make things a little easier, we'll first reduce 3SAT to **NAE4SAT** and then reduce NAE4SAT to NAE3SAT. (See Moret (1998) for a similar reduction from 3SAT to NAE3SAT.) The simplest thing to do to would be to add the constant literal FALSE to every clause. That would create a 4-literal clause that can only be satisfied by a truth assignment that sets one of the three original literals to TRUE. Unfortunately, we are not allowed to have constants in a clause. We can, however, achieve the same effect by creating a new variable b and adding b to every clause.

Suppose t is a truth assignment that satisfies the NAE4SAT instance. Notice that when any NAE4SAT instance is satisfied by a truth assignment, it is also satisfied by the complement of the truth assignment, so we can assume that $t(b) = $ FALSE. (If not, start with the complement of t instead.) Since $t(b) = $ FALSE and since b is included in every clause, t must assign TRUE to at least one of the three original literals in every clause. Therefore, t also satisfies the 3SAT instance.

Next, suppose t is a truth assignment that satisfies all of the clauses in the 3SAT instance. Extend t to include an assignment for b and set $t(b) = $ FALSE. This extended version of t satisfies the NAE4SAT instance. To see this, note that because t satisfies the 3SAT instance, t assigns TRUE to some literal in every clause of the NAE4SAT instance. Since $t(b) = $ FALSE and b appears in every clause, t also assigns FALSE to a literal in every clause of the NAE4SAT instance. Therefore, the extended version of t satisfies the NAE4SAT instance without setting all of the literals in any clause to TRUE.

We can conclude, then, that the 3SAT instance is satisfiable if and only if the NAE4SAT instance created by the reduction can be satisfied without setting all of the literals in any clause to TRUE. That the reduction can be computed in polynomial time is easy to see because the reduction makes only a minor modification to each clause in the 3SAT instance. Since NAE4SAT is also clearly in NP, NAE4SAT is NP-complete.

A reduction of NAE4SAT to NAE3SAT can be accomplished using the SAT to 3SAT reduction from Figure 7.1. In particular, to split the 4-literal clause $c_j = (l_1 \vee l_2 \vee l_3 \vee l_4)$ into two 3-literal clauses, add another variable, u_j, and create two 3-literal clauses $(l_1 \vee l_2 \vee u_j)$ and $(\overline{u_j} \vee l_3 \vee l_4)$.

Suppose t is a truth assignment that satisfies the NAE4SAT instance. Extend t to include an assignment for each variable u_j in the NAE3SAT such that:

$$t(u_j) = \begin{cases} \overline{t(l_1)} & \text{if } t(l_1) = t(l_2) \\ t(l_4) & \text{otherwise} \end{cases}$$

There are two cases to consider. If $t(l_1) = t(l_2)$, it must be the case that either $t(l_3) \neq t(l_1)$ or $t(l_4) \neq t(l_1)$; otherwise all four literals would be assigned the same value, contradicting the assumption that t satisfies the NAE4SAT instance without setting all four literals in any clause to TRUE. Assume $t(l_4) \neq t(l_1)$. (A similar argument works for $t(l_3) \neq t(l_1)$.) Since $t(u_j) = t(l_4)$, which is not equal to $t(l_1)$, the first NAE3SAT clause is satisfied properly. Furthermore, $t(\overline{u}) = t(l_1) \neq t(l_4)$, so the second NAE3SAT clause is satisfied properly.

On the other hand, if $t(l_1) \neq t(l_2)$, then the first NAE3SAT clause is satisfied properly. Since $t(u_j)$ is set to $t(l_4)$, $t(\overline{u_j}) \neq t(l_4)$, which implies that the second NAE3SAT clause is also satisfied properly. Therefore, if the NAE4SAT instance can be satisfied without assigning the same value to all four literals in any clause, the NAE3SAT instance can be satisfied without assigning the same value to all three literals in any clause.

Next, suppose t is a truth assignment that satisfies the NAE3SAT instance. Again, we have two cases to consider. If $t(l_1) \neq t(l_2)$, then t satisfies the NAE4SAT clause $(l_1 \vee l_2 \vee l_3 \vee l_4)$ without assigning the same value to all four of the literals. If $t(l_1) = t(l_2)$, then $t(u_j) \neq t(l_1)$ since t satisfies the NAE3SAT instance without assigning the same value to all three literals in any clause. But this implies that $t(\overline{u_j}) = t(l_1)$, so one of $t(l_3)$ and $t(l_4)$ must not be equal to $t(l_1)$. Consequently, t satisfies $(l_1 \vee l_2 \vee l_3 \vee l_4)$ without assigning the same value to all four of the literals. Therefore, if the NAE3SAT instance can be satisfied without assigning the same value to all three literals in any clause, the NAE4SAT instance can be satisfied without assigning the same value to all four literals in any clause.

Since the reduction can certainly be computed in polynomial time, we can conclude that NAE3SAT is NP-complete.

Solution to Exercise 7.5   *Complete the reduction from SAT to DIRECTED HAMILTONIAN CYCLE*

The reduction as we left it in Chapter 7, creates a beginning vertex B, an ending vertex E, a clause vertex for each clause, and a truth-setting component for each variable. We connect B to the truth-setting component for x_1, connect x_1's truth-setting component to x_2's truth-setting component, connect x_2's to x_3's, and so on, until we connect x_n's truth-setting component to E, and then connect E back to B.

The truth-setting component for a variable x_i consists of two vertices, L_i and R_i, and two directed edges, (L_i, R_i) and (R_i, L_i). Only one of these edges can be traversed in any Hamiltonian cycle. Our intended interpretation of the truth-setting component is that if the Hamiltonian cycle traverses the truth-setting component from left to right, then the value of x_i is TRUE, while if the Hamiltonian cycle traverses the truth-setting component from right to left, then the value of x_i is FALSE. The idea was to connect each clause vertex to the truth-setting components corresponding to the literals in the clause in such a way that the clause vertex can only be included in a cycle if the truth-setting component of one of the clause's constituent variables is traversed in the direction that corresponds to satisfying the clause.

For example, Figure S.23 shows the graph created for the SAT instance consisting of the single clause $(x_1 \vee \overline{x_2})$. If the truth-setting component for x_1

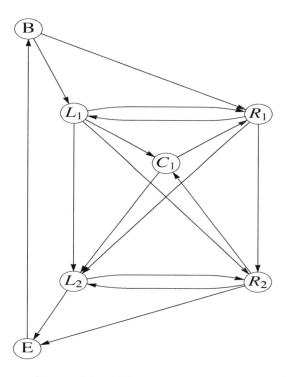

Figure S.23: The graph created for the formula with a single clause $(x_1 \vee \overline{x_2})$. C_1 can be included in the cycle either by inserting it between L_1 and R_1 or by inserting it in between R_2 and L_2.

is traversed from left to right, which corresponds to x_1 being assigned TRUE, then we can include C_1 by going from L_1 to C_1 to R_1. Similarly, if the truth-setting component for x_2 is traversed from right to left, which corresponds to x_2 being assigned FALSE, then we can include C_1 by going from R_2 to C_1 to L_2. Thus, our intent is for the clause vertex to be included only if the cycle is one we interpret as satisfying the clause.

We discovered, however, that C_1 could be included incorrectly, as shown in

Figure S.24. Notice that the clause vertex, C_1, is entered from L_1 even though x_1's truth-setting component is traversed right to left. The clause vertex is being used as a bridge from x_1's truth-setting component to x_2's truth-setting component. It is this problem that we need to correct.

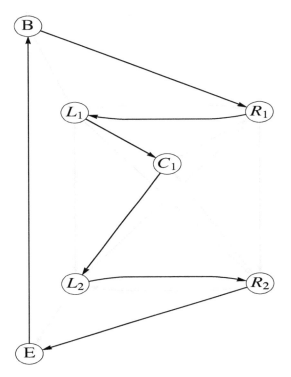

Figure S.24: A Hamiltonian cycle, shown in darker edges, that we do not want to allow for the formula $(x_1 \vee \overline{x_2})$. C_1 is used to bridge between the truth-setting component for x_1 and the truth-setting component for x_2. This allows C_1 to be included in a Hamiltonian cycle even though the corresponding truth assignment does not satisfy the clause that C_1 represents.

To prevent this sort of bridge from occurring, we will add vertices to both ends of each variable's truth-setting component. If a cycle leaves a truth-setting component prematurely by bridging through a clause vertex to another variable's truth-setting component, one of these vertices bookending the variable's truth-setting component will be left behind. In particular, on the left end of the truth-setting component for variable x_i, we will add a vertex T_i; on the right end of the truth-setting component for variable x_i, we will add a vertex F_i. Our interpretation of the truth-setting component is now even simpler: if T_i appears earlier than F_i in a Hamiltonian cycle starting at B, x_i is assigned TRUE; otherwise, x_i is assigned FALSE. (See Figure S.25.)

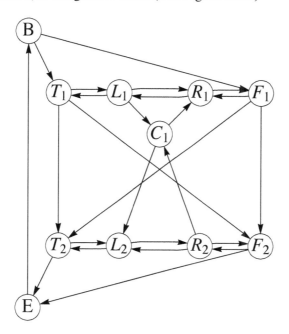

Figure S.25: The DIRECTED HAMILTONIAN CYCLE instance with T and F vertices added to bookend each variable's truth-setting component. If a cycle leaves the truth-setting component for x_1 prematurely by bridging through C_1, it will not be able to include both T_1 and F_1.

The T and F vertices of a variable's truth-setting component will be connected to the T and F vertices of the next variable's truth-setting component. Because they will not be connected to any clause vertices, we cannot use a clause vertex as a bridge out of a variable's truth-setting component to the next variable's truth-setting component without leaving one of the T and F vertices behind.

This looks great for a single clause, but will this work when we have multiple clauses? For example, suppose x_1 appears as a positive literal in two clauses, c_1 and c_2. Then we will have the left side of x_1's truth-setting component connected to both C_1 and C_2, as in Figure S.26.

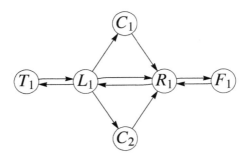

Figure S.26: A variable's truth-setting component connected to two clauses – a bad thing.

It is possible for the truth assignment to rely on x_1 to satisfy both clauses, but the x_1 component cannot take a detour through both C_1 and C_2. This is a problem. We are going to need a separate truth-setting component for each clause in which x_1 is represented by a literal. At the same time, we are going to need to make sure we cannot have one of these components setting x_1 to TRUE and another one setting x_1 to FALSE. These components, therefore, have to be connected in some way to maintain consistency. We can maintain consistency by connecting the truth-setting components for each variable together in a chain, as shown in Figure S.27.

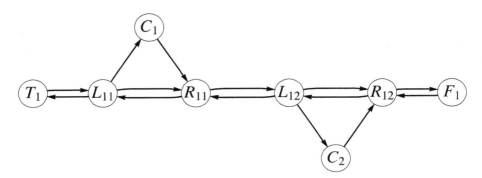

Figure S.27: A variable's truth-setting component expanded into a chain to connect multiple clauses.

With that many links to clause vertices, however, we again have the potential to bridge out to another variable's truth-setting component and then back again in a different direction through another clause vertex. See Figure S.28 for a possible example of a rogue Hamiltonian cycle.

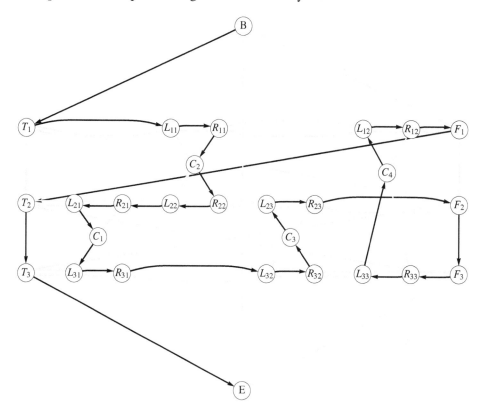

Figure S.28: A rogue Hamiltonian cycle in the DIRECTED HAMILTONIAN CY-CLE instance created for the formula $(x_2 \vee \overline{x_3}) \wedge (\overline{x_1} \vee x_2) \wedge (\overline{x_2} \vee \overline{x_3}) \wedge (\overline{x_1} \vee x_3)$. The dark edges show the cycle; the light edges show the rest of the edges in the graph. While the formula is satisfiable, this Hamiltonian cycle uses the clause vertices as bridges between truth-setting components of different variables, which is something we do not want to allow. As an additional exercise, expand this example to create an unsatisfiable formula such that the corresponding graph has a Hamiltonian cycle.

To prevent these rogue Hamiltonian cycles from occurring, we need additional vertices to separate the links in a variable's truth-setting component. These separator vertices will not be connected to any clause vertices. Their existence in the chain forces any cycle to go through all of the links in a variable's truth-setting component before going to another variable's truth-setting component. For the formula $(x_1 \vee \overline{x_2}) \wedge (\overline{x_1} \vee x_2)$, we would create the DIRECTED HAMILTONIAN CYCLE instance depicted in Figure S.29.

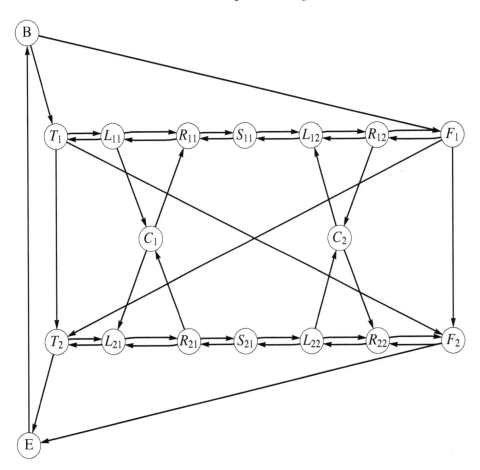

Figure S.29: The DIRECTED HAMILTONIAN CYCLE instance created for the formula $(x_1 \vee \overline{x_2}) \wedge (\overline{x_1} \vee x_2)$. S_{i1} denotes the first separator vertex for x_i's truth-setting component.

To see how the separator vertices prevent bridging from one truth-setting component to another and then back again later, consider the two possible ways for such a bridge to occur. First, a cycle may enter a clause vertex from one side of a link in the chain but not immediately return to the chain. For example, as Figure S.30 illustrates, a cycle could move from T_1 to L_{11}, from L_{11} to C_1, and then from C_1 to L_{21}.

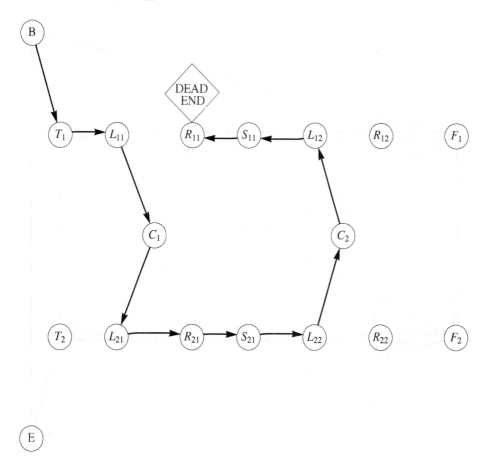

Figure S.30: The first type of bridge from x_1's truth-setting component to x_2's truth-setting component. The darker edges indicated a path that leaves the $L_{11} - R_{11}$ truth-setting component without visiting R_{11}. R_{11} becomes a dead end.

Since we moved to x_2's truth-setting component before going to R_{11}, we must follow a path back to R_{11} at some point to include it in the cycle. R_{11}, however, has become a dead end. We may be able to get back to it through S_{11}, but then there is no way out of R_{11} without going to a vertex that is already in the cycle.

The second way we could use a clause vertex as a bridge is by moving to the clause vertex after we have already included both ends of the corresponding link in the chain. For example, suppose we moved from F_2 to R_{22}, from R_{22} to L_{22}, and then from L_{22} to C_2. This creates a dead end at S_{21}, as illustrated in Figure S.31. We may be able to find a path back to S_{21}, but there is no new vertex to which the cycle can go from there.

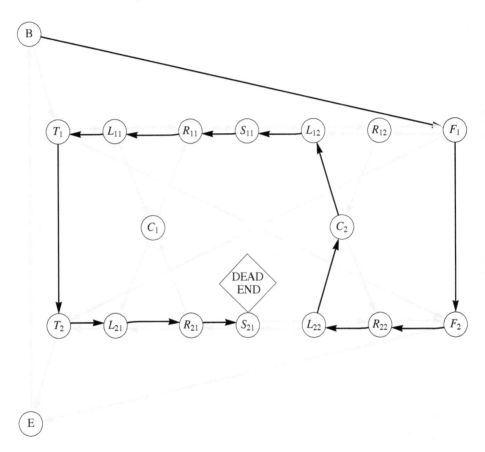

Figure S.31: The second type of bridge, this time going from x_2's truth-setting component to x_1's truth-setting component. The darker edges indicated a path that visits both R_{22} and L_{22} but does not immediately move to the separator vertex S_{21}. S_{21} becomes a dead end.

Let's summarize our argument showing that this is a valid reduction. We need to make sure we argue both ways of the if and only if in the definition of instance mapping reduction: YES instances of SAT are transformed into YES instances of DIRECTED HAMILTONIAN CYCLE and YES instances of HAMILTONIAN CYCLE must have been created from YES instances of SAT.

First, suppose there is a truth assignment t that satisfies every clause in the SAT instance. Create a Hamiltonian cycle in the graph as follows. If $t(x_1)$ is TRUE, then take the edge from B to T_1; otherwise, take the edge from B to F_1. For each variable x_i, if $t(x_i) =$ TRUE, then move left to right through the chain for x_i; otherwise move right to left through the chain for x_i. As we move through each chain, take a detour through every clause vertex C_j that has not been taken by a previous variable (i.e., a variable with a lower index). To connect the chains together, take the edge from the exiting side of the chain for x_i to the entering side of the chain for x_{i+1}. For example, if $t(x_i)$ is FALSE and $t(x_{i+1})$ is TRUE, take the edge (T_i, T_{i+1}). Finally, connect the exiting vertex in the chain for x_n to E, and connect E to B. This construction guarantees that every chain is entered and exited properly, and since every clause is satisfied by t, each clause vertex is included. Since the path created is a cycle in which each vertex is included exactly once, it is a Hamiltonian cycle.

We have argued that if the clause is satisfiable, then there is a Hamiltonian cycle. In other words, if the SAT instance is a YES instance then the DIRECTED HAMILTONIAN CYCLE instance created is also a YES instance. We now need to prove that if the DIRECTED HAMILTONIAN CYCLE instance created is a YES instance, then the SAT instance we started with is a YES instance.

Suppose there is a Hamiltonian cycle in the graph. We can create a truth assignment for the SAT instance by assigning $t(x_i)$ to TRUE if T_i appears before F_i in the cycle beginning at B and assigning $t(x_i)$ to FALSE if F_i appears before T_i in the cycle beginning at B. The Hamiltonian cycle must pass through each clause vertex. As argued above, to pass through a clause vertex, the cycle must move through the truth-setting component of one of the variables represented in the clause in the direction that corresponds to satisfying the clause, left to right if the literal is positive and right to left otherwise. This implies that the truth assignment satisfies each clause. We can conclude that the SAT instance is satisfiable if and only if the graph created contains a Hamiltonian cycle.

To complete the proof that DIRECTED HAMILTONIAN CYCLE is NP-complete, we have to argue that our reduction can be performed in polynomial time. Since we are not doing anything complicated in the creation of each vertex and each edge in the graph, the time taken will be polynomial in the size of the graph created. We need to make sure, then, that the number of vertices and edges in the graph is polynomial in the size of the SAT instance, which has n variables and m clauses.

We could encode the SAT instance by listing the literals in each clause using the index of each literal and indicating whether the literal is positive or negative. Writing down the index of a literal takes about $\log n$ bits because there are n numbers to write down. We would need one bit to indicate whether each literal is positive or negative and we would need at least one bit to separate the clauses. If n_L is the total number of literals in the formula, a reasonable encoding of the SAT instance would be $\theta(n_L \log n + m)$ bits long.

How big is the graph? We have m clause vertices, one for each clause. We have T and F vertices for each variable's truth-setting component, giving us $2n$ of these vertices overall. Inside each vertex's truth-setting component, we have three vertices for each occurrence of the variable in the formula, one each for L, R, and S. Actually, this overstates the number by n since there is no need for the last separator vertex in each variable's truth-setting component because the F vertex serves the same purpose. If there are n_L literals in the entire formula, then we have $3n_L - n$ of these vertices overall.

Since we also have one B and one E vertex, the total number of vertices is $m + n + n_L + 2$. Is this number polynomial in the size of the SAT instance, which is $\theta(n_L \log n + m)$? That n in the number of vertices makes me nervous. Why? Because n only appears in the size of the SAT instance as $\log n$ and n is exponential in $\log n$. Luckily, we can assume that each variable appears somewhere in the formula. If not, we can preprocess the formula to check for variables that do not occur. If a variable does not occur in the formula, we do not need to include a truth-setting component for that variable in the graph. This means we can assume the total number of variables is $O(n_L)$. The graph then has $O(n_L + m)$ vertices, which is certainly polynomial in $n_L \log n + m$. Since the number of edges in the graph is no more than the square of the number of vertices, the total size of the graph is polynomial in $n_L \log n + m$. This proves that our reduction of SAT to DIRECTED HAMILTONIAN CYCLE is a polynomial time reduction.

We have previously argued that HAMILTONIAN CYCLE is in NP. The same argument shows that DIRECTED HAMILTONIAN CYCLE is in NP, so we have proven that DIRECTED HAMILTONIAN CYCLE is NP-complete.

Solution to Exercise 7.6 *Prove that HAMILTONIAN CYCLE is* NP-*complete.*

This solution is based on the proof in Hopcroft and Ullman (1979).

We will reduce DIRECTED HAMILTONIAN CYCLE to the HAMILTONIAN CYCLE problem. These problems differ only in that the graph given in the DIRECTED HAMILTONIAN CYCLE problem is directed, while the just plain HAMILTONIAN CYCLE problem deals with undirected graphs. We need to create something that is equivalent to direction in the undirected HAMILTONIAN CYCLE instance created by our reduction.

Let D be the directed graph given in the instance of DIRECTED HAMILTONIAN CYCLE. We can think of a Hamiltonian cycle in an undirected graph as entering a vertex and then leaving the vertex just entered. So, for each vertex v in the DIRECTED HAMILTONIAN CYCLE instance, let's create two vertices, v^{in} and v^{out}, in the undirected HAMILTONIAN CYCLE instance. In other words, given D, create an undirected graph H as the instance of the undirected HAMILTONIAN CYCLE problem as follows:

1. For each vertex v in D, create two vertices, v^{in} and v^{out}, and one edge, (v^{in}, v^{out}), to be included in H.

2. For each edge (u, v) in D, create an edge (u^{out}, v^{in}) in H.

We would like any Hamiltonian cycle in H to be forced to go through v^{out} immediately after it goes through v^{in}. That way when we write down any Hamiltonian cycle in H starting at some vertex v_1^{in}, we'll know that it then goes through v_1^{out}, followed by some other v_2^{in}, then v_2^{out}, and so on. Figure S.32 shows an instance of the DIRECTED HAMILTONIAN CYCLE problem and the corresponding undirected graph created.

It looks like we might have a problem that we didn't anticipate. Because v_4^{in} is connected to both v_2^{out} and v_3^{out} in the example shown in Figure S.32(b), it is possible to create a Hamiltonian cycle that includes the sequence, v_2^{out}, v_4^{in}, v_3^{out}, as shown in Figure S.33. This is not a good thing.

To prevent this sort of Hamiltonian cycle from occurring, we need to have a vertex in each *in-out* component that is not connected to any other in-out component. This can be done by placing an additional vertex in between v^{in} and v^{out}. Let's call this new vertex v^{mid}. So in addition to the vertices and edges described above, for each vertex v in D, create a vertex v^{mid} in H and

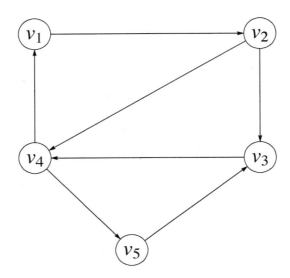

a) A DIRECTED HAMILTONIAN CYCLE instance.

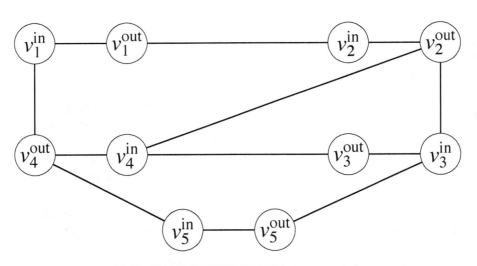

b) The HAMILTONIAN CYCLE instance created.

Figure S.32: A instance of the DIRECTED HAMILTONIAN CYCLE problem and the corresponding undirected graph created by splitting vertices into *in* and *out* vertices.

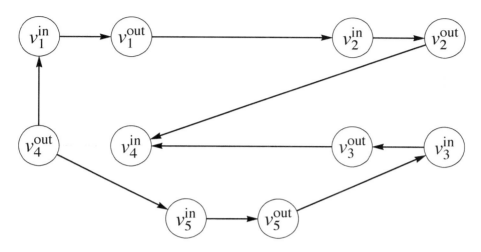

Figure S.33: A cycle, shown with dark edges, that we do not want to allow. The cycle moves to from v_4^{in} to v_3^{out} rather than proceeding directly from v_4^{in} to v_4^{out} as desired.

add edges (v^{in}, v^{mid}) and (v^{mid}, v^{out}) to H. Figure S.34 shows the new instance of HAMILTONIAN CYCLE created from the DIRECTED HAMILTONIAN CYCLE instance in Figure S.32(a).

To prove more formally that our reduction works, suppose first that D contains a Hamiltonian cycle, $v_1, v_2, \ldots, v_n$. Then H contains a cycle, v_1^{in}, v_1^{mid}, $v_1^{out}, v_2^{in}, v_2^{mid}, v_2^{out}, \ldots, v_n^{in}, v_n^{mid}, v_n^{out}$. Because of the way H is constructed from D, this cycle is a Hamiltonian cycle.

Next suppose that H contains a Hamiltonian cycle. Since we can view a cycle as starting at any vertex, let's start at v_1^{in}. If the cycle does not go directly to v_1^{mid}, then v_1^{mid} must be reached later in the cycle by crossing the edge from v_1^{out}. This, however, would leave v_1^{mid} as a dead end. Therefore, the cycle proceeds from v_1^{in} to v_1^{mid} and then goes directly to v_1^{out} since there is nowhere else to go from v_1^{mid}. Because of the way the graph is constructed, from v_1^{out} the cycle must go to some v_i^{in}. By the same argument we used for v_1, from vertex v_i^{in}, the cycle must move to v_i^{mid}, then to v_i^{out}, and then to some other v_k^{in}. We can see, then, that any Hamiltonian cycle in H will have the form: v_1^{in}, v_1^{mid}, $v_1^{out}, v_2^{in}, v_2^{mid}, v_2^{out}, \ldots, v_n^{in}, v_n^{mid}, v_n^{out}$. If H contains such a cycle, then $v_1, v_2, \ldots, v_n$ is a Hamiltonian cycle in D.

We can conclude that D is a YES instance of DIRECTED HAMILTONIAN CYCLE if and only if H is a YES instance of HAMILTONIAN CYCLE. All

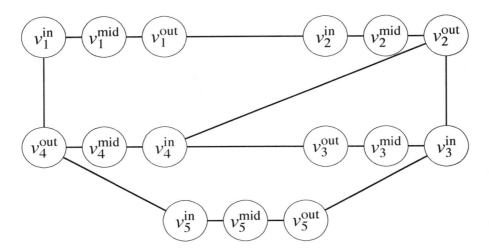

Figure S.34: The final HAMILTONIAN CYCLE instance using v^{mid} to ensure the proper movement through each vertex's component.

that is left to do is to show that the reduction can be computed in polynomial time. For each vertex v in D, the reduction creates 3 vertices and 2 edges for the v^{in}-v^{mid}-v^{out} component in H. For each edge (u, v) in D, the reduction creates one additional edge, (u_{out}, v_{in}), in H. Therefore, the total amount of time needed to construct H is $O(m + n)$, where n is the number of vertices and m is the number of edges in D. This is polynomial in the size of D.

Solutions for Chapter 8: Approximation Algorithms

Solution to Exercise 8.1 *Design a polynomial time verifier for 0-1 KNAP-SACK to show that 0-1 KNAPSACK is in* NP.

The verifier takes a subset of the objects as the certificate. It simply verifies that the sum of the values of the objects in the subset is at least V and that the sum of the costs of the objects in the subset is at most B. This requires one simple pass through the objects that can be done in polynomial time.

Solution to Exercise 8.2 *Provide a formal instance mapping reduction of SUBSET-SUM to 0-1 KNAPSACK.*

Given an instance of SUBSET-SUM consisting of numbers $x_1, x_2, \ldots, x_n$ and target value T, create an instance of 0-1 KNAPSACK consisting of objects $a_1, a_2, \ldots, a_n$ with target value T, budget T, object values $v(a_i) = x_i$ for each i, and costs $c(a_i) = x_i$ for each i. Now, suppose the SUBSET-SUM instance is a YES instance. Then there is a subset S of the numbers such that the sum of the numbers in the subset is exactly T. Since the numbers in the subset correspond to the values and costs of the objects in the 0-1 KNAPSACK instance, the sum of the numbers in S is equal to both the sum of the costs and the sum of the values of the corresponding objects. Therefore, we have:

$$\sum_{x \in S} v(x) = T \qquad \text{and} \qquad \sum_{x \in S} c(x) = T$$

Since the target value and the budget in the 0-1 KNAPSACK instance are both T, S is a solution to the 0-1 KNAPSACK instance.

Next, suppose the reduction creates a YES instance of the 0-1 KNAP-SACK problem. Then there is a subset S of the objects such that the sum of the values of the objects in S is at least T and the sum of the costs of the objects in S is at most T. But since the value of an object is equal to the cost of the object, the sum of the values of the objects in S must be exactly T. Furthermore, since the value of each object corresponds to a number in the SUBSET-SUM instance, the corresponding subset of numbers must sum to T. Therefore, the SUBSET-SUM instance must be a YES instance.

Solution to Exercise 8.3   *Show that the TRAVELING SALESMAN OPTI-MIZATION PROBLEM is* NP-*hard.*

A simple Turing reduction will suffice. If we had an algorithm to solve the TRAVELING SALESMAN OPTIMIZATION PROBLEM, we could simply run that algorithm and compare the total cost of the solution to the budget. If the total cost of the optimal solution is less than the budget, then the TSP instance is a YES instance; otherwise, it is a NO instance. The TRAVELING SALESMAN OPTIMIZATION PROBLEM is therefore NP-hard.

Solution to Exercise 8.4   *It is generally straightforward to show that an op-timization version of an* NP-*complete decision problem is* NP-*hard. How-ever, an optimization problem may be "harder" than the corresponding deci-sion problem. For example, consider an optimization version of 2SAT called* **MAX2SAT**:

GIVEN: 1. *a set of Boolean variables;*
              2. *a collection of distinct clauses, each containing ex-actly two literals constructed from two different vari-ables.*

OBJECTIVE: *Find an assignment of values to the Boolean variables such that the number of satisfied clauses is maximized.*

To solve 2SAT, we must determine whether there exists a truth assignment that satisfies every clause. In Exercise 6.3, we showed that this could be done in polynomial time. To solve MAX2SAT, we need to return a truth assignment that satisfies the maximum number of clauses possible. Show that MAX2SAT is NP-*hard.*

This solution was inspired by the final exam solutions of two students, Bill Stitson and Ari Morse, from my Theory of Computation class in the spring of 2009.

Let's try a reduction from NAE3SAT, which we proved is NP-complete in Exercise 7.4. NAE3SAT is defined formally as follows:

GIVEN: 1. a set of Boolean variables;

    2.   a collection of clauses formed from these variables and containing three distinct literals each.

QUESTION: Is there an assignment of values to the variables that satisfies every clause but does not set all of the literals in any clause to TRUE?

There are two obvious differences between NAE3SAT and MAX2SAT. First, NAE3SAT has to set a literal in each clause to TRUE *and* a literal in each clause to FALSE, while MAX2SAT can satisfy a clause in the typical way by setting at least one literal in the clause to TRUE. The second difference is that NAE3SAT has three literals in each clause, while MAX2SAT only has two. (Note that we will assume that x_i and $\overline{x}_i$ never appear in the same NAE3SAT clause for any i. If they do, that clause is satisfied by every truth assignment and can be ignored. If necessary, we can preprocess the NAE3SAT instance to remove such clauses.)

To deal with the first difference, consider any clause $(l_1 \vee l_2 \vee l_3)$ in the NAE3SAT instance, where each l_i represents a literal. To satisfy this clause without setting all three of the literals to TRUE, at least one of the literals must be set to TRUE and at least one must be set to FALSE. This is equivalent to satisfying two clauses: $(l_1 \vee l_2 \vee l_3)$ and $(\overline{l}_1 \vee \overline{l}_2 \vee \overline{l}_3)$. So, for every clause $(l_1 \vee l_2 \vee l_3)$ in the NAE3SAT instance, we will consider the instance to include two clauses – the original clause and a companion clause: $(\overline{l}_1 \vee \overline{l}_2 \vee \overline{l}_3)$.

To deal with the difference in clause size, we need to create a set of 2-literal clauses for each pair of clauses $(l_1 \vee l_2 \vee l_3)$ and $(\overline{l}_1 \vee \overline{l}_2 \vee \overline{l}_3)$ representing a single NAE3SAT clause. We would like a fixed number of the MAX2SAT clauses in the set to be satisfied whenever both clauses in the NAE3SAT pair are satisfied. For example, for the pair $(l_1 \vee l_2 \vee l_3)$ and $(\overline{l}_1 \vee \overline{l}_2 \vee \overline{l}_3)$, we could create six clauses: $(l_1 \vee l_2)$, $(l_1 \vee l_3)$, $(l_2 \vee l_3)$, $(\overline{l}_1 \vee \overline{l}_2)$, $(\overline{l}_1 \vee \overline{l}_3)$, $(\overline{l}_2 \vee \overline{l}_3)$. While these six clauses are not equivalent to the original three clauses, we have maintained a connection between each pair of literals that appear together in a NAE3SAT clause. Figure S.35 shows the number of clauses in this set that are satisfied for each possible assignment to the three literals l_1, l_2, and l_3.

As we can from the figure, 5 of the 6 clauses will be satisfied by a truth assignment when the NA3SAT clause is satisfied, but only 3 of the 6 clauses will be satisfied when the NAE3SAT clause is not satisfied by a truth assignment. This is the kind of correspondence we need between satisfying a clause in the NAE3SAT instance and satisfying a fixed fraction of the clauses in the MAX2SAT instance.

	TTT	TTF	TFT	TFF	FTT	FTF	FFT	FFF
$(l_1 \vee l_2)$	T	T	T	T	T	T	F	F
$(l_1 \vee l_3)$	T	T	T	T	T	F	T	F
$(l_2 \vee l_3)$	T	T	T	F	T	T	T	F
$(\overline{l_1} \vee \overline{l_2})$	F	F	T	T	T	T	T	T
$(\overline{l_1} \vee \overline{l_3})$	F	T	F	T	T	T	T	T
$(\overline{l_2} \vee \overline{l_3})$	F	T	T	T	F	T	T	T
Number satisfied	3	5	5	5	5	5	5	3

Figure S.35: A table detailing the number of clauses in the MAX2SAT instance that are satisfied by each possible truth assignment for literals l_1, l_2, and l_3. The columns represent assignments to the three variables. For example TFT indicates that l_1 is assigned TRUE, l_2 is assigned FALSE, and l_3 is assigned TRUE. The rows indicate whether the corresponding clause evaluates to TRUE or FALSE, with the final row indicating the number of clauses in the set that are satisfied.

We still need to be careful because clauses do not exist in isolation. If the NAE3SAT instance contains clause $c_1 = (x_1 \vee x_2 \vee x_3)$ and clause $c_2 = (x_1 \vee x_2 \vee \overline{x_3})$, our current reduction will create the 2-literal clause $(x_1 \vee x_2)$ twice, once for c_1 and once for c_2. However, we do not allow duplicate clauses in our MAX2SAT instances.

To avoid duplicates, we need to make sure we have distinct variables for each clause. For example, for clause $c_j = (x_1 \vee x_2 \vee x_3)$, we need to create three new variables, x_{1j}, x_{2j}, and x_{3j}, and six 2-literal clauses:

$$(x_{1j} \vee x_{2j}), (x_{1j} \vee x_{3j}), (x_{2j} \vee x_{3j}), (\overline{x_{1j}} \vee \overline{x_{2j}}), (\overline{x_{1j}} \vee \overline{x_{3j}}), (\overline{x_{2j}} \vee \overline{x_{3j}}).$$

With this construction, we will never have duplicate clauses because each set of six clauses has unique variables.

Having unique variables in each set, however, leads to another problem. We need to make sure that the truth assignments returned as solutions for MAX2SAT consistently assign values to the variables whenever the NAE3SAT instance is a YES instance. For example, if there are two clauses, $c_1 = (x_1 \vee x_2 \vee x_3)$ and $c_2 = (x_1 \vee x_4 \vee x_5)$ in the NAE3SAT instance, our reduction will create the following two sets of six clauses:

$$(x_{11} \vee x_{21}), (x_{11} \vee x_{31}), (x_{21} \vee x_{31}), (\overline{x_{11}} \vee \overline{x_{21}}), (\overline{x_{11}} \vee \overline{x_{31}}), (\overline{x_{21}} \vee \overline{x_{31}})$$

$$(x_{12} \vee x_{42}), (x_{12} \vee x_{52}), (x_{42} \vee x_{52}), (\overline{x_{12}} \vee \overline{x_{42}}), (\overline{x_{12}} \vee \overline{x_{52}}), (\overline{x_{42}} \vee \overline{x_{52}})$$

The variable x_1 is represented in the first set by x_{11} and in the second set by x_{12}. We would like any truth assignments returned by our MAX2SAT algorithm to be forced, or at least strongly encouraged, to set these two variables to the same value. This can be accomplished by having an extra variable, z_i, in the MAX2SAT instance for each variable, x_i, in the NAE3SAT instance. The z_i's will be tightly coupled with each of the corresponding x_{ij}'s by including the clauses $(\overline{z_i} \vee x_{ij})$ and $(z_i \vee \overline{x_{ij}})$. These clauses are equivalent to the logical statements $z_i \Rightarrow x_{ij}$ and $\overline{z_i} \Rightarrow \overline{x_{ij}}$. Taken together, the clauses represent the statement $z_i = x_{ij}$.

We will have a total of $6m$ of these *truth-setting* clauses, two for each of the $3m$ literals in the NAE3SAT instance. We can satisfy each of the $6m$ truth-setting clauses simply by assigning the same value to z_i and x_{ij}, for each i and j. As we determined from Figure S.35, we can satisfy at most five clauses in each set of six clauses representing a single NAE3SAT clause. Since there is one set of these six MAX2SAT clauses for each of the m NAE3SAT clauses, that adds a total of $5m$ clauses that can be satisfied. The maximum number of clauses that can be satisfied in the MAX2SAT instance is therefore $11m$.

Consider a truth assignment t^{NAE} that satisfies the NAE3SAT instance without assigning TRUE to all three of the literals in any clause. Create a truth assignment t^{MAX} for the MAX2SAT instance by setting $t^{MAX}(x_{ij}) = t^{NAE}(x_i)$ for each i and j, and setting $t^{MAX}(z_i) = t^{NAE}(x_i)$, for each i. Since $t^{MAX}(z_i) = t^{MAX}(x_{ij})$ for each i and j, t^{MAX} satisfies all $6m$ of the truth-setting clauses. Furthermore, since t^{NAE} satisfies each NAE3SAT clause without setting all three of the literals in any clause to TRUE and since $t^{MAX}(x_{ij}) = t^{NAE}(x_i)$ for each i and j, t^{MAX} satisfies five out of every set of six clauses representing a single NAE3SAT clause, as demonstrated in Figure S.35. Therefore, t^{MAX} satisfies $11m$ clauses.

Next, suppose t^{MAX} is a truth assignment that satisfies $11m$ of the MAX-2SAT clauses. Since t^{MAX} can satisfy at most five out of every set of six clauses representing a single NAE3SAT clause for a total of $5m$ clauses, it must satisfy all of the $6m$ truth-setting clauses. That means $t^{MAX}(x_{ij}) = t^{MAX}(z_i)$ for every i and j. Let t^{NAE} be a truth assignment for the NAE3SAT instance such that $t^{NAE}(x_i) = t^{MAX}(z_i)$. Since $t^{MAX}(x_{ij}) = t^{MAX}(z_i)$ for every i and j, $t^{MAX}(x_{ij}) = t^{NAE}(x_i)$ for every i and j, As Figure S.35 shows, when t^{MAX} satisfies five out of every set of six clauses representing a single NAE3SAT clause, t^{NAE} satisfies the NAE3SAT instance without setting all three of the literals in any clause to TRUE.

Since there is a truth assignment that satisfies the NAE3SAT instance without setting all three of the literals in any clause to TRUE if and only if $11m$ is the maximum number of clauses that can be satisfied in the MAX2SAT instance, we can use an algorithm for MAX2SAT to solve NAE3SAT by simply comparing the number of clauses satisfied by the returned solution to $11m$. Therefore, MAX2SAT is NP-hard.

Solution to Exercise 8.5 *Show the approximation ratio of GreedyKnapsack, the algorithm without the a_{max} modification, is arbitrarily bad.*

This solution is based on Example 2.1 in Ausiello et al. (1999).

We need to show that for any constant d, there is an instance for which the approximation ratio, $\frac{OPT}{Value(G)}$, is at least d. A bad instance for GreedyKnapsack would be one in which the most valuable item is extremely valuable but also extremely costly, while there are a number of items with little value but which have a higher value to cost ratio than the item with the highest value. Let's let the cost of the most valuable item be equal to the budget so there is no money left to pay for any other item once the most valuable item is taken. Let's also set things up so that the value to cost ratio of the most valuable item is a little less than 1, while the value to cost ratio of all of the other items is 1. Setting the value of the most valuable item to $B-1$ and setting the cost and value of every other item to 1 does this trick. In other words, let:

$$v(a_i) = 1 \qquad \text{for } i = 1, \ldots, n-1$$
$$c(a_i) = 1 \qquad \text{for } i = 1, \ldots, n-1$$
$$v(a_n) = B - 1$$
$$c(a_n) = B$$

To complete the specification of the instance, the only thing left to do is to choose a value for B. We need B to be really large since $B-1$ will be the value of the optimal solution. If B is at least $n-1$, then GreedyKnapsack will choose the first $n-1$ items as the solution. This would result in a value of $n-1$ since the first $n-1$ items each have a value of 1. The approximation ratio would then be $(B-1)/(n-1)$. We want this ratio to be at least d, so let's let $B = dn$. The approximation ratio is then $(dn-1)/(n-1)$, which is bigger than d.

Solution to Exercise 8.6 *Design an algorithm that uses the MinCost and Take tables returned by SolveMaximumKnapsack from Figure 8.8 to construct* *the corresponding optimal set of objects for the given instance of MAXIMUM KNAPSACK.*

First find the value of the optimal solution by looking in row n of the *MinCost* table for the largest target value that can be achieved at a cost of at most B. If that cost appears in column t, then t is the value of the corresponding optimal solution. For example, Figure S.36 shows the *MinCost* table for the example in Figure 8.1. The largest target value that can be achieved at a cost of at most 100 is 150.

	0	1	...	76	...	103	...	150	151	...	178	...	253
						target value						
$i=1$	0	51	...	51	...	∞	...	∞	∞	...	∞	...	∞
$i=2$	0	50	...	51	...	101	...	101	101	...	∞	...	∞
$i=3$	0	50	...	51	...	100	...	100	101	...	151	...	∞

Figure S.36: The *MinCost* table for the example in Figure 8.1. In the example, $v(a_1) = 102$, $c(a_1) = 51$, $v(a_2) = 75$, $c(a_2) = 50$, $v(a_3) = 75$, and $c(a_3) = 50$. The columns shown are the points at which the minimum cost changes. A target value of 253 is unachievable even with all three object available. The maximum achievable value with all three objects available and a budget of 100 is 150. This can be seen from the last row, which at column 151 shows a switch from a minimum cost of 100, which fits into the budget, to a minimum cost of 101, which does not.

We can use this information along with the *Take* table to construct the corresponding solution. *Take*$[n,t]$ indicates whether object n is included in the solution. If *Take*$[n,t]$ is NO, then we must achieve a value of t using a subset of the first $n-1$ objects. To determine whether object $n-1$ is included in our solution when n is not included, we can look at *Take*$[n-1,t]$. If *Take*$[n,t]$ is YES, then n is included and the next target to consider is $t-v(n)$. In other words, since n adds $v(n)$ to the value of the solution, the total value of the other objects in our solution must be $t-v(n)$. Therefore, to determine whether object $n-1$ is included in our solution when n is included, we can look at *Take*$[n-1,t-v(n)]$. This process repeats with objects $n-2$, $n-3$, and so on, until we have considered every object. Figure S.37 shows the *Take* table corresponding to the *MinCost* table from Figure S.36. The pseudocode for the algorithm to construct the solution appears in Figure S.38.

	0	1	...	75	76	...	103	...	150	151	...	178	...
$i=1$	N	Y	...	Y	Y	...	N	...	N	N	...	N	...
$i=2$	N	Y	...	Y	N	...	Y	...	Y	Y	...	N	...
$i=3$	N	N	...	N	N	...	Y	...	Y	N	...	Y	...

target value

Figure S.37: The *Take* table corresponding to the *MinCost* table in Figure S.36. The circled cells show the cells that need to be considered when building the solution. With a budget of 100, the maximum achievable target value is 150. Since *Take*[3, 150] is YES, the solution includes the third object. Subtracting the value of object 3, which is 75, away from 150 tells us the next column we need to consider. *Take*[2, 75] is YES, which indicates the solution includes object 2. Finally, *Take*[1, 0] tells us that the solution does not include object 1.

ConstructMaxKnapsackSolution$(A, n, v, c, B, MinCost, Take)$

1 Set a_{max} to index of object with max value (break ties however you like)
2 Initialize *optimalValue* to $n \cdot v(a_{max})$
3 **while** *optimalValue* > 0 AND *MinCost*$[n, optimalValue] > B$
4   Decrement *optimalValue* by 1
5 **end while**
6 Let *Solution* be a list that is initially empty
7 Set $i = n$
8 Set $t = optimalValue$
9 **while** $i > 0$ AND $t > 0$
10   **if** *Take*$[i, t]$ is YES
11   **then begin**
12   Append i to *Solution*   // object i was chosen for *MinCost*$[i, t]$
13   Set $t = t - v(i)$ // update t to indicate value received for i
14   **end**
15   Set $i = i - 1$
16 **end while**
17 **return** *Solution* and *optimalValue*

Figure S.38: An algorithm that returns the list of objects taken in the optimal solution computed by SolveMaximumKnapsack, from Figure 8.8. The algorithm takes as parameters an instance of the MAXIMUM KNAPSACK problem as well as the *MinCost* and *Take* arrays computed by SolveMaximumKnapsack on that instance.

Solution to Exercise 8.7 *Prove Theorem 8.4.*

We need to prove that if B is strongly NP-complete, then B cannot be solved by a pseudo-polynomial time algorithm unless $P = NP$. Consider a pseudo-polynomial time algorithm for B. If the largest magnitude of any number in a problem instance is M, then the running time of a pseudo-polynomial time algorithm on that problem instance is $O(n^c M^d)$, for some constants c and d. Since B is strongly NP-hard, it is NP-hard even when restricted to instances in which M is $O(n^k)$ for some constant k. On these restricted instances of B, the pseudo-polynomial time algorithm runs in $O(n^c (n^k)^d)$ time. Since c, d, and k are constants and $n^c (n^k)^d = n^{c+kd}$, this running time is polynomial in the size of the problem instance. Therefore, a pseudo-polynomial time algorithm for B is a polynomial time algorithm on the restricted instances of B. Because B is strongly NP-hard, no such algorithm exists unless $P = NP$.

Solution to Exercise 8.8 *Develop a polynomial time c-approximation algorithm for the METRIC TRAVELING SALESMAN PROBLEM. A polynomial time $\frac{3}{2}$-approximation algorithm is known, but there are a couple of simpler 2-approximations. You may want to review what you know (or don't know) about* **minimum spanning trees**.

This solution is based on the presentations in Cormen, Leiserson, Rivest, and Stein (2009) and Williamson and Shmoys (2011).

The key insight into developing approximation algorithms for METRIC TSP is that when we remove any single edge from a TSP tour, we are left with a path that touches every vertex in the graph. Such a path is said to *span* the graph. Since there are no cycles in the path, the path is a tree. A tree that spans the graph is called a **spanning tree**. The cost of the optimal tour, then, must be at least as large as the cost of a minimum cost spanning tree. A minimum spanning tree can be found in polynomial time, using Prim's algorithm for example. (See Cormen, Leiserson, Rivest, and Stein (2009).) Might there be a way to build a decent tour based on a minimum spanning tree? Consider the graph in Figure S.39, which satisfies the triangle inequality. A minimum spanning tree for the graph appears in Figure S.40.

Now imagine that in our tour through the vertices we are only allowed to traverse edges in this minimum spanning tree. Figure S.41 shows the way in which the tour would proceed. Starting at v_1, the tour would go to v_2, then

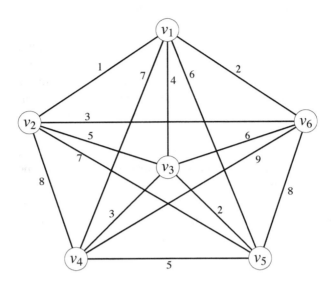

Figure S.39: A METRIC TSP instance. You can verify that the edges satisfy the triangle inequality.

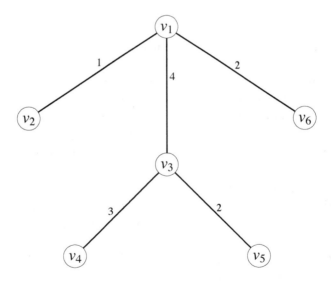

Figure S.40: A minimum spanning tree for the METRIC TSP instance in Figure S.39.

back to v_1, to v_3, to v_4, back to v_3, to v_5, back to v_3 again, back to v_1 again, on to v_6, and finally back to v_1 to conclude the tour. Notice that each edge in the minimum spanning tree is covered twice, so the cost of this tour is twice the cost of the minimum spanning tree.

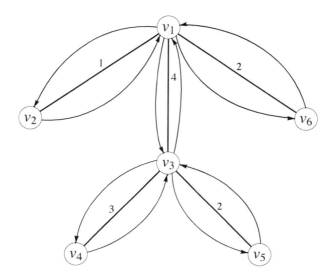

Figure S.41: The arrows indicate the steps required to walk through the vertices of the graph using only the edges in the minimum spanning tree shown in Figure S.40. (As a practical exercise, recreate this figure as a balloon puppet.)

In constructing a TSP tour, however, we are not restricted to use only the edges in a given minimum spanning tree. Instead, we can take shortcuts through the minimum spanning tree. For example, rather than backtracking from v_2 to v_1 to get to v_3, we can go directly to v_3. The tour created by shortcutting our way through the minimum spanning tree is shown in Figure S.42.

Notice that the cost of the edge from v_2 to v_3 is no more than the cost of the path from v_2 through v_1 to v_3. This is because of the triangle inequality. The same type of shortcut can be taken from v_5 to v_6. Again, the cost of the edge from v_5 to v_6 is no more than the cost of the path from v_5, through v_3 and v_1, to v_6. Because of the triangle inequality, the TSP tour found by "shortcutting" a minimum spanning tree has a cost that is no more than the cost of the tour created by backtracking our way through the minimum spanning tree. The cost of the backtracking tour is no more than twice the cost of the minimum

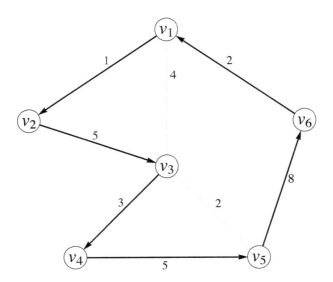

Figure S.42: The TSP tour found by "shortcutting" the minimum spanning tree in Figure S.41. The darker edges with arrows show the edges in the tour, while the lighter edges show edges in the minimum spanning tree that are not in the tour. The cost of this tour is 24. The optimal tour, which is shown in Figure S.43 is 22.

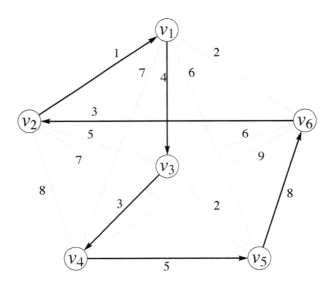

Figure S.43: The optimal TSP tour for the graph in Figure S.39. The darker edges with arrows show the edges in the tour. The cost of the optimal tour is 22.

spanning tree. Since the cost of the minimum spanning tree is a lower bound on the cost of the optimal TSP tour, the TSP tour found by shortcutting a minimum spanning tree has a cost that is at most twice the cost of the optimal TSP tour. Thus, the algorithm that finds a minimum spanning tree and then traverses the tree using shortcuts rather than backtracking is a 2-approximation for METRIC TSP.

   This shortcutting technique can be improved to develop a $\frac{3}{2}$-approximation algorithm known as Christofides' Algorithm. See Williamson and Shmoys (2011) for details.

Solutions for Chapter 9: Heuristics

Solution to Exercise 9.1   *Design a local search algorithm for the problem below, which is known as* **SCHEDULING ON IDENTICAL PARALLEL MACHINES**. *Show that your algorithm is a 2-approximation.*

GIVEN: 1. m identical machines that each can process one job at a time;

2. n jobs, where each job j has a processing time p_j.

OBJECTIVE: Find an assignment of jobs to machines so that the time the last job completes is minimized. Note that each machine will be given a set of jobs. The total amount of processing time assigned to a machine is the time at which the last job on that machine is completed.

For example, if we have 2 machines and 5 jobs with processing times 2, 4, 5, 8, *and* 10, *the optimal schedule is to assign the jobs with processing times 4 and 10 to one machine and to assign the jobs with processing times 2, 5, and 8 to the other machine. The first machine finishes at time* 14, *while the second machine finishes at time* 15. *The last job, then, completes at time 15. A suboptimal solution would be to assign the jobs with times 10 and 8 to one machine and the jobs with times 2, 4, and 5 to the other. In this suboptimal schedule, the last job completes at time 18.*

This solution is adapted from Williamson and Shmoys (2011).

To describe a local search algorithm, we need to describe the candidate solutions and specify the neighborhood relation and the selection mechanism. In this algorithm, a candidate solution consists of an assignment of jobs to machines. The neighbors of any candidate solution consist of all schedules in which the last job to complete on any machine is switched to another machine. The selection mechanism chooses the neighbor with the greatest decrease in completion time for the job that is switched. In other words, the selection mechanism will switch the job to the machine that becomes idle earliest.

The algorithm starts with a randomly chosen assignment of jobs to machines, moving to new candidate solutions as specified by the selection mechanism until there is no way to decrease the completion time of the last job processed. We need to analyze the running time of this algorithm and prove that it is a 2-approximation.

First, let's consider the running time. The algorithm moves the job with the latest completion time to the machine with the earliest completion time. Let *From* be the machine from which the job was moved and *To* be the machine to which the job was moved. *From*'s completion time has increased, while *To*'s completion time has decreased. However, the completion time of *To* must be at least as large as *From*'s completion time was prior to the move. If not, the job would not have been moved at all because the job's completion time would not have decreased. Figure S.44 illustrates this point. This means that the earliest completion time among the machines does not decrease during the execution of the algorithm.

Machine	Scheduled Jobs

Figure S.44: When job j moves from machine *From* to machine *To*, the completion time of j decreases. Time is shown, starting at zero, along the top of each bar representing a machine's schedule, where C_T is the completion time of machine *To* before the move and C_F is the completion time of machine *From* after the move. Because the completion time of j decreases, it must be the case that $C_T \leq C_F$. Since the completion time of no other machine changes during this move, the earliest completion time among all of the machines cannot decrease.

Because the earliest completion time among the machines does not decrease, the completion of any job can only decrease when it is moved for the first time. (This argument is illustrated in Figure S.45.) But the selection mechanism will not move a job unless the job's completion time decreases. Therefore, no job can be moved twice. Consequently, the number of iterations of the algorithm must be $O(n)$.

In each iteration, the algorithm needs to find the earliest completion time among the m machines. This can easily be done in $O(m)$ time. Since there are $O(n)$ iterations, this gives us a total running time of $O(mn)$. We can assume that m is $O(n)$; otherwise there are more machines than jobs and there is little to do as far as scheduling goes. The running time is therefore $O(n^2)$, which is

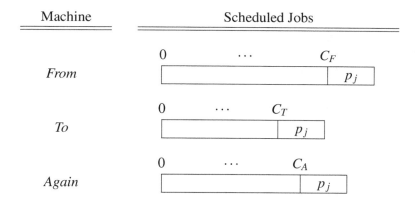

Figure S.45: Before the iteration in which job j moves from machine *From* to machine *To*, the completion time of *To*, C_T, is the earliest completion time among the machines. To move j again, say to machine *Again*, the completion time of *Again*, C_A, must be at least as large as C_T because the earliest completion time among the machines does not decrease after any iteration. But then the completion time for job j will not decrease with j's move to *Again*. Since the selection mechanism will only move j if j's completion time is decreased, j cannot be moved a second time.

polynomial in the size of the problem instance.

Next we need to argue that this local search algorithm returns a schedule with an overall completion time that is no more than twice the completion time of the optimal schedule. To do that, we need to come up with upper bounds on the optimal solution and show that the completion time of the solution returned is no more than twice the upper bound.

Let j be the job in the solution returned that finishes last. Since j cannot be switched to another machine to facilitate an earlier completion time for j, none of the machines are idle before j starts. Let $Start_j$ be j's starting time. Since none of the machines are idle at time $Start_j$, the sum of all of the processing times must be at least $m \cdot Start_j$. Thus we have $m \cdot Start_j \leq \sum_{i=1}^{n} p_i$, which implies:

$$Start_j \leq \frac{1}{m} \sum_{i=1}^{n} p_i$$

This means that $Start_j$ is no more than the average processing time of the machines. But the completion time of some machine in any solution, including the optimal solution, must be at least as large as the average processing time of the machines. Therefore, $Start_j \leq$ OPT. Furthermore, OPT is at least as large as the processing time for j since the optimal solution must run j on some machine. Since j's completion time is $Start_j + p_j$ and both the start time and the processing time are no more than OPT, j's completion time is no more than $2 \cdot$ OPT. The local search algorithm is therefore a 2-approximation.

Solution to Exercise 9.2   *Implement the DPPL algorithm in your favorite programming language and run experiments on randomly generated 3SAT instances with varying ratios of clauses to variables. Keep track of the running time of your program and plot the running time against the clause to variable ratio. Pay particular attention to the behavior of the algorithm near the critical point.*

You didn't really expect me to include code in a real programming language here, did you?

Solutions for Chapter 10: Space

Solution to Exercise 10.1   *Reduce 3SAT to QSAT to show that QSAT is* NP-*hard.*

This one is so easy it may be hard. Determining whether a 3SAT instance consisting of variables x_1, x_2, ..., x_n and clauses $c_1, c_2, \ldots, c_m$ is satisfiable is equivalent to determining whether the following quantified Boolean formula is TRUE:

$$\exists x_1 \exists x_2 \ldots \exists x_n [c_1 \wedge c_2 \wedge \ldots \wedge c_m]$$

We can read this quantified Boolean formula as: do there exist values for x_1 through x_n such that all of the clauses are satisfied? This is exactly the question we ask in 3SAT. To put this into the correct form for QSAT, the existial quantifiers must alternate with universal quantifiers. So, create n new variables, $y_1, y_2, \ldots, y_n$, and n new clauses, $(y_1 \vee \overline{y_1})$, $(y_2 \vee \overline{y_2})$, ..., $(y_n \vee \overline{y_n})$. Since each of these new clauses is TRUE for each i no matter what value we assign to y_i, determining whether the 3SAT instance is satisfiable is equivalent to determining where the following quantified formula is TRUE:

$$\exists x_1 \forall y_1 \exists x_2 \forall y_2 \ldots \exists x_n \forall y_n [c_1 \wedge c_2 \wedge \ldots \wedge c_m \wedge (y_1 \vee \overline{y_1}) \wedge (y_2 \vee \overline{y_2}) \ldots (y_n \vee \overline{y_n})].$$

Solution to Exercise 10.2   *Design an algorithm to solve QSAT using* $O(n)$ *space.*

The algorithm in Figure 10.2 uses $\Theta(n \log n)$ space because it uses $\Theta(\log n)$ bits to store the local variable i in binary on the stack. We can eliminate the $\log n$ in the running time by making i a global variable. At the beginning of each subroutine, we will increment i. Prior to returning from each subroutine, we will decrement i. The revised pseudocode for the Exists subroutine is shown in Figure S.46. The changes required for the ForAll subroutine would be similar. By making i a global variable, we eliminate the need to store the current value of i on the stack, leaving only a constant amount of space in each stack entry. The total space used is then proportional to the number of recursive calls, which is $O(n)$.

Exists()

```
1    if i is n        // we have assigned a value to every variable
2      then if all clauses are satisfied by the truth assignment t
3              then return TRUE
4              else return FALSE
5      else begin
6              Increment i by 1.
7              Set t[xi] to TRUE
8              if ForAll() returns TRUE
9                 then begin
10                      Decrement i by 1
11                      return TRUE
12                  end
13                 else begin
14                      Set t[xi] to FALSE
15                      if ForAll() returns TRUE
16                         then begin
17                              Decrement i by 1
18                              return TRUE
19                          end
20                         else begin
21                              Decrement i by 1
22                              return FALSE
23                          end
24                  end
25          end
```

SolveQSAT($n, clauses$)

```
1    for i = 1 to n
2        Initialize t[xi] to undefined        // truth assignment t is a global variable
3    end for
4    Set i to 0
5    return Exists()
```

Figure S.46: A recursive algorithm to solve QSAT using $O(n)$ space, where n is the number of variables and *clauses* is the set of clauses. The ForAll() subroutine is not shown. The revisions to ForAll() would be similar to the revisions shown for Exists(), with i being incremented at the beginning and decremented before each **return** statement.

Solution to Exercise 10.3 *Consider any problem that can be solved by a Turing machine with k work tapes such that the maximum number of tape squares accessed on any single work tape is S(n). Show that that problem can solved using S(n) space by a Turing machine with a read-only input tape and a single work tape.*

The idea here is similar to the idea used in the solution to Exercise 3.8, where we showed that a machine with one tape can simulate a machine with k tapes. In the tape alphabet of the one-tape machine, we can include compound symbols to represent the contents on the k work tapes. Because k doesn't depend on the size of the input string, the size of the tape alphabet for the machine with one work tape is still constant. Each of the compound symbols takes up a single tape square on the work tape. Since the maximum number of tape squares used on any single work tape by the machine with k work tapes is $S(n)$, the total number of tape squares used by the machine with a single work tape is also $S(n)$.

Solution to Exercise 10.4 *Show that the problem of determining whether a string is a palindrome is in* L.

The algorithm, which is shown in Figure S.47, counts the number of symbols in the string and uses this count as an index to find pairs of strings that must be compared. Each variable in the algorithm would be maintained on a separate work tape. The algorithm proceeds by first counting the number of pairs of symbols that need to be compared based on the length of the string. Note that the integer division by 2 in Line 6 can be done by shifting the binary integer representing the length one bit to the right. Once the number of pairs is determined, the algorithm moves left from the end of the input to the appropriate comparison position in the string. This symbol is stored on a work tape. The algorithm then moves all the way to the left of the input string, works back to the correct comparison position, and compares the symbol on the tape with the symbol stored. If the symbols do not match, the algorithm returns No. If the symbols do match, the algorithm moves on to the next pair. If the algorithm never finds a mismatched pair, the string is a palindrome.

Since each work tape either maintains a counter or a single symbol, the space used by the algorithm is the number of bits in the counter that achieves the maximum value. The maximum value is achieved by *lengthCounter*, which is n. Therefore, the space used by the algorithm is $O(\log n)$.

Palindrome()

1   Set *lengthCounter* to 0
2   **while** head on the input tape is not β
3   Move Right
4   Increment *lengthCounter* by 1
5   **end while**
    // we now have the length of the string stored in *lengthCounter*
6   Set *numPairs* to *lengthCounter*/2   // shift right 1 bit to divide by 2
7   **for** *compareIndex* = 1 to *numPairs*
8   // We are at the blank immediately after the last symbol of input string
9   **for** *tempCounter* = 1 to *compareIndex*
10   Move Left
11   **end for**
12   Set *matchSymbol* to the symbol on the input tape.
        // Move back to left most tape square using *lengthCounter* to guide
13   **while** head on the input tape is not β
14   Move Right
15   **end while**
16   **for** *tempCounter* = 1 to *lengthCounter*
17   Move Left
18   **end for**
        // Find the symbol to compare from the left side
19   **for** *tempCounter* = 1 to *compareIndex* − 1
20   Move Right
21   **end for**
22   **if** head on input tape does not match symbol stored on work tape
23   **then return** No
        // Move to the end of input again to set up to compare next pair
24   **while** head on input tape is not β
25   Move Right
26   **end while**
27 **end for**
    // if we have gotten this far without returning No, we have a palindrome.
28 **return** YES

Figure S.47: An algorithm that uses $O(\log n)$ space on a Turing machine to determine whether an input string is a palindrome.

Solution to Exercise 10.5 *Design a Turing machine that writes exactly n^2 symbols to the work tape when given any string of length n on the input tape.*

The idea behind the algorithm is simple: for each symbol of the input string, append the entire input string to the work tape. We have to be careful, though, to do this while using exactly n^2 space. We could move through the input tape, writing a 1 to the result tape for each symbol read. Then we could move back to the leftmost square of the input tape and repeat the process n times. Remember, though, there is no way to know when you get back to the beginning of the input tape. We figured out a general way to get around that problem in Exercise 3.3, but our solution required us to write a left end of tape marker to the input tape. Here we have a read-only input tape, so we can't write to the input tape at all.

From Exercise 10.3, we know that anything we do with multiple work tapes can be done with one work tape using the exact same amount of space. Having multiple tapes makes things a little easier, so we will use three work tapes. One work tape, called the result tape, will be the tape on which we write exactly n^2 symbols. The result tape uses the most space of all of the work tapes. Recall that we measure the space on a machine with multiple work tapes as the maximum number of tape squares accessed on any single work tape, so we measure the amount of space used by our machine as the space used on the result tape.

We will have two other work tapes: the increment tape to keep track of how many times we have written n strings to the result tape and the copy tape to keep track of how many symbols we have written in our current increment. We will initialize these tape with n symbols, writing * at the beginning of each to mark the beginning of the tape. In the initialization process, we will also write n symbols to the result tape, so we will have $n-1$ copies left to make after the initialization is complete. In the code, which appears in Figure S.48, Lines 1 through 14 perform the initialization and handle the special cases when $n=0$ and $n=1$. The loop beginning on Line 16 walks back through the increment tape until it reaches the beginning, which is marked with *. In each iteration of this outer loop, the inner loop beginning on Line 18 walks through the copy tape and writes a 1 on the result tape for each symbol on the copy tape.

A trace of the execution of this algorithm on a string of length 3 appears in Figure S.49. The trace shows the contents of the three tapes after executing the line number indicated on the left. After two iterations of the loop beginning on Line 18, the algorithm has written n^2 symbols to the result tape.

ConstructSquareOfLength()

1   **if** head on input tape is blank   **then return**   // $0^2 = 0$
    // Walk through input to initialize the increment, copy, and result tapes
2   Write * on the increment tape to indicate the leftmost square
3   Write * on the copy tape to indicate the leftmost square
4   Write 1 on result tape
5   Move Right on the input tape.
6   **if** head on input tape is β **then return**   // length of input is 1
7   **while** head on the input tape is not β
8   Move Right on the increment tape
9   Move Right on the copy tape
10   Move Right on the result tape
11   Write 1 on the increment tape
12   Write 1 on the copy tape
13   Write 1 on result tape
14 **end while**

    // We now have *11111 on the increment and copy tapes
    //   where the number of 1's is $n - 1$.
    // The result tape now has n 1's.
    // The heads on all three tapes will be at the last 1.
    // We need to make $n - 1$ more copies
15 Move Right on copy tape   // need to start at β to run copy loop n times
16 **while** head on increment tape is not *
17   Move Left on increment tape
18   **while** head on copy tape is not *
19   Move Left on the copy tape
20   Move Right on the result tape
21   Write 1 on the result tape
22   **end while**
        // move back to the end of the copy tape
23   **while** head on copy tape is not β
24   Move Right on copy tape
25   **end while**
26 **end while**

Figure S.48: An algorithm to construct n^2 1's on the result tape.

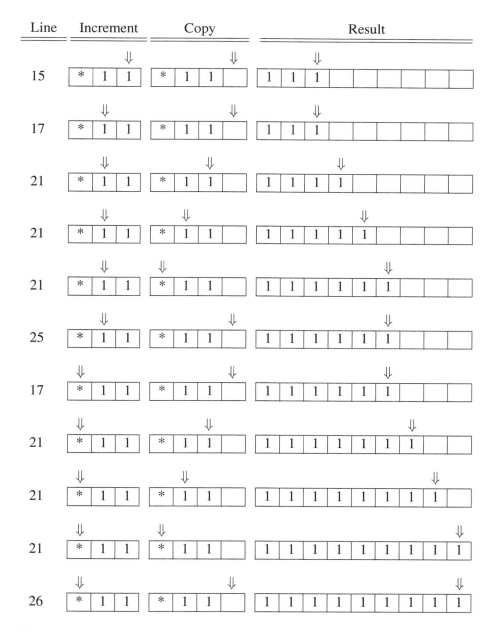

Figure S.49: The execution of our Turing machine program from Figure S.48 with an input string of length 3. The figure shows the contents of each work tape after the line number indicated on the left has been executed.

Solution to Exercise 10.6 *Wait a minute!! In Chapter 6 we said that encoding schemes for inputs to our programs must "not create inputs that are unnecessarily large." Haven't we violated that principle by padding the source code for* Match *with useless instructions in the proof of the Space Hierarchy Theorem?*

Well, not really. The padding of the source code for Match is just an illustration. The point is that there are infinitely many different versions of the source code for Match, so there must be some version that is large enough to get past the asymptotic trap in the proof. Still, you could argue that the encoding scheme should provide Strange with the minimum size source code that is equivalent to whatever long, convoluted source code is given. However, the other part of our encoding scheme requirement is that the encoding has to be easy to compute. The problem of finding equivalent source code of minimum size is undecidable, so at some point Strange will be given a long, convoluted version of the source code for Match as input and we will have no way to compress it. Since the outputs of Strange and the long version of Match do not match, the proof is legitimate.

Solution to Exercise 10.7 *All of the relationships in the list on page 178 were either established earlier in the book or are straightforward to prove. Make sure you understand why each of the classes is a subset of the subsequent class, paying particular attention to the subsets that are proper subsets. You'll need to prove that* Regular $\subsetneq$ L *and that* L $\subseteq$ P.

First note that a language that is decided by a finite automaton uses $O(1)$ space because the finite automaton has a fixed amount of memory. Therefore, Regular $\subset$ L. We know that this subset is proper because we showed that $\{0^n1^n : n \geq 0\}$ is not regular but is in L.

Next to show that L $\subseteq$ P, the key is to realize that $d^{\log n} = n^{\log d}$. Any machine that uses $O(\log n)$ space can enter at most $d^{\log n}$ distinct configurations, where d is some number that depends on the size of the machine's tape alphabet, the number of lines in the program, and the constant hidden inside the $O()$. This number does not, however, depend on the size of the input. Therefore, for any input of size n, the machine must halt before executing $d^{\log n}$ instructions. But $d^{\log n} = n^{\log d}$, which is polynomial in n because d is constant. Therefore, the running time of any machine that uses $\log n$ space is polynomial, so L $\subseteq$ P.

The Space Hierarchy Theorem implies that PSPACE is a proper subset of the decidable languages – there are decidable problems that require more than polynomial space. The remainder of the relationships were previously established – Decidable is a proper subset of Recognizable, for example, because the ACCEPTANCE PROBLEM is recognizable but not decidable.

Chapter Notes

Notes on Chapter 1: Introduction

The Mathematical Theorem problem is a somewhat loosely stated form of what is referred to as the **Entsheidungsproblem**. According to Davis (1973), the great mathematician David Hilbert considered developing an algorithm to solve this problem to be the "central problem of mathematical logic." In other words, this problem was a big deal in the early 20th century and it played a seminal role in the early development of the theory of computation.

Notes on Chapter 2: Finite Automata

The proof in Section 2.3 is a proof of a more general result, the Myhill-Nerode Theorem (Myhill, 1957; Nerode, 1958), tailored to the specific example of $L = \{0^n 1^n : n \geq 0\}$. See Hopcroft and Ullman (1979) for a proof of the general result. Other books on the theory of computation provide a much more extensive treatment of finite automata and regular languages. Hopcroft and Ullman (1979) is the classic reference on Automata Theory and much of the theory of computation. (See Hopcroft, Motwani, and Ullman (2006) for an updated version.) Sipser (2006) provides an excellent treatment of finite automata and regular languages.

Notes on Chapter 3: Turing Machines

Turing (1936) defined the machine that has come to be known as the Turing machine. Church (1936) and Post (1936) defined models of computation that are equivalent in power to Turing machines. The description of Turing machines as programs is based on Davis, Sigal, and Weyuker (1994), which is an excellent book. For more information on the Church-Turing Thesis, see Copeland (2008) and Yao (2003). Random access machines are discussed in Aho, Hopcroft, and Ullman (1974), Cook and Reckhow (1973) and Hartmanis (1971).

Notes on Chapter 4: Unsolvable Problems

The presentation in this chapter was heavily influenced by Sipser (2006), which provides an excellent and very readable introduction to unsolvable problems. In particular, the proofs that the ACCEPTANCE PROBLEM and the NON-REGULARITY TESTING PROBLEM are undecidable are based on proofs of the undecidability of similar problems in Sipser (2006), as well as Hopcroft and Ullman (1979). The proof of Rice's Theorem is adapted from Hopcroft and Ullman (1979). Many books provide extensive coverage of unsolvable problems, including Davis (1973), Davis, Sigal, and Weyuker (1994), Sipser (2006), and Hopcroft and Ullman (1979). Definition 4.3 is based on Garey and Johnson (1979).

Notes on Chapter 5: Nondeterminism

The idea of presenting nondeterminism as a model of free-will came from the last line of Floyd (1967), which also discusses nondeterminism in relation to search. See Russell and Norvig (2010) and Nilsson (1998) for discussions of breadth-first search and depth-first search in relation to Artificial Intelligence. The proof of the equivalence of NFAs and DFAs is based on Hopcroft and Ullman (1979).

Notes on Chapter 6: Computational Complexity

See Chapter 2 of Cormen, Leiserson, Rivest, and Stein (2009) for a brief but good discussion about using the RAM model to evaluate the running time of algorithms. The proof of the Cook-Levin Theorem in Section 6.6 is based on the treatment given in Garey and Johnson (1979), which is the classic reference on computational complexity theory. (Thank you to an anonymous reviewer who suggested going with that approach.) A number of other books provide good, short introductions to computational complexity, including Kleinberg and Tardos (2005), Cormen, Leiserson, Rivest, and Stein (2009), and Sipser (2006). Papadimitriou (1994) and Arora and Barak (2009) provide much more comprehensive treatments of the subject. As of June 2013, information on the Clay Mathematics Institute's Millennium Prize for the P vs NP problem can be found at http://www.claymath.org/millennium/P_vs_NP/.

Notes on Chapter 7: Reduce, Reuse, Recycle

Moret (1998) provides an excellent introduction to reductions. The reduction of SAT to DIRECTED HAMILTONIAN CYCLE is based on the reduction in Arora and Barak (2009). The reduction of SAT to 3SAT is based on the reduction in Garey and Johnson (1979). The reduction of 1in3SAT to SUBSET-SUM is based on the reduction from 3SAT to SUBSET-SUM in Cormen, Leiserson, Rivest, and Stein (2009).

Notes on Chapter 8: Approximation Algorithms

The initial discussion of the 0-1 KNAPSACK and FRACTIONAL KNAPSACK problems is based on Jay Aslam's unpublished lecture notes. The proof that the GreedyKnapsack algorithm is a 2-approximation is based on Ausiello, Protasi, Marchetti-Spaccamela, Gambosi, Crescenzi, and Kann (1999). The FPTAS for MAXIMUM KNAPSACK is based on Garey and Johnson (1979), Vazirani (2001), and Kleinberg and Tardos (2005). Cormen, Leiserson, Rivest, and Stein (2009) includes an excellent chapter on approximation algorithms. Vazirani (2001), Ausiello, Protasi, Marchetti-Spaccamela, Gambosi, Crescenzi, and Kann (1999), and Williamson and Shmoys (2011) provide comprehensive treatments of the subject.

Notes on Chapter 9: Heuristics

GSAT is from Selman, Levesque, and Mitchell (1992). The description of GSAT in the chapter differs from the actual algorithm in that the actual GSAT algorithm allows "sideways moves" – moves that do not decrease the number of unsatisfied clauses. According to Selman, Levesque, and Mitchell (1992), these sideways moves are an important part of GSAT's success. See Hoos and Stützle (2004) for a survey of local search algorithms and applications. Michiels, Aarts, and Korst (2007) discusses the theoretical foundations of local search. Gomes, Kautz, Sabharwal, and Selman (2008) provides a survey of SAT solvers with a good discussion of the critical region. (See also Biere, Heule, van Maaren, and Walsh (2009).) Cook and Mitchell (1998) discusses hard instances of SAT and Kirkpatrick and Selman (1994) discusses the critical region.

Notes on Chapter 10: Space

The definition of QSAT is from Papadimitriou (1994). The proof of Savitch's Theorem is based on the presentations in Sipser (2006), Hopcroft and Ullman (1979), and Papadimitriou (1994). The Time Hierarchy Theorem is from Hartmanis and Stearns (1965) and the Space Hierarchy Theorem is from Stearns, Hartmanis, and Lewis (1965). The proof of the Space Hierarchy Theorem is based on the proofs in Hopcroft and Ullman (1979), Arora and Barak (2009), and Sipser (2006), as well as many discussions with Dick Stearns.

Stuff you need to know.

Miscellaneous

The Battle of Hastings occurred in 1066.

Algorithms

A course on Algorithms and Data Structures should provide sufficient background to understand the material in this book. Below we review some basic terminology. (See Cormen, Leiserson, Rivest, and Stein (2009) for more details.)

Asymptotics

The running times of algorithms are compared using asymptotic notation, with $O()$ analogous to $\leq$, $\Omega()$ analogous to $\geq$, and $\Theta()$ analogous to $=$. These are defined formally below. It is important to understand that asymptotic comparisons are not absolute. For example, $1000n$ is $O(n^2)$, but $1000n$ is actually greater than n^2 when n is below 1000. Most of the time we can use asymptotics safely without having to worry about this level of detail, but it is critical to understand asymptotics well so that we know when to be more careful. For example, in the proof of the Space Hierarchy Theoremin Chapter 10, there is an asymptotic trap.

Definition S.5 (Upper Bound) *A function $f(n)$ is $O(g(n))$ if there is a constant c and a number BigEnough such that $f(n) \leq cg(n)$ whenever n is bigger than BigEnough.*

Definition S.6 (Lower Bound) *A function $f(n)$ is $\Omega(g(n))$ if there is a constant c and a number BigEnough such that $f(n) \geq cg(n)$ whenever n is bigger than BigEnough.*

Definition S.7 (Asymptotically Equal) *A function $f(n)$ is $\Theta(g(n))$ if $f(n)$ is $O(g(n))$ and $f(n)$ is $\Omega(g(n))$.*

A function $f(n)$ is $O(1)$ if it is bounded above by a constant. For example, $f(n) = 2/n$ is $O(1)$ because $2/n$ is at most 2 for all $n \geq 1$.

Definition S.8 (Asymptotically Smaller) *When we say that a function $f(n)$ is **asymptotically smaller** than a function $g(n)$, we mean that for every constant $c > 0$, there is a number BigEnough such that $f(n) < cg(n)$ when $n > BigEnough$. In this case, we also say that $f(n)$ is $o(g(n))$, which is read as "$f(n)$ is little-oh of $g(n)$."*

Dynamic programming

In Chapter 8, we use a dynamic programmingalgorithm for the 0-1 KNAP-SACK problem. Dynamic programming is a general technique for solving optimization problems. The idea is to define the value of an optimal solution recursively and then compute the value "bottom up". The usefulness of "bottom up" computation is easy to see when computing the Fibonacci numbers. The Fibonacci numbers are defined recursively as follows:

$$F(0) = 1$$
$$F(1) = 1$$
$$F(n) = F(n-1) + F(n-2) \qquad \text{when } n \geq 2$$

A simple recursive algorithm can be used to compute the n-the Fibonacci number:

FiboRecursive(n)

1 **if** n is 0 or 1
2   **then return** 1
3   **else return** FiboRecursive$(n-1)$+ FiboRecursive$(n-2)$

Figure S.50 shows a tree representation of the recursive calls when using this algorithm to compute the 8th Fibonacci number. The function will call

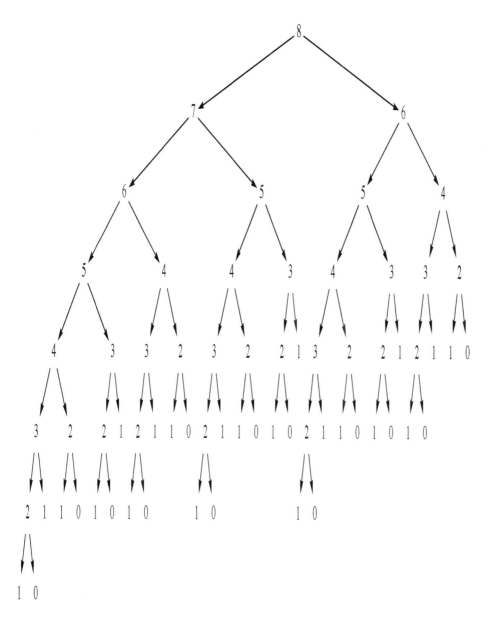

Figure S.50: A tree representation of the calls made by the recursive algorithm to compute the 8th Fibonacci numbers. Each node in the tree represents a recursive call. The numbers represent the value of the parameters passed in to each call.

itself twice, once with $n = 7$ and once with $n = 6$. Each of these invocations of the function will make two recursive calls, each of those calls will in turn make two recursive calls, and so on. The recursion terminates when $n = 1$ or $n = 0$. Even with $n = 8$, we can see the inefficiency of the recursive algorithm, which has exponential running time.

To improve the efficiency, we can compute the function from the bottom up instead of the top down. In other words, we know that $F(0)$ and $F(1)$ are 1. From these, we can compute $F(2)$; then using $F(1)$ and $F(2)$, we can compute $F(3)$; using $F(2)$ and $F(3)$, we can compute $F(4)$; etc. We can repeat this process until we reach $F(n)$. Here is the algorithm:

FiboBottomUp(n)

```
1   Let F be an array of size n.
2   Set F[0] to 1
3   Set F[1] to 1
4   for i = 2 to n
5       Set F[i] = F[i − 1] + F[i − 2]
6   end for
7   return F[n]
```

The running time for this algorithm is $\Theta(n)$, which is quite a bit faster than the exponential time algorithm to compute the Fibonacci numbers recursively.

Logic

Having a fundamental understanding of Boolean logic is essential to understanding the theory of computation, which grew out of the field of mathematical logic. For the purposes of understanding the material in this book, a few basics are sufficient.

Boolean variables can take one of two values: TRUE or FALSE. Boolean formulas are created from Boolean variables using the AND, OR and NOT operators. We use $\wedge$ for AND, $\vee$ for OR, and $\bar{x}$ to represent NOT x, which is TRUE only when x is FALSE. The AND and OR operators can be described using a **truth table**, which specifies the result of the operation given the inputs. The truth tables for AND and OR appear in Figure S.51.

Another Boolean operator that we use throughout the book is the implication: $x \Rightarrow y$. We interpret the statement $x \Rightarrow y$ to mean that whenever x is

x	y	$x \wedge y$
FALSE	FALSE	FALSE
TRUE	FALSE	FALSE
FALSE	TRUE	FALSE
TRUE	TRUE	TRUE

x	y	$x \vee y$
FALSE	FALSE	FALSE
TRUE	FALSE	TRUE
FALSE	TRUE	TRUE
TRUE	TRUE	TRUE

Figure S.51: The truth tables for AND and OR.

TRUE, y must also be TRUE. But when x is FALSE the statement $x \Rightarrow y$ doesn't tell us anything about the value of y; it could be either TRUE or FALSE. For example, the statement "If it is 2:00PM Eastern Standard Time, then it is afternoon in Manhattan" is TRUE. Knowing that it is not 2:00PM doesn't tell us anything about whether it is afternoon in Manhattan. Even if it is not 2:00PM and it is not afternoon in Manhattan, the statement "If it is 2:00PM Eastern Standard Time, then it is afternoon in Manhattan" is still TRUE. The only way that statement could be FALSE is for it to be 2:00PM and for it not to be afternoon in Manhattan. This is reflected in the truth table for $x \Rightarrow y$, shown in Figure S.52. The figure also shows the equivalence between $x \Rightarrow y$ and $\bar{x} \vee y$, which we use multiple times in the book.

x	y	$x \Rightarrow y$
FALSE	FALSE	TRUE
TRUE	FALSE	FALSE
FALSE	TRUE	TRUE
TRUE	TRUE	TRUE

x	y	$\bar{x}$	$\bar{x} \vee y$
FALSE	FALSE	TRUE	TRUE
TRUE	FALSE	FALSE	FALSE
FALSE	TRUE	TRUE	TRUE
TRUE	TRUE	FALSE	TRUE

Figure S.52: The truth tables for $x \Rightarrow y$ and $\bar{x} \vee y$, showing that the two formulas are equivalent.

   De Morgan's laws, which we use in the proof of the Cook-Levin Theorem, provide a way to distribute NOTs into expressions consisting of ANDs or ORs. The two laws are: $\overline{x \wedge y} = \bar{x} \vee \bar{y}$ and $\overline{x \vee y} = \bar{x} \wedge \bar{y}$.

Acknowledgements

First, I would like to thank Dick Stearns for everything he has taught me.[1] I would also like to thank Dick for providing me with his lecture notes, taking the time to read many drafts of this book, and providing insightful comments as usual. I could not have written this book without Dick's abundant help and guidance.

S. S. Ravi has always been a great support and I am grateful for all he has done for me over the years, including providing detailed comments on Chapter 8. I would like to thank Jay Aslam for teaching me how to teach and for making the suggestion that I emphasize computational complexity in my Theory of Computation course. Jay also gave me his unpublished lecture notes for Algorithms, which have had a tremendous influence on the way I present material. The discussion of the KNAPSACK problem is based on those notes, as is the discussion of the Fibonacci sequence in the Stuff You Need To Know Section. Prasad Jayanti graciously provided me with his handwritten lecture notes when I first taught Theory at Dartmouth College. Some of my initial lecture notes, from which this book was born, were based on Prasad's notes. Thanks to Tom Cormen for fielding my questions about publishing and for distributing the clrscode package, which I used to typeset the algorithms in this book. Mark Huibregtse suggested in an offhand comment at the printer one day that I turn my lecture notes into a book – it seemed like a good idea, so I did. Thanks, Mark. Scot Drysdale and Ada Brunstein provided some much needed encouragement at a time when this book was close to being added to my List Of Things I Wish I Had Completed. Haoran Ma ran DPLL experiments for me

---

[1] It is somewhat surreal to be writing these words while sitting at a picnic table with the GE Research and Development Center looming over me from across the Mohawk River. As I look up at those buildings, I imagine Dick and his colleagues walking through the halls discussing the ideas that became the foundation of computational complexity theory.

that were very helpful. Thanks to Howard Silverman for the gift to Skidmore College that supported the sabbatical during which I first began working on this book. Thanks also to Mark Hofmann for making sure that sabbatical happened.

A number of people were kind enough to read and comment on drafts of this book in various stages, including Andrew Matusiwiecz (who read my "final" draft and provided many insightful comments), Andrew Cencini, Dave Gill, Michael Duda, Flip Phillips, Eileen O'Connell, Greg Granquist, Christina Ellingson, and Kevin O'Connell. Mike Eckmann and Phil Markowitz used the book for an independent study; their questions and comments were invaluable. Several students over the years read this book when it was a work in progress, found typos, and made suggestions or comments, including Matt Leo, Alex Danilevksy, Steve Anton, Max Levine, Nick Moran, Chris Sacca, Wes Jossey, Andrei Margea, Ari Morse, Bill Stitson, Oliver Layton, Takehiko Yamaguchi, Kat Sullivan, Sarah Llewelyn, and Aaron Miller. There are surely many others whom I have inadvertently omitted; to them I apologize.

I am grateful to Jane Spurr of College Publications for being very patient with me as I went through the process of publishing this book. I would also like to thank Laraine Welch for the cover design. (That pig is awesome.)

For putting up with the endless hours I spent toiling over this book, I would like to thank my kids, who repeatedly asked if it was fun to write a book and who received various confusing responses. Finally, I would like to thank my wife, who often seemed to care more about this book than I did. Without my wife, I would have nothing.

Bibliography

Aho, A. V., J. E. Hopcroft, and J. Ullman (1974). *The Design and Analysis of Computer Algorithms* (1st ed.). Addison-Wesley Longman Publishing Co., Inc., Boston, MA, USA.

Arora, S. and B. Barak (2009). *Computational Complexity: A Modern Approach* (1st ed.). Cambridge University Press, New York, NY, USA.

Ausiello, G., M. Protasi, A. Marchetti-Spaccamela, G. Gambosi, P. Crescenzi, and V. Kann (1999). *Complexity and Approximation: Combinatorial Optimization Problems and Their Approximability Properties* (1st ed.). Springer-Verlag New York, Inc., Secaucus, NJ, USA.

Biere, A., M. J. H. Heule, H. van Maaren, and T. Walsh Eds. (2009). *Handbook of Satisfiability*, Volume 185 of *Frontiers in Artificial Intelligence and Applications*. IOS Press, Amsterdam, The Netherlands.

Church, A. (1936). An unsolvable problem of elementary number theory. *American Journal of Mathematics 58*, 345–363.

Cook, S. A. and D. G. Mitchell (1998). Finding hard instances of the satisfiability problem: A survey. In *Satisfiability Problem: Theory and Applications, DIMACS Series in Discrete Mathematics and Theoretical Computer Science. 35*, pp. 1–17. American Mathematical Society.

Cook, S. A. and R. A. Reckhow (1973). Time bounded random access machines. *Journal of Computer and System Sciences 7*, 354–375. Fourth Annual ACM Symposium on the Theory of Computing (Denver, Colo., 1972).

Copeland, B. J. (2008). The Church-Turing Thesis. In *The Stanford Encyclopedia of Philosophy* (Fall 2008 ed.). (E. N. Zalta Ed.). http://plato.stanford.edu/entries/church-turing/.

Cormen, T., C. Leiserson, R. Rivest, and C. Stein (2009). *Introduction to Algorithms* (3rd ed.). MIT Press, Cambridge, MA.

Davis, M. (1973). *Computability and Unsolvability*. Dover Books on Advanced Mathematics. Dover Publications, Inc., Mineola, NY.

Davis, M., R. Sigal, and E. Weyuker (1994). *Computability, Complexity, and Languages Fundamentals of Theoretical Computer Science*. Academic Press, San Diego, CA.

Floyd, R. W. (1967, October). Nondeterminstic algorithms. *Journal of the Association of Computing Machinery 14*(4), 636–644.

Garey, M. and D. Johnson (1979). *Computers and Intractability: A Guide to the Theory of NP-Completeness*. W. H. Freeman, New York, NY.

Gomes, C. P., H. Kautz, A. Sabharwal, and B. Selman (2008). Satisfiability solvers. In *Handbook of Knowledge Representation*, Volume 3 of *Foundations of Artificial Intelligence*, pp. 89–134. Amsterdam, The Netherlands: Elsevier.

Hartmanis, J. (1971). Computational complexity of random acess stored program machines. *Mathematical Systems Theory 5*(3), 232–245.

Hartmanis, J. and R. Stearns (1965). On the computational complexity of algorithms. *Transactions of the American Mathematical Society 117*, 285–305.

Hoos, H. H. and T. Stützle (2004). *Stochastic Local Search: Foundations & Applications*. Elsevier / Morgan Kaufmann, San Francisco, CA.

Hopcroft, J. and J. Ullman (1979). *Introduction to Automata Theory, Languages, and Computation*. Addison-Wesley, Reading, MA.

Hopcroft, J. E., R. Motwani, and J. D. Ullman (2006). *Introduction to Automata Theory, Languages, and Computation (3rd Edition)*. Addison-Wesley Longman Publishing Co., Inc., Boston, MA, USA.

Kaplan, J. Ed. (1950). *Dialogues of Plato*. Simon and Schuster, New York, NY.

Kirkpatrick, S. and B. Selman (1994). Critical behavior in the satisfiability of random boolean expressions. *Science 264*(5163), 1297–1301.

Kleinberg, J. and E. Tardos (2005). *Algorithm Design*. Addison-Wesley Longman Publishing Co., Inc., Boston, MA, USA.

Michiels, W., E. Aarts, and J. Korst (2007). *Theoretical Aspects of Local Search (Monographs in Theoretical Computer Science. An EATCS Series)*. Springer-Verlag New York, Inc., Secaucus, NJ, USA.

Moret, B. M. (1998). *The Theory of Computation*. Addison-Wesley, Reading, MA.

Myhill, J. (1957). Finite automata and the representation of events. *WADD TR-57-624*, 112–137.

Nerode, A. (1958). Linear automaton transformations. In *Proceedings of the American Mathematical Society*, pp. 541–544.

Nilsson, N. (1998). *Artificial Intelligence: A New Synthesis*. The Morgan Kaufmann Series in Artificial Intelligence. Morgan Kaufmann Publishers, San Francisco, CA, USA.

Papadimitriou, C. M. (1994). *Computational Complexity*. Addison-Wesley, Reading, Massachusetts.

Post, E. L. (1936). Finite combinatory processes-formulation, I. *Journal of Symbolic Logic 1*, 103–105.

Russell, S. J. and P. Norvig (2010). *Artificial Intelligence: A Modern Approach*. Prentice-Hall, Inc., Upper Saddle River, NJ, USA.

Sagan, C. (1985). *Contact*. Pocket Books, New York, NY.

Selman, B., H. Levesque, and D. Mitchell (1992). A new method for solving hard satisfiability problems. In *Proceedings of the Tenth National Conference on Artificial Intelligence*, AAAI'92, pp. 440–446. AAAI Press.

Sipser, M. (2006). *Introduction to the Theory of Computation* (2nd ed.). International Thomson Publishing, Boston, MA.

Stearns, R. E., J. Hartmanis, and P. M. Lewis (1965). Hierarchies of memory limited computations. In *Proceedings of the 6th Annual Symposium on Switching Circuit Theory and Logical Design (SWCT 1965)*, FOCS '65, Washington, DC, USA, pp. 179–190. IEEE Computer Society.

Turing, A. M. (1936). On computable numbers, with an application to the Entscheidungsproblem. *Proceedings of the London Mathematical Society 42*(2), 230–265.

Vazirani, V. V. (2001). *Approximation Algorithms*. Springer Verlag, New York, NY.

White, E. B. (1952). *Charlotte's Web*. Harper and Brothers Publishers, New York, NY.

Williamson, D. P. and D. B. Shmoys (2011). *The Design of Approximation Algorithms*. Cambridge University Press, New York, NY.

Yao, A. C.-C. (2003). Classical physics and the Church–Turing Thesis. *Journal of the ACM 50*(1), 100–105.

Index

∃, *see* existential quantifier
∀, *see* universal quantifier
$\leq_T$, *see* Turing reduction
$\leq_T^p$, *see* Turing reduction (polynomial time)
$\leq_m$, *see* instance mapping reduction
$\leq_m^p$, *see* instance mapping reduction (polynomial time)
0-1 KNAPSACK, 126–128, 251
1in3SAT, 113–116, 141, 142, 232–234, 281
2-SATISFIABILITY, *see* 2SAT
2SAT, 74–77, 79, 129, 130, 223–225, 252
3SAT, 102–106, 108–113, 116, 231–235, 281

ACCEPTANCE PROBLEM, 39–51, 214, 215, 280
accepting state, 19
alphabet, 4
approximation algorithm, 135
    for MAXIMUM KNAPSACK, 135
    for METRIC TSP, 259
    for SCHEDULING ON IDENTICAL PARALLEL MACHINES, 265
approximation ratio, 135, 256
asymptotically smaller, 284

breadth-first search, 3, 55, 56, 58, 59, 69, 71, 222, 225, 280

certificate, 84

Church-Turing Thesis, 35, 38, 53, 78, 280
    extended, 78
    strong form, 78
clause, 74
concatenation, 62
configuration, 68
configuration graph, 69–71, 93, 94, 176, 177, 222
Cook-Levin Theorem, 93
critical point, 161

data stream, 10
Davis Putnam Logemann Loveland, *see* DPPL
De Morgan's laws, 97, 287
decidable, 38
decides, 6
    a language, 6
    a problem, 6
    see also solves, 6
decision problems, 2
depth-first search, 55, 56, 59, 158, 280
deterministic Turing machine, 54
DIRECTED HAMILTONIAN CYCLE, 117–122, 239, 241, 242, 245–249, 281
DPLL, 158, 160, 161
dynamic programming, 139–142, 145

empty language, 6
Entsheidungsproblem, 279
enumerator, 217, 218
existential quantifier, 165

295

feasible solution, 126, 129, 131
finite state automaton, 19, 20
    nondeterministic, 60
finite state machine, 10, 12, 13, 15–18,
    20, 21
FPTAS, *see* fully polynomial time ap-
    proximation scheme
FRACTIONAL KNAPSACK, 130–133
fully polynomial time approximation
    scheme, 137
    for MAXIMUM KNAPSACK, 143
fully space-constructible, 174, 175
fully time-constructible, 175

GSAT, 150, 152, 281

HALTING PROBLEM, 44, 45, 47
HAMILTONIAN CYCLE, 83–85, 87–91,
    102, 117, 122, 145, 146, 166,
    227, 245–250
Hamiltonian cycle, 81
head, 24

instance mapping reduction, 46, 47, 90,
    101, 102, 111, 127, 245, 251
    polynomial time, 91
instance of a problem, 3

L, *see* logarithmic space
language, 5
lexicographic ordering, 217, 218
literal, 74
local optimum, 152
local search, 150–153, 161, 282
logarithmic space, 276

many-one reduction, 46
MAX2SAT, 75, 129, 130, 223, 252–254
maximization problem, 129
MAXIMUM KNAPSACK, 123–126, 128–
    135, 137, 139–143, 258
METRIC TRAVELING SALESMAN, *see*
    TRAVELING SALESMAN

minimization problem, 129
minimum spanning tree, 259
minimum spanning trees, 148, 259
multi-tape Turing machine, 34, 203
Myhill-Nerode Theorem, 21, 22, 279

NAE3SAT, *see* Not-All-Equal-3SAT
NAE4SAT, *see* Not-All-Equal-4SAT
neighborhood relation, 150
NON-REGULARITY TESTING, 47–49,
    280
nondeterministic finite state automaton,
    60
nondeterministic polynomial time, 84
nondeterministic search algorithm, 56
nondeterministic Turing machine, *see* Tur-
    ing machine
Not-All-Equal-3SAT, 116, 234–236, 252
Not-All-Equal-4SAT, 234–236
NP, 84
NP-complete, 93, 129, 252
NP-completeness proofs
    for 0-1 KNAPSACK, 126–128, 251
    for 1in3SAT, 232–234
    for DIRECTED HAMILTONIAN
        CYCLE, 117–122, 236–246
    for HAMILTONIAN CYCLE, 246–
        250
    for NAE3SAT, 235–236
    for NAE4SAT, 234–235
    for SAT, 93–99
    for SUBSET-SUM, 108–116
    for TRAVELING SALESMAN, 86–
        91, 122
    for 3SAT, 103–105
NP-hard, 128–130, 139, 141, 252
    strongly, 145
NP-hardness proofs
    for MAX2SAT, 252–256
    for QSAT, 269
    for TRAVELING SALESMAN, 251–
        252

NPSPACE, 176

OPEN list
in breadth-first search, 55, 71
in depth-first search, 55
optimization problems, 129

P, 77
palindrome, 190
parrot, 16
recipes, 16
pig, 73, 74, 164, 165, 182
Plato, 80
polynomial time, 77
pseudo-polynomial time, 141, 142, 145, 146, 259
PSPACE, 171

QSAT, 166, 167, 169, 171, 269, 270, 282
quantified Boolean formula, 165

RAM, *see* Random Access Machine
Random Access Machine, 78, 79, 223, 280
recognizable, 38
recognizable language, 38
recognizes, 38
recursive language, 217
recursively enumerable (r.e.), 217
regular language, 20, 178
REJECTION PROBLEM, 51, 214, 215
Rice's Theorem, 49, 50, 213, 280
running time, 76, 84

SAT, *see* SATISFIABILITY, 235
SATISFIABILITY, 92–99, 101–106, 117–122, 152–156, 158, 161, 231, 232, 236–246, 281, 282
Savitch's Theorem, 177, 178, 282
SCHEDULING ON IDENTICAL PARALLEL MACHINES, 151, 265
search tree, 56
selection mechanism, 150–152
solves, 4, 41
nondeterministically in time, 84
using space, 170
using time, 76
space, 170
Space Hierarchy Theorem, 175, 276, 277, 282
spanning tree, 259
spider, 181, 182
state, 9
state transition diagram, 19
streaming model, 10
string over an alphabet, 4
SUBSET-SUM, 108–116, 126, 127, 141, 142, 166, 251, 281

Tabu Search, 152
tabu tenure, 152
tape alphabet, 31
Time Hierarchy Theorem, 175, 282
TRAVELING SALESMAN PROBLEM, 86–91, 101, 122, 145, 146, 227
METRIC, 148, 259, 260, 263
optimization version, 129, 145, 146, 252
triangle inequality, 148
trivial property, 49, 50, 213
truth table, 286
TSP, *see* TRAVELING SALESMAN
Turing machine, 24–38, 49, 51, 53, 54, 60, 66, 68, 71, 76–79, 84, 95, 170, 171, 175, 176, 189–207, 221, 228
multi-tape, 34, 203
nondeterministic, 54, 61, 66, 71, 84, 93, 176, 221
Turing reduction, 47, 128, 129, 223, 252
polynomial time, 128

undecidability proofs
for the ACCEPTANCE PROBLEM, 41–43

for the HALTING PROBLEM, 44–
45
for the NON-REGULARITY TEST-
ING PROBLEM, 47–49
for the USELESS LANGUAGE
PROBLEM, 45–46
undecidable, 43
unit clause, 154–158
unit propagation, 155–158
universal quantifier, 165
universal Turing machine, 36, 40, 203–
207, 215, 216
unrecognizability proofs
for the REJECTION PROBLEM,
214–215
unrecognizable, 50, 214
USELESS LANGUAGE PROBLEM, 45–
46

verifiable, 84
verifier, 83
for 0-1 KNAPSACK, 251
for 3SAT, 103
for HAMILTONIAN CYCLE, 83
for SUBSET-SUM, 108
for TRAVELING SALESMAN, 86

www.ingramcontent.com/pod-product-compliance
Lightning Source LLC
Chambersburg PA
CBHW071104050326
40690CB00008B/1115